Gia

MEN'S ALPINE SKI
WORLD CUP

EVERY PODIUM
EVERY RACE
EVERY CUP

1967-2023

ISBN Code: 9798864990605
Independently published

1967

CUPS

OVERALL

1.	**JEAN-CLAUDE KILLY**	**(FRA)**
2.	Heini Messner	(AUT)
3.	Guy Périllat	(FRA)

SLALOM

1.	**JEAN-CLAUDE KILLY**	**(FRA)**
2.	Guy Périllat	(FRA)
3.	Heini Messner	(AUT)

GIANT SLALOM

1.	**JEAN-CLAUDE KILLY**	**(FRA)**
2.	Georges Mauduit	(FRA)
3.	Jimmy Heuga	(USA)

DOWNHILL

1.	**JEAN-CLAUDE KILLY**	**(FRA)**
2.	Guy Périllat	(FRA)
3.	Franz Vogler	(FRG)

RACES

05/01/1967, Berchtesgaden (FRG)
SLALOM

1.	**HEINI MESSNER**	**(AUT)**
2.	Jules Melquiond	(FRA)
3.	Dumeng Giovanoli	(SUI)

06/01/1967, Berchtesgaden (FRG)
GIANT SLALOM

1.	**GEORGES MAUDUIT**	**(FRA)**
2.	Léo Lacroix	(FRA)
3.	Jean-Claude Killy	(FRA)

09/01/1967, Adelboden (SUI)
GIANT SLALOM

1.	**JEAN-CLAUDE KILLY**	**(FRA)**
2.	Willy Favre	(FRA)
3.	Georges Mauduit	(FRA)

14/01/1967, Wengen (SUI)
DOWNHILL

1.	**JEAN-CLAUDE KILLY**	**(FRA)**
2.	Léo Lacroix	(FRA)
3.	Jean-Daniel Dätwyler	(SUI)

15/01/1967, Wengen (SUI)
SLALOM

1.	**JEAN-CLAUDE KILLY**	**(FRA)**
2.	Heini Messner	(AUT)
3.	Jules Melquiond	(FRA)

21/01/1967, Kitzbühel (AUT)
DOWNHILL

1.	**JEAN-CLAUDE KILLY**	**(FRA)**
2.	Franz Vogler	(FRG)
3.	Heini Messner	(AUT)

22/01/1967, Kitzbühel (AUT)
SLALOM

1.	**JEAN-CLAUDE KILLY**	**(FRA)**
2.	Bengt-Erik Grahn	(SWE)
3.	Louis Jauffret	(FRA)

27/01/1967, Megève (FRA)
DOWNHILL

1.	**JEAN-CLAUDE KILLY**	**(FRA)**
2.	Hans Peter Rohr	(SUI)
3.	Franz Vogler	(FRG)

29/01/1967, Megève (FRA)
SLALOM

1.	**GUY PÉRILLAT**	**(FRA)**
2.	Jean-Claude Killy	(FRA)
3.	Karl Schranz	(AUT)

05/02/1967, Madonna di Campiglio (ITA)
SLALOM

1.	**GUY PÉRILLAT**	**(FRA)**
2.	Louis Jauffret	(FRA)
3.	Léo Lacroix	(FRA)

03/03/1967, Sestriere (ITA)
DOWNHILL

1.	**JEAN-CLAUDE KILLY**	**(FRA)**
2.	Bernard Orcel	(FRA)
3.	Guy Périllat	(FRA)

10/03/1967, Franconia (USA)
DOWNHILL

1.	**JEAN-CLAUDE KILLY**	**(FRA)**
2.	Guy Périllat	(FRA)
3.	Jim Barrows	(USA)

11/03/1967, Franconia (USA)
SLALOM

1.	**JEAN-CLAUDE KILLY**	**(FRA)**

2. Jimmy Heuga (USA)
3. Herbert Huber (AUT)

12/03/1967, Franconia (USA)
GIANT SLALOM
1. **JEAN-CLAUDE KILLY** **(FRA)**
2. Georges Mauduit (FRA)
3. Dumeng Giovanoli (SUI)

19/03/1967, Vail (USA)
GIANT SLALOM
1. **JEAN-CLAUDE KILLY** **(FRA)**
2. Jimmy Heuga (USA)
3. Heini Messner (AUT)

25/03/1967, Jackson Hole (USA)
GIANT SLALOM
1. **JEAN-CLAUDE KILLY** **(FRA)**
2. Jimmy Heuga (USA)
3. Werner Bleiner (AUT)

26/03/1967, Jackson Hole (USA)
SLALOM
1. **HERBERT HUBER** **(AUT)**
2. Georges Mauduit (FRA)
3. Werner Bleiner (AUT)

1968

CUPS

OVERALL
1. **JEAN-CLAUDE KILLY** **(FRA)**
2. Dumeng Giovanoli (SUI)
3. Herbert Huber (AUT)

SLALOM
1. **DUMENG GIOVANOLI** **(SUI)**
2. Jean-Claude Killy (FRA)
3. Patrick Russel (FRA)

GIANT SLALOM
1. **JEAN-CLAUDE KILLY** **(FRA)**
2. Edmund Bruggmann (SUI)
3. Herbert Huber (AUT)

DOWNHILL
1. **GERHARD NENNING** **(AUT)**
2. Jean-Claude Killy (FRA)
3. Karl Schranz (AUT)

RACES

04/01/1968, Bad Hindelang (FRG)
GIANT SLALOM
1. **EDMUND BRUGGMANN** **(SUI)**
2. Jean-Claude Killy (FRA)
3. Dumeng Giovanoli (SUI)

08/01/1968, Adelboden (SUI)
GIANT SLALOM
1. **JEAN-CLAUDE KILLY** **(FRA)**
2. Edmund Bruggmann (SUI)
3. Stefan Kälin (SUI)

13/01/1968, Wengen (SUI)
DOWNHILL
1. **GERHARD NENNING** **(AUT)**
2. Karl Schranz (AUT)
3. Edmund Bruggmann (SUI)

14/01/1968, Wengen (SUI)
SLALOM
1. **DUMENG GIOVANOLI** **(SUI)**
2. Håkon Mjøen (NOR)
3. Alfred Matt (AUT)

20/01/1968, Kitzbühel (AUT)
DOWNHILL

1. **GERHARD NENNING** **(AUT)**
2. Jean-Claude Killy (FRA)
3. Andreas Sprecher (SUI)

21/01/1968, Kitzbühel (AUT)
SLALOM

1. **DUMENG GIOVANOLI** **(SUI)**
2. Alfred Matt (AUT)
3. Jean-Claude Killy (FRA)

09/02/1968, Grenoble (FRA)
DOWNHILL

1. **JEAN-CLAUDE KILLY** **(FRA)**
2. Guy Périllat (FRA)
3. Jean-Daniel Dätwyler (SUI)

12/02/1968, Grenoble (FRA)
GIANT SLALOM

1. **JEAN-CLAUDE KILLY** **(FRA)**
2. Willy Favre (SUI)
3. Heini Messner (AUT)

17/02/1968, Grenoble (FRA)
SLALOM

1. **JEAN-CLAUDE KILLY** **(FRA)**
2. Herbert Huber (AUT)
3. Alfred Matt (AUT)

24/02/1968, Chamonix (FRA)
DOWNHILL

1. **BERNARD ORCEL** **(FRA)**
2. Kurt Huggler (SUI)
3. Guy Périllat (FRA)

24/02/1968, Oslo (NOR)
GIANT SLALOM

1. **WERNER BLEINER** **(AUT)**
2. Dumeng Giovanoli (SUI)
3. Edmund Bruggmann (SUI)

25/02/1968, Oslo (NOR)
SLALOM

1. **PATRICK RUSSEL** **(FRA)**
2. Dumeng Giovanoli (SUI)
3. Håkon Mjøen (NOR)

01/03/1968, Kranjska Gora (YUG)
SLALOM

1. **PATRICK RUSSEL** **(FRA)**

2. Franz Digruber (AUT)
3. Stefan Kälin (SUI)

10/03/1968, Méribel (FRA)
GIANT SLALOM

1. **JEAN-CLAUDE KILLY** **(FRA)**
2. Georges Mauduit (FRA)
3. Guy Périllat (FRA)

15/03/1968, Aspen (USA)
DOWNHILL

1. **GERHARD NENNING** **(AUT)**
2. Heini Messner (AUT)
3. Jean-Claude Killy (FRA)

16/03/1968, Aspen (USA)
SLALOM

1. **BILLY KIDD** **(USA)**
2. Herbert Huber (AUT)
3. Alfred Matt (AUT)

29/03/1968, Rossland (CAN)
SLALOM

1. **JEAN-CLAUDE KILLY** **(FRA)**
2. Jean-Pierre Augert (FRA)
3. Rick Chaffee (USA)

31/03/1968, Rossland (CAN)
GIANT SLALOM

1. **HERBERT HUBER** **(AUT)**
2. Reinhard Tritscher (AUT)
3. Guy Périllat (FRA)

06/04/1968, Heavenly Valley (USA)
GIANT SLALOM

1. **HERBERT HUBER** **(AUT)**
2. Georges Mauduit (FRA)
3. Reinhard Tritscher (AUT)

07/04/1968, Heavenly Valley (USA)
SLALOM

1. **SPIDER SABICH** **(USA)**
2. Herbert Huber (AUT)
3. Rick Chaffee (USA)

1968-69

CUPS

OVERALL
1. **KARL SCHRANZ** (AUT)
2. Jean-Noël Augert (FRA)
3. Reinhard Tritscher (AUT)

SLALOM
1. **JEAN-NOËL AUGERT** (FRA)
= **ALFRED MATT** (AUT)
= **ALAIN PENZ** (FRA)
= **PATRICK RUSSEL** (FRA)

GIANT SLALOM
1. **KARL SCHRANZ** (AUT)
2. Reinhard Tritscher (AUT)
3. Jean-Noël Augert (FRA)

DOWNHILL
1. **KARL SCHRANZ** (AUT)
2. Henri Duvillard (FRA)
= Heini Messner (AUT)

RACES

12/12/1968, Val-d'Isère (FRA)
GIANT SLALOM
1. **KARL SCHRANZ** (AUT)
2. Bernard Orcel (FRA)
3. Henri Duvillard (FRA)

03/01/1969, Berchtesgaden (FRG)
SLALOM
1. **ALFRED MATT** (AUT)
2. Karl Schranz (AUT)
3. Patrick Russel (FRA)

06/01/1969, Adelboden (SUI)
GIANT SLALOM
1. **JEAN-NOËL AUGERT** (FRA)
2. Jean-Pierre Augert (FRA)
3. Karl Schranz (AUT)

11/01/1969, Wengen (SUI)
DOWNHILL
1. **KARL SCHRANZ** (AUT)
2. Heini Messner (AUT)
3. Karl Cordin (AUT)

12/01/1969, Wengen (SUI)
SLALOM
1. **REINHARD TRITSCHER** (AUT)
2. Spider Sabich (USA)
3. Peter Frei (SUI)

18/01/1969, Kitzbühel (AUT)
DOWNHILL
1. **KARL SCHRANZ** (AUT)
2. Jean-Daniel Dätwyler (SUI)
3. Karl Cordin (AUT)
= Henri Duvillard (FRA)

19/01/1969, Kitzbühel (AUT)
SLALOM
1. **PATRICK RUSSEL** (FRA)
2. Herbert Huber (AUT)
3. Dumeng Giovanoli (SUI)

24/01/1969, Megève (FRA)
DOWNHILL
1. **HENRI DUVILLARD** (FRA)
2. Heini Messner (AUT)
3. Alfred Matt (AUT)

26/01/1969, Megève (FRA)
SLALOM
1. **ALAIN PENZ** (FRA)
2. Herbert Huber (AUT)
3. Spider Sabich (USA)

01/02/1969, Sankt Anton am Arlberg (AUT)
DOWNHILL
1. **KARL SCHRANZ** (AUT)
2. Heini Messner (AUT)
3. Franz Vogler (FRG)

08/02/1969, Åre (SWE)
GIANT SLALOM
1. **JEAN-NOËL AUGERT** (FRA)
2. Jakob Tischhauser (SUI)
3. Alain Penz (FRA)

09/02/1969, Åre (SWE)
SLALOM
1. **PATRICK RUSSEL** (FRA)
2. Jean-Noël Augert (FRA)
3. Alfred Matt (AUT)

09/02/1969, Cortina d'Ampezzo (ITA)

DOWNHILL
1.	**JOS MINSCH**	**(SUI)**
2.	Jean-Pierre Augert	(FRA)
3.	Hans Peter Rohr	(SUI)

14/02/1969, Val Gardena (ITA)
DOWNHILL
1.	**JEAN-DANIEL DÄTWYLER**	**(SUI)**
2.	Henri Duvillard	(FRA)
3.	Rudi Sailer	(AUT)

16/02/1969, Kranjska Gora (YUG)
GIANT SLALOM
1.	**REINHARD TRITSCHER**	**(AUT)**
2.	Alfred Matt	(AUT)
3.	Franz Digruber	(AUT)

17/02/1969, Kranjska Gora (YUG)
SLALOM
1.	**EDMUND BRUGGMANN**	**(SUI)**
2.	Alain Penz	(FRA)
3.	Herbert Huber	(AUT)

28/02/1969, Squaw Valley (USA)
SLALOM
1.	**BILLY KIDD**	**(USA)**
2.	Alain Penz	(FRA)
3.	Patrick Russel	(FRA)

01/03/1969, Squaw Valley (USA)
GIANT SLALOM
1.	**REINHARD TRITSCHER**	**(AUT)**
2.	Jakob Tischhauser	(SUI)
3.	Heini Messner	(AUT)

15/03/1969, Mont-Sainte-Anne (CAN)
GIANT SLALOM
1.	**KARL SCHRANZ**	**(AUT)**
2.	Dumeng Giovanoli	(SUI)
3.	Jakob Tischhauser	(SUI)

16/03/1969, Mont-Sainte-Anne (CAN)
SLALOM
1.	**ALFRED MATT**	**(AUT)**
2.	Jean-Noël Augert	(FRA)
3.	Billy Kidd	(USA)

21/03/1969, Waterville Valley (USA)
GIANT SLALOM
1.	**DUMENG GIOVANOLI**	**(SUI)**
2.	Karl Schranz	(AUT)
3.	Jakob Tischhauser	(SUI)

22/03/1969, Waterville Valley (USA)
SLALOM
1.	**JEAN-NOËL AUGERT**	**(FRA)**
2.	Herbert Huber	(AUT)
3.	Patrick Russel	(FRA)

1969-70

CUPS

OVERALL
1. **KARL SCHRANZ** **(AUT)**
2. Patrick Russel (FRA)
3. Gustav Thöni (ITA)

SLALOM
1. **ALAIN PENZ** **(FRA)**
= **PATRICK RUSSEL** **(FRA)**
3. Jean-Noël Augert (FRA)

GIANT SLALOM
1. **GUSTAV THÖNI** **(ITA)**
2. Dumeng Giovanoli (SUI)
= Patrick Russel (FRA)

DOWNHILL
1. **KARL SCHRANZ** **(AUT)**
= **KARL CORDIN** **(AUT)**
3. Henri Duvillard (FRA)

RACES

11/12/1969, Val-d'Isère (FRA)
GIANT SLALOM
1. **GUSTAV THÖNI** **(ITA)**
2. Patrick Russel (FRA)
3. Jean-Noël Augert (FRA)

14/12/1969, Val-d'Isère (FRA)
DOWNHILL
1. **MALCOLM MILNE** **(AUS)**
2. Jean-Daniel Dätwyler (SUI)
3. Karl Schranz (AUT)

20/12/1969, Lienz (AUT)
GIANT SLALOM
1. **PATRICK RUSSEL** **(FRA)**
2. Gustav Thöni (ITA)
3. Jakob Tischhauser (SUI)

21/12/1969, Lienz (AUT)
SLALOM
1. **JEAN-NOËL AUGERT** **(FRA)**
2. Herbert Huber (AUT)
3. Spider Sabich (USA)

04/01/1970, Bad Hindelang (FRG)
SLALOM
1. **GUSTAV THÖNI** **(ITA)**
2. Patrick Russel (FRA)
3. Jean-Noël Augert (FRA)

05/01/1970, Adelboden (SUI)
GIANT SLALOM
1. **KARL SCHRANZ** **(AUT)**
2. Sepp Heckelmiller (FRG)
3. Dumeng Giovanoli (SUI)

10/01/1970, Wengen (SUI)
DOWNHILL
1. **HENRI DUVILLARD** **(FRA)**
2. Karl Cordin (AUT)
3. Heini Messner (AUT)

11/01/1970, Wengen (SUI)
SLALOM
1. **PATRICK RUSSEL** **(FRA)**
2. Dumeng Giovanoli (SUI)
3. Henri Bréchu (FRA)

17/01/1970, Kitzbühel (AUT)
GIANT SLALOM
1. **DUMENG GIOVANOLI** **(SUI)**
2. Andrzej Bachleda (POL)
3. Karl Schranz (AUT)

18/01/1970, Kitzbühel (AUT)
SLALOM
1. **PATRICK RUSSEL** **(FRA)**
2. Gustav Thöni (ITA)
3. Jean-Noël Augert (FRA)

20/01/1970, Kranjska Gora (YUG)
GIANT SLALOM
1. **DUMENG GIOVANOLI** **(SUI)**
2. Patrick Russel (FRA)
3. Georges Mauduit (FRA)

23/01/1970, Megève (FRA)
DOWNHILL
1. **KARL SCHRANZ** **(AUT)**
2. Heini Messner (AUT)
3. Henri Duvillard (FRA)

25/01/1970, Megève (FRA)
SLALOM
1. **PATRICK RUSSEL** **(FRA)**

2.	Alain Penz	(FRA)
3.	Henri Bréchu	(FRA)

29/01/1970, Madonna di Campiglio (ITA)
GIANT SLALOM

1.	**GUSTAV THÖNI**	**(ITA)**
2.	Dumeng Giovanoli	(SUI)
3.	Jean-Noël Augert	(FRA)

30/01/1970, Madonna di Campiglio (ITA)
GIANT SLALOM

1.	**GUSTAV THÖNI**	**(ITA)**
2.	Edmund Bruggmann	(SUI)
3.	Jean-Noël Augert	(FRA)

31/01/1970, Madonna di Campiglio (ITA)
SLALOM

1.	**HENRI BRÉCHU**	**(FRA)**
2.	Gustav Thöni	(ITA)
3.	Dumeng Giovanoli	(SUI)

01/02/1970, Garmisch-Partenkirchen (FRG)
DOWNHILL

1.	**KARL SCHRANZ**	**(AUT)**
2.	Karl Cordin	(AUT)
3.	Franz Vogler	(FRG)

08/02/1970, Val Gardena (ITA)
SLALOM

1.	**JEAN-NOËL AUGERT**	**(FRA)**
2.	Patrick Russel	(FRA)
3.	Billy Kidd	(USA)

10/02/1970, Val Gardena (ITA)
GIANT SLALOM

1.	**KARL SCHRANZ**	**(AUT)**
2.	Werner Bleiner	(AUT)
3.	Dumeng Giovanoli	(SUI)

15/02/1970, Val Gardena (ITA)
DOWNHILL

1.	**BERNHARD RUSSI**	**(SUI)**
2.	Karl Cordin	(AUT)
3.	Malcolm Milne	(AUS)

21/02/1970, Jackson Hole (USA)
DOWNHILL

1.	**KARL CORDIN**	**(AUT)**
2.	Bernard Orcel	(FRA)
3.	Henri Duvillard	(FRA)

22/02/1970, Jackson Hole (USA)
SLALOM

1.	**ALAIN PENZ**	**(FRA)**
2.	Henri Bréchu	(FRA)
3.	Gustav Thöni	(ITA)

27/02/1970, Vancouver (CAN)
GIANT SLALOM

1.	**ALAIN PENZ**	**(FRA)**
2.	Werner Bleiner	(AUT)
3.	Patrick Russel	(FRA)

28/02/1970, Vancouver (CAN)
SLALOM

1.	**ALAIN PENZ**	**(FRA)**
2.	Gustav Thöni	(ITA)
3.	Patrick Russel	(FRA)

06/03/1970, Heavenly Valley (USA)
SLALOM

1.	**ALAIN PENZ**	**(FRA)**
2.	Rick Chaffee	(USA)
3.	Heini Messner	(AUT)

08/03/1970, Heavenly Valley (USA)
GIANT SLALOM

1.	**PATRICK RUSSEL**	**(FRA)**
2.	Werner Bleiner	(AUT)
3.	Karl Schranz	(AUT)

13/03/1970, Voss (NOR)
GIANT SLALOM

1.	**WERNER BLEINER**	**(AUT)**
2.	Jean-Noël Augert	(FRA)
3.	Karl Schranz	(AUT)

15/03/1970, Voss (NOR)
SLALOM

1.	**PATRICK RUSSEL**	**(FRA)**
2.	Jean-Noël Augert	(FRA)
3.	Henri Bréchu	(FRA)

1970-71

CUPS

OVERALL

1. **GUSTAV THÖNI** **(ITA)**
2. Henri Duvillard (FRA)
3. Patrick Russel (FRA)

SLALOM

1. **JEAN-NOËL AUGERT** **(FRA)**
2. Gustav Thöni (ITA)
3. Tyler Palmer (USA)

GIANT SLALOM

1. **GUSTAV THÖNI** **(ITA)**
= **PATRICK RUSSEL** **(FRA)**
3. Edmund Bruggmann (SUI)

DOWNHILL

1. **BERNHARD RUSSI** **(SUI)**
2. Bernard Orcel (FRA)
3. Karl Cordin (AUT)

RACES

13/12/1970, Sestriere (ITA)
DOWNHILL
1. **HENRI DUVILLARD** **(FRA)**
2. Bernard Orcel (FRA)
3. Karl Schranz (AUT)

17/12/1970, Val-d'Isère (FRA)
GIANT SLALOM
1. **PATRICK RUSSEL** **(FRA)**
2. Jean-Noël Augert (FRA)
3. Gustav Thöni (ITA)

20/12/1970, Val-d'Isère (FRA)
DOWNHILL
1. **KARL CORDIN** **(AUT)**
2. Bernard Orcel (FRA)
3. Karl Schranz (AUT)

05/01/1971, Berchtesgaden (FRG)
GIANT SLALOM
1. **EDMUND BRUGGMANN** **(SUI)**
2. Patrick Russel (FRA)
3. David Zwilling (AUT)

06/01/1971, Berchtesgaden (FRG)
SLALOM
1. **JEAN-NOËL AUGERT** **(FRA)**
2. Heini Messner (AUT)
3. Max Rieger (FRG)

09/01/1971, Madonna di Campiglio (ITA)
GIANT SLALOM
1. **HENRI DUVILLARD** **(FRA)**
2. Patrick Russel (FRA)
3. Gustav Thöni (ITA)

10/01/1971, Madonna di Campiglio (ITA)
SLALOM
1. **GUSTAV THÖNI** **(ITA)**
2. Jean-Noël Augert (FRA)
3. Patrick Russel (FRA)

16/01/1971, Sankt Moritz (SUI)
DOWNHILL
1. **WALTER TRESCH** **(SUI)**
2. Bernhard Russi (SUI)
3. Andreas Sprecher (SUI)

17/01/1971, Sankt Moritz (SUI)
SLALOM
1. **TYLER PALMER** **(USA)**
2. Harald Rofner (AUT)
3. Gustav Thöni (ITA)

18/01/1971, Adelboden (SUI)
GIANT SLALOM
1. **PATRICK RUSSEL** **(FRA)**
2. Gustav Thöni (ITA)
3. Henri Duvillard (FRA)

24/01/1971, Kitzbühel (AUT)
SLALOM
1. **JEAN-NOËL AUGERT** **(FRA)**
2. Alain Penz (FRA)
3. Harald Rofner (AUT)

29/01/1971, Megève (FRA)
DOWNHILL
1. **JEAN-DANIEL DÄTWYLER** **(SUI)**
2. Bernard Orcel (FRA)
3. Walter Tresch (SUI)

30/01/1971, Megève (FRA)
SLALOM

1.	**JEAN-NOËL AUGERT**	**(FRA)**
2.	Gustav Thöni	(ITA)
3.	Christian Neureuther	(FRG)

31/01/1971, Megève (FRA)
DOWNHILL

1.	**BERNHARD RUSSI**	**(SUI)**
2.	Franz Vogler	(FRG)
3.	Michel Dätwyler	(SUI)

07/02/1971, Mürren (SUI)
SLALOM

1.	**JEAN-NOËL AUGERT**	**(FRA)**
2.	Tyler Palmer	(USA)
3.	Patrick Russel	(FRA)

13/02/1971, Mont-Sainte-Anne (CAN)
GIANT SLALOM

1.	**BERNHARD RUSSI**	**(SUI)**
2.	Edmund Bruggmann	(SUI)
3.	Werner Bleiner	(AUT)

14/02/1971, Mont-Sainte-Anne (CAN)
SLALOM

1.	**PATRICK RUSSEL**	**(FRA)**
2.	Gustav Thöni	(ITA)
3.	Alain Penz	(FRA)

18/02/1971, Sugarloaf (USA)
DOWNHILL

1.	**BERNHARD RUSSI**	**(SUI)**
2.	Henri Duvillard	(FRA)
3.	Stefano Anzi	(ITA)

19/02/1971, Sugarloaf (USA)
DOWNHILL

1.	**STEFANO ANZI**	**(ITA)**
2.	Karl Cordin	(AUT)
3.	Gustav Thöni	(ITA)

21/02/1971, Sugarloaf (USA)
GIANT SLALOM

1.	**GUSTAV THÖNI**	**(ITA)**
2.	Edmund Bruggmann	(SUI)
3.	Henri Duvillard	(FRA)

25/02/1971, Heavenly Valley (USA)
SLALOM

1.	**GUSTAV THÖNI**	**(ITA)**
2.	Christian Neureuther	(FRG)
3.	Tyler Palmer	(USA)

27/02/1971, Heavenly Valley (USA)
GIANT SLALOM

1.	**GUSTAV THÖNI**	**(ITA)**
2.	Henri Duvillard	(FRA)
3.	Sepp Heckelmiller	(FRG)

13/03/1971, Åre (SWE)
GIANT SLALOM

1.	**DAVID ZWILLING**	**(AUT)**
2.	Sepp Heckelmiller	(FRG)
3.	Patrick Russel	(FRA)

14/03/1971, Åre (SWE)
SLALOM

1.	**JEAN-NOËL AUGERT**	**(FRA)**
2.	Gustav Thöni	(ITA)
3.	Edmund Bruggmann	(SUI)

1971-72

CUPS

OVERALL
1. **GUSTAV THÖNI** **(ITA)**
2. Henri Duvillard (FRA)
3. Edmund Bruggmann (SUI)

SLALOM
1. **JEAN-NOËL AUGERT** **(FRA)**
2. Andrzej Bachleda (POL)
3. Roland Thöni (ITA)

GIANT SLALOM
1. **GUSTAV THÖNI** **(ITA)**
2. Edmund Bruggmann (SUI)
3. Roger Rossat-Mignod (FRA)

DOWNHILL
1. **BERNHARD RUSSI** **(SUI)**
2. Karl Schranz (AUT)
3. Mike Lafferty (USA)

RACES

05/12/1971, Sankt Moritz (SUI)
DOWNHILL
1. **BERNHARD RUSSI** **(SUI)**
2. Heini Messner (AUT)
3. Walter Tresch (SUI)

09/12/1971, Val-d'Isère (FRA)
GIANT SLALOM
1. **ERIK HÅKER** **(NOR)**
2. Jean-Noël Augert (FRA)
3. Henri Duvillard (FRA)

12/12/1971, Val-d'Isère (FRA)
DOWNHILL
1. **KARL SCHRANZ** **(AUT)**
2. Heini Messner (AUT)
3. Michel Dätwyler (SUI)

19/12/1971, Sestriere (ITA)
SLALOM
1. **TYLER PALMER** **(USA)**
2. Jean-Noël Augert (FRA)
3. Harald Rofner (AUT)

09/01/1972, Berchtesgaden (FRG)
SLALOM
1. **HENRI DUVILLARD** **(FRA)**
2. Max Rieger (FRG)
3. Andrzej Bachleda (POL)

10/01/1972, Berchtesgaden (FRG)
GIANT SLALOM
1. **ROGER ROSSAT-MIGNOD** **(FRA)**
2. Gustav Thöni (ITA)
3. Walter Tresch (SUI)

14/01/1972, Kitzbühel (AUT)
DOWNHILL
1. **KARL SCHRANZ** **(AUT)**
2. Henri Duvillard (FRA)
3. Bernhard Russi (SUI)

15/01/1972, Kitzbühel (AUT)
DOWNHILL
1. **KARL SCHRANZ** **(AUT)**
2. Henri Duvillard (FRA)
3. Heini Messner (AUT)

16/01/1972, Kitzbühel (AUT)
SLALOM
1. **JEAN-NOËL AUGERT** **(FRA)**
2. Edmund Bruggmann (SUI)
3. Andrzej Bachleda (POL)

23/01/1972, Wengen (SUI)
SLALOM
1. **JEAN-NOËL AUGERT** **(FRA)**
2. Gustav Thöni (ITA)
3. Bob Cochran (USA)

24/01/1972, Adelboden (SUI)
GIANT SLALOM
1. **WERNER MATTLE** **(SUI)**
2. Adolf Rösti (SUI)
3. Gustav Thöni (ITA)

18/02/1972, Banff (CAN)
GIANT SLALOM
1. **ERIK HÅKER** **(NOR)**
2. Sepp Heckelmiller (FRG)
3. Helmuth Schmalzl (ITA)

19/02/1972, Banff (CAN)
SLALOM
1. **ANDRZEJ BACHLEDA** **(POL)**

2.	Jean-Noël Augert	(FRA)
3.	Gustav Thöni	(ITA)

25/02/1972, Crystal Mountain (USA)
DOWNHILL
1.	**BERNHARD RUSSI**	**(SUI)**
2.	Mike Lafferty	(USA)
3.	Jean-Daniel Dätwyler	(SUI)

26/02/1972, Crystal Mountain (USA)
DOWNHILL
1.	**FRANZ VOGLER**	**(FRG)**
2.	Bernhard Russi	(SUI)
3.	Jean-Daniel Dätwyler	(SUI)

02/03/1972, Heavenly Valley (USA)
GIANT SLALOM
1.	**GUSTAV THÖNI**	**(ITA)**
2.	Henri Duvillard	(FRA)
3.	David Zwilling	(AUT)

15/03/1972, Val Gardena (ITA)
DOWNHILL
1.	**BERNHARD RUSSI**	**(SUI)**
2.	René Berthod	(SUI)
3.	Mike Lafferty	(USA)

16/03/1972, Val Gardena (ITA)
GIANT SLALOM
1.	**EDMUND BRUGGMANN**	**(SUI)**
2.	Reinhard Tritscher	(AUT)
3.	Roland Thöni	(ITA)

17/03/1972, Madonna di Campiglio (ITA)
SLALOM
1.	**ROLAND THÖNI**	**(ITA)**
2.	Alain Penz	(FRA)
3.	Andrzej Bachleda	(POL)

18/03/1972, Pra Loup (FRA)
SLALOM
1.	**ROLAND THÖNI**	**(ITA)**
2.	Gustav Thöni	(ITA)
3.	Edmund Bruggmann	(SUI)

19/03/1972, Pra Loup (FRA)
GIANT SLALOM
1.	**EDMUND BRUGGMANN**	**(SUI)**
2.	Gustav Thöni	(ITA)
3.	Roger Rossat-Mignod	(FRA)

1972-73

CUPS

OVERALL
1.	**GUSTAV THÖNI**	**(ITA)**
2.	David Zwilling	(AUT)
3.	Roland Collombin	(SUI)

SLALOM
1.	**GUSTAV THÖNI**	**(ITA)**
2.	Christian Neureuther	(FRG)
3.	Jean-Noël Augert	(FRA)

GIANT SLALOM
1.	**HANSI HINTERSEER**	**(AUT)**
2.	Erik Håker	(NOR)
3.	Adolf Rösti	(SUI)

DOWNHILL
1.	**ROLAND COLLOMBIN**	**(SUI)**
2.	Bernhard Russi	(SUI)
3.	Marcello Varallo	(ITA)

RACES

08/12/1972, Val-d'Isère (FRA)
GIANT SLALOM
1.	**PIERO GROS**	**(ITA)**
2.	Erik Håker	(NOR)
3.	Helmuth Schmalzl	(ITA)

10/12/1972, Val-d'Isère (FRA)
DOWNHILL
1.	**REINHARD TRITSCHER**	**(AUT)**
2.	David Zwilling	(AUT)
3.	Marcello Varallo	(ITA)

15/12/1972, Val Gardena (ITA)
DOWNHILL
1.	**ROLAND COLLOMBIN**	**(SUI)**
2.	Karl Cordin	(AUT)
3.	David Zwilling	(AUT)

17/12/1972, Madonna di Campiglio (ITA)
SLALOM
1.	**PIERO GROS**	**(ITA)**
2.	Gustav Thöni	(ITA)
3.	Christian Neureuther	(FRG)

19/12/1972, Madonna di Campiglio (ITA)
GIANT SLALOM
1. **DAVID ZWILLING** **(AUT)**
2. Adolf Rösti (SUI)
3. Helmuth Schmalzl (ITA)

06/01/1973, Garmisch-Partenkirchen (FRG)
DOWNHILL
1. **ROLAND COLLOMBIN** **(SUI)**
2. Philippe Roux (SUI)
= Marcello Varallo (ITA)

07/01/1973, Garmisch-Partenkirchen (FRG)
DOWNHILL
1. **ROLAND COLLOMBIN** **(SUI)**
2. Marcello Varallo (ITA)
3. Bernhard Russi (SUI)

13/01/1973, Grindelwald (SUI)
DOWNHILL
1. **BERNHARD RUSSI** **(SUI)**
2. Roland Collombin (SUI)
3. Reinhard Tritscher (AUT)

14/01/1973, Wengen (SUI)
SLALOM
1. **CHRISTIAN NEUREUTHER** **(FRG)**
2. Walter Tresch (SUI)
3. Claude Perrot (FRA)

15/01/1973, Adelboden (SUI)
GIANT SLALOM
1. **GUSTAV THÖNI** **(ITA)**
2. Hansi Hinterseer (AUT)
3. Erik Håker (NOR)

19/01/1973, Megève (FRA)
GIANT SLALOM
1. **HENRI DUVILLARD** **(FRA)**
2. Hansi Hinterseer (AUT)
3. Gustav Thöni (ITA)

21/01/1973, Megève (FRA)
SLALOM
1. **CHRISTIAN NEUREUTHER** **(FRG)**
2. Gustav Thöni (ITA)
3. Walter Tresch (SUI)

27/01/1973, Kitzbühel (AUT)
DOWNHILL
1. **ROLAND COLLOMBIN** **(SUI)**

2. Bernhard Russi (SUI)
3. Bob Cochran (USA)

28/01/1973, Kitzbühel (AUT)
SLALOM
1. **JEAN-NOËL AUGERT** **(FRA)**
2. Gustav Thöni (ITA)
3. Andrzej Bachleda (POL)

03/02/1973, Sankt Anton am Arlberg (AUT)
DOWNHILL
1. **BERNHARD RUSSI** **(SUI)**
2. Franz Klammer (AUT)
3. Philippe Roux (SUI)

04/02/1973, Sankt Anton am Arlberg (AUT)
SLALOM
1. **GUSTAV THÖNI** **(ITA)**
2. Christian Neureuther (FRG)
3. Henri Duvillard (FRA)

11/02/1973, Sankt Moritz (SUI)
DOWNHILL
1. **WERNER GRISSMANN** **(AUT)**
2. Josef Walcher (AUT)
3. Franz Klammer (AUT)

02/03/1973, Mont-Sainte-Anne (CAN)
GIANT SLALOM
1. **MAX RIEGER** **(FRG)**
2. Hansi Hinterseer (AUT)
3. Franz Klammer (AUT)

04/03/1973, Mont-Sainte-Anne (CAN)
SLALOM
1. **GUSTAV THÖNI** **(ITA)**
2. Ilario Pegorari (ITA)
3. Christian Neureuther (FRG)

08/03/1973, Anchorage (USA)
GIANT SLALOM
1. **HANSI HINTERSEER** **(AUT)**
2. Adolf Rösti (SUI)
3. Josef Pechtl (AUT)

12/03/1973, Naeba (JPN)
GIANT SLALOM
1. **ERIK HÅKER** **(NOR)**
2. Hansi Hinterseer (AUT)
3. Adolf Rösti (SUI)

15/03/1973, Naeba (JPN)
SLALOM
1.	**JEAN-NOËL AUGERT**	**(FRA)**
2.	Christian Neureuther	(FRG)
3.	Ilario Pegorari	(ITA)

23/03/1973, Heavenly Valley (USA)
SLALOM
1.	**JEAN-NOËL AUGERT**	**(FRA)**
2.	Bob Cochran	(USA)
3.	Tino Pietrogiovanna	(ITA)

24/03/1973, Heavenly Valley (USA)
GIANT SLALOM
1.	**BOB COCHRAN**	**(USA)**
2.	Erwin Stricker	(ITA)
3.	Jean-Noël Augert	(FRA)

1973-74

CUPS

OVERALL
1.	**PIERO GROS**	**(ITA)**
2.	Gustav Thöni	(ITA)
3.	Hansi Hinterseer	(AUT)

SLALOM
1.	**GUSTAV THÖNI**	**(ITA)**
2.	Christian Neureuther	(FRG)
3.	Johann Kniewasser	(AUT)

GIANT SLALOM
1.	**PIERO GROS**	**(ITA)**
2.	Hansi Hinterseer	(AUT)
3.	Gustav Thöni	(ITA)

DOWNHILL
1.	**ROLAND COLLOMBIN**	**(SUI)**
2.	Franz Klammer	(AUT)
3.	Herbert Plank	(ITA)

RACES

08/12/1973, Val-d'Isère (FRA)
GIANT SLALOM
1.	**HANSI HINTERSEER**	**(AUT)**
2.	Helmuth Schmalzl	(ITA)
3.	Piero Gros	(ITA)

10/12/1973, Val-d'Isère (FRA)
DOWNHILL
1.	**HERBERT PLANK**	**(ITA)**
2.	Werner Grissmann	(AUT)
3.	Franz Klammer	(AUT)

16/12/1973, Saalbach (AUT)
GIANT SLALOM
1.	**HUBERT BERCHTOLD**	**(AUT)**
2.	Thomas Hauser	(AUT)
3.	Hansi Hinterseer	(AUT)

17/12/1973, Vipiteno (ITA)
SLALOM
1.	**PIERO GROS**	**(ITA)**
2.	Hans Kniewasser	(AUT)
3.	Christian Neureuther	(FRG)

18/12/1973, Zell am See (AUT)
DOWNHILL

1.	**KARL CORDIN**	**(AUT)**
2.	Roland Collombin	(SUI)
3.	Peter Feyersinger	(AUT)
=	Manfred Grabler	(AUS)
=	Josef Walcher	(AUT)

22/12/1973, Schladming (AUT)
DOWNHILL

1.	**FRANZ KLAMMER**	**(AUT)**
2.	Roland Collombin	(SUI)
3.	Bernhard Russi	(SUI)

05/01/1974, Garmisch-Partenkirchen (FRG)
SLALOM

1.	**CHRISTIAN NEUREUTHER**	**(FRG)**
2.	Gustav Thöni	(ITA)
3.	Hansjörg Schlager	(FRG)

06/01/1974, Garmisch-Partenkirchen (FRG)
DOWNHILL

1.	**ROLAND COLLOMBIN**	**(SUI)**
2.	Franz Klammer	(AUT)
3.	Herbert Plank	(ITA)

07/01/1974, Berchtesgaden (FRG)
GIANT SLALOM

1.	**PIERO GROS**	**(ITA)**
2.	Gustav Thöni	(ITA)
3.	Erwin Stricker	(ITA)

12/01/1974, Avoriaz (FRA)
DOWNHILL

1.	**ROLAND COLLOMBIN**	**(SUI)**
2.	Franz Klammer	(AUT)
3.	Philippe Roux	(SUI)

13/01/1974, Morzine (FRA)
GIANT SLALOM

1.	**PIERO GROS**	**(ITA)**
2.	Hansi Hinterseer	(AUT)
3.	Gustav Thöni	(ITA)

19/01/1974, Wengen (SUI)
DOWNHILL

1.	**ROLAND COLLOMBIN**	**(SUI)**
2.	Franz Klammer	(AUT)
3.	Herbert Plank	(ITA)

20/01/1974, Wengen (SUI)
SLALOM

1.	**CHRISTIAN NEUREUTHER**	**(FRG)**
2.	Fausto Radici	(ITA)
3.	David Zwilling	(AUT)

21/01/1974, Adelboden (SUI)
GIANT SLALOM

1.	**GUSTAV THÖNI**	**(ITA)**
2.	Piero Gros	(ITA)
3.	Hansi Hinterseer	(AUT)

26/01/1974, Kitzbühel (AUT)
DOWNHILL

1.	**ROLAND COLLOMBIN**	**(SUI)**
2.	Stefano Anzi	(ITA)
=	Giuliano Besson	(ITA)

27/01/1974, Kitzbühel (AUT)
SLALOM

1.	**HANSI HINTERSEER**	**(AUT)**
2.	Hans Kniewasser	(AUT)
3.	Gustav Thöni	(ITA)

02/03/1974, Voss (NOR)
GIANT SLALOM

1.	**GUSTAV THÖNI**	**(ITA)**
2.	Hansi Hinterseer	(AUT)
3.	Ingemar Stenmark	(SWE)

03/03/1974, Voss (NOR)
SLALOM

1.	**PIERO GROS**	**(ITA)**
2.	Ingemar Stenmark	(SWE)
3.	Hans Kniewasser	(AUT)

06/03/1974, Zakopane (POL)
SLALOM

1.	**FRANCISCO FERNÁNDEZ OCHOA**	**(ESP)**
2.	Gustav Thöni	(ITA)
3.	Hansi Hinterseer	(AUT)

09/03/1974, Vysoké Tatry (TCH)
GIANT SLALOM

1.	**PIERO GROS**	**(ITA)**
2.	Ingemar Stenmark	(SWE)
3.	Hansi Hinterseer	(AUT)

10/03/1974, Vysoké Tatry (TCH)
SLALOM

1.	**GUSTAV THÖNI**	**(ITA)**

2.	Ingemar Stenmark	(SWE)
3.	Francisco Fernández Ochoa	(ESP)

1974-75

CUPS

OVERALL

1.	**GUSTAV THÖNI**	**(ITA)**
2.	Ingemar Stenmark	(SWE)
3.	Franz Klammer	(AUT)

SLALOM

1.	**INGEMAR STENMARK**	**(SWE)**
2.	Gustav Thöni	(ITA)
3.	Piero Gros	(ITA)

GIANT SLALOM

1.	**INGEMAR STENMARK**	**(SWE)**
2.	Piero Gros	(ITA)
3.	Erik Håker	(NOR)

DOWNHILL

1.	**FRANZ KLAMMER**	**(AUT)**
2.	Werner Grissmann	(AUT)
3.	Herbert Plank	(ITA)

RACES

05/12/1974, Val-d'Isère (FRA)
GIANT SLALOM

1.	**PIERO GROS**	**(ITA)**
2.	Ingemar Stenmark	(SWE)
3.	Erik Håker	(NOR)

08/12/1974, Val-d'Isère (FRA)
DOWNHILL

1.	**FRANZ KLAMMER**	**(AUT)**
2.	Werner Grissmann	(AUT)
3.	Michael Veith	(FRG)

15/12/1974, Sankt Moritz (SUI)
DOWNHILL

1.	**FRANZ KLAMMER**	**(AUT)**
2.	Herbert Plank	(ITA)
3.	Werner Grissmann	(AUT)

17/12/1974, Madonna di Campiglio (ITA)
SLALOM

1.	**INGEMAR STENMARK**	**(SWE)**
2.	Paolo De Chiesa	(ITA)
3.	Fausto Radici	(ITA)

18/12/1974, Madonna di Campiglio (ITA)
GIANT SLALOM
1. **PIERO GROS** **(ITA)**
2. Greg Jones (USA)
3. Tino Pietrogiovanna (ITA)

05/01/1975, Garmisch-Partenkirchen (FRG)
DOWNHILL
1. **FRANZ KLAMMER** **(AUT)**
2. Werner Grissmann (AUT)
3. Josef Walcher (AUT)

06/01/1975, Garmisch-Partenkirchen (FRG)
SLALOM
1. **PIERO GROS** **(ITA)**
2. Gustav Thöni (ITA)
3. Fausto Radici (ITA)

11/01/1975, Wengen (SUI)
DOWNHILL
1. **FRANZ KLAMMER** **(AUT)**
2. Herbert Plank (ITA)
3. Erik Håker (NOR)

12/01/1975, Wengen (SUI)
SLALOM
1. **INGEMAR STENMARK** **(SWE)**
2. Piero Gros (ITA)
3. Paolo De Chiesa (ITA)

12/01/1975, Wengen (SUI)
COMBINED
1. **GUSTAV THÖNI** **(ITA)**
2. David Zwilling (AUT)
3. Walter Tresch (SUI)

13/01/1975, Adelboden (SUI)
GIANT SLALOM
1. **PIERO GROS** **(ITA)**
2. Gustav Thöni (ITA)
3. Werner Mattle (SUI)

18/01/1975, Kitzbühel (AUT)
DOWNHILL
1. **FRANZ KLAMMER** **(AUT)**
2. Gustav Thöni (ITA)
3. Werner Grissmann (AUT)

19/01/1975, Kitzbühel (AUT)
SLALOM
1. **PIERO GROS** **(ITA)**
2. Ingemar Stenmark (SWE)
3. Paolo De Chiesa (ITA)

19/01/1975, Kitzbühel (AUT)
COMBINED
1. **GUSTAV THÖNI** **(ITA)**
2. Francisco Fernández Ochoa (ESP)
3. Franz Klammer (AUT)

21/01/1975, Fulpmes (AUT)
GIANT SLALOM
1. **ERIK HÅKER** **(NOR)**
2. Ingemar Stenmark (SWE)
3. Hansi Hinterseer (AUT)

26/01/1975, Innsbruck (AUT)
DOWNHILL
1. **FRANZ KLAMMER** **(AUT)**
2. Bernhard Russi (SUI)
3. Herbert Plank (ITA)

30/01/1975, Chamonix (FRA)
SLALOM
1. **GUSTAV THÖNI** **(ITA)**
2. Ingemar Stenmark (SWE)
3. Hansi Hinterseer (AUT)

01/02/1975, Megève (FRA)
DOWNHILL
1. **WALTER VESTI** **(SUI)**
2. René Berthod (SUI)
3. Philippe Roux (SUI)

30/01-01/02/1975, Chamonix/Megève (FRA)
COMBINED
1. **GUSTAV THÖNI** **(ITA)**
2. Francisco Fernández Ochoa (ESP)
3. Erik Håker (NOR)

21/02/1975, Naeba (JPN)
SLALOM
1. **HANSI HINTERSEER** **(AUT)**
2. Ingemar Stenmark (SWE)
3. Christian Neureuther (FRG)

23/02/1975, Naeba (JPN)
GIANT SLALOM
1. **INGEMAR STENMARK** **(SWE)**
2. Erik Håker (NOR)
3. Hansi Hinterseer (AUT)

02/03/1975, Garibaldi (CAN)
GIANT SLALOM

1.	**INGEMAR STENMARK**	**(SWE)**
2.	Heini Hemmi	(SUI)
3.	Gustav Thöni	(ITA)

09/03/1975, Jackson Hole (USA)
DOWNHILL

1.	**FRANZ KLAMMER**	**(AUT)**
2.	Michael Veith	(FRG)
3.	René Berthod	(SUI)

13/03/1975, Sun Valley (USA)
GIANT SLALOM

1.	**INGEMAR STENMARK**	**(SWE)**
2.	Piero Gros	(ITA)
3.	Gustav Thöni	(ITA)

15/03/1975, Sun Valley (USA)
SLALOM

1.	**GUSTAV THÖNI**	**(ITA)**
2.	Piero Gros	(ITA)
3.	Ingemar Stenmark	(SWE)

21/03/1975, Val Gardena (ITA)
DOWNHILL

1.	**FRANZ KLAMMER**	**(AUT)**
2.	Erik Håker	(NOR)
3.	Bernhard Russi	(SUI)

23/03/1975, Val Gardena (ITA)
PARALLEL SLALOM

1.	**GUSTAV THÖNI**	**(ITA)**
2.	Ingemar Stenmark	(SWE)
3.	Walter Tresch	(SUI)

1975-76

CUPS

OVERALL

1.	**INGEMAR STENMARK**	**(SWE)**
2.	Piero Gros	(ITA)
3.	Gustav Thöni	(ITA)

SLALOM

1.	**INGEMAR STENMARK**	**(SWE)**
2.	Piero Gros	(ITA)
3.	Gustav Thöni	(ITA)
=	Hansi Hinterseer	(AUT)

GIANT SLALOM

1.	**INGEMAR STENMARK**	**(SWE)**
2.	Gustav Thöni	(ITA)
3.	Piero Gros	(ITA)

DOWNHILL

1.	**FRANZ KLAMMER**	**(AUT)**
2.	Herbert Plank	(ITA)
3.	Bernhard Russi	(SUI)

COMBINED

1.	**WALTER TRESCH**	**(SUI)**
2.	Gustav Thöni	(ITA)
3.	Jim Hunter	(CAN)

RACES

05/12/1975, Val-d'Isère (FRA)
GIANT SLALOM

1.	**GUSTAV THÖNI**	**(ITA)**
2.	Ingemar Stenmark	(SWE)
3.	Piero Gros	(ITA)

07/12/1975, Val-d'Isère (FRA)
DOWNHILL

1.	**KEN READ**	**(CAN)**
2.	Herbert Plank	(ITA)
3.	Bernhard Russi	(SUI)

12/12/1975, Madonna di Campiglio (ITA)
DOWNHILL

1.	**FRANZ KLAMMER**	**(AUT)**
2.	Philippe Roux	(SUI)
3.	Erik Håker	(NOR)

14/12/1975, Madonna di Campiglio (ITA)
GIANT SLALOM
1. **ENGELHARD PARGÄTZI** **(SUI)**
2. Ernst Good (SUI)
3. Piero Gros (ITA)

15/12/1975, Vipiteno (ITA)
SLALOM
1. **INGEMAR STENMARK** **(SWE)**
2. Hansi Hinterseer (AUT)
3. Piero Gros (ITA)

20/12/1975, Schladming (AUT)
DOWNHILL
1. **DAVE IRWIN** **(CAN)**
2. Klaus Eberhard (AUT)
3. Herbert Plank (ITA)

21/12/1975, Schladming (AUT)
SLALOM
1. **HANSI HINTERSEER** **(AUT)**
2. Ingemar Stenmark (SWE)
3. Piero Gros (ITA)

05/01/1976, Garmisch-Partenkirchen (FRG)
SLALOM
1. **FAUSTO RADICI** **(ITA)**
2. Piero Gros (ITA)
3. Ingemar Stenmark (SWE)

09/01/1976, Wengen (SUI)
DOWNHILL
1. **HERBERT PLANK** **(ITA)**
2. Franz Klammer (AUT)
3. Bernhard Russi (SUI)

*05-09/01/1976, Garmisch-Partenkirchen
(FRG)/Wengen (SUI)*
COMBINED
1. **WALTER TRESCH** **(SUI)**
2. Piero Gros (ITA)
3. Gustav Thöni (ITA)

10/01/1976, Wengen (SUI)
DOWNHILL
1. **FRANZ KLAMMER** **(AUT)**
2. Philippe Roux (SUI)
3. Jim Hunter (CAN)

11/01/1976, Wengen (SUI)
SLALOM
1. **INGEMAR STENMARK** **(SWE)**
2. Piero Gros (ITA)
3. Christian Neureuther (FRG)

11/01/1976, Wengen (SUI)
COMBINED
1. **FRANZ KLAMMER** **(AUT)**
2. Gustav Thöni (ITA)
3. Walter Tresch (SUI)

12/01/1976, Adelboden (SUI)
GIANT SLALOM
1. **GUSTAV THÖNI** **(ITA)**
2. Ingemar Stenmark (SWE)
3. Engelhard Pargätzi (SUI)

17/01/1976, Morzine (FRA)
DOWNHILL
1. **FRANZ KLAMMER** **(AUT)**
2. Bernhard Russi (SUI)
3. Anton Steiner (AUT)

18/01/1976, Morzine (FRA)
GIANT SLALOM
1. **FRANCO BIELER** **(ITA)**
2. Piero Gros (ITA)
3. Ingemar Stenmark (SWE)

24/01/1976, Kitzbühel (AUT)
SLALOM
1. **INGEMAR STENMARK** **(SWE)**
2. Gustav Thöni (ITA)
3. Piero Gros (ITA)

25/01/1976, Kitzbühel (AUT)
DOWNHILL
1. **FRANZ KLAMMER** **(AUT)**
2. Erik Håker (NOR)
3. Josef Walcher (AUT)

25/01/1976, Kitzbühel (AUT)
COMBINED
1. **WALTER TRESCH** **(SUI)**
2. Jim Hunter (CAN)
3. Gustav Thöni (ITA)

27/01/1976, Zwiesel (FRG)
GIANT SLALOM
1. **INGEMAR STENMARK** **(SWE)**
2. Gustav Thöni (ITA)
3. Hansi Hinterseer (AUT)

05/03/1976, Copper Mountain (USA)
GIANT SLALOM

1. **GREG JONES** **(USA)**
2. Phil Mahre (USA)
3. Engelhard Pargätzi (SUI)

07/03/1976, Copper Mountain (USA)
SLALOM

1. **INGEMAR STENMARK** **(SWE)**
2. Steve Mahre (USA)
3. Gustav Thöni (ITA)

12/03/1976, Aspen (USA)
DOWNHILL

1. **FRANZ KLAMMER** **(AUT)**
2. René Berthod (SUI)
3. Ernst Winkler (AUT)

14/03/1976, Aspen (USA)
SLALOM

1. **INGEMAR STENMARK** **(SWE)**
2. Phil Mahre (USA)
3. Gustav Thöni (ITA)

18/03/1976, Mont-Sainte-Anne (CAN)
GIANT SLALOM

1. **HEINI HEMMI** **(SUI)**
2. Piero Gros (ITA)
3. Ernst Good (SUI)

1976-77

CUPS

OVERALL

1. **INGEMAR STENMARK** **(SWE)**
2. Klaus Heidegger (AUT)
3. Franz Klammer (AUT)

SLALOM

1. **INGEMAR STENMARK** **(SWE)**
2. Klaus Heidegger (AUT)
3. Paul Frommelt (LIE)

GIANT SLALOM

1. **HEINI HEMMI** **(SUI)**
2. Ingemar Stenmark (SWE)
3. Klaus Heidegger (AUT)

DOWNHILL

1. **FRANZ KLAMMER** **(AUT)**
2. Josef Walcher (AUT)
3. Bernhard Russi (SUI)

RACES

10/12/1976, Val-d'Isère (FRA)
GIANT SLALOM

1. **PHIL MAHRE** **(USA)**
2. Ingemar Stenmark (SWE)
3. Klaus Heidegger (AUT)

12/12/1976, Val-d'Isère (FRA)
GIANT SLALOM

1. **HEINI HEMMI** **(SUI)**
2. Piero Gros (ITA)
3. Phil Mahre (USA)

17/12/1976, Val Gardena (ITA)
DOWNHILL

1. **FRANZ KLAMMER** **(AUT)**
2. Herbert Plank (ITA)
3. Erik Håker (NOR)

18/12/1976, Val Gardena (ITA)
DOWNHILL

1. **FRANZ KLAMMER** **(AUT)**
2. Josef Walcher (AUT)
3. Bernhard Russi (SUI)

19/12/1976, Madonna di Campiglio (ITA)
SLALOM

1.	**FAUSTO RADICI**	**(ITA)**
2.	Piero Gros	(ITA)
3.	Gustav Thöni	(ITA)

02/01/1977, Ebnat-Kappel (SUI)
GIANT SLALOM

1.	**HEINI HEMMI**	**(SUI)**
2.	Christian Hemmi	(SUI)
3.	Gustav Thöni	(ITA)

03/01/1977, Laax (SUI)
SLALOM

1.	**INGEMAR STENMARK**	**(SWE)**
2.	Paul Frommelt	(LIE)
3.	Walter Tresch	(SUI)

08/01/1977, Garmisch-Partenkirchen (FRG)
DOWNHILL

1.	**FRANZ KLAMMER**	**(AUT)**
2.	Ernst Winkler	(AUT)
3.	Peter Wirnsberger	(AUT)

09/01/1977, Garmisch-Partenkirchen (FRG)
GIANT SLALOM

1.	**KLAUS HEIDEGGER**	**(AUT)**
2.	Heini Hemmi	(SUI)
3.	Willi Frommelt	(LIE)

10/01/1977, Berchtesgaden (FRG)
SLALOM

1.	**INGEMAR STENMARK**	**(SWE)**
2.	Klaus Heidegger	(AUT)
3.	Alois Morgenstern	(AUT)

15/01/1977, Kitzbühel (AUT)
DOWNHILL

1.	**FRANZ KLAMMER**	**(AUT)**
2.	René Berthod	(SUI)
3.	Bernhard Russi	(SUI)

16/01/1977, Kitzbühel (AUT)
SLALOM

1.	**INGEMAR STENMARK**	**(SWE)**
2.	Piero Gros	(ITA)
3.	Franco Bieler	(ITA)

16/01/1977, Kitzbühel (AUT)
COMBINED

1.	**GUSTAV THÖNI**	**(ITA)**
2.	Walter Tresch	(SUI)
3.	Anton Steiner	(AUT)

22/01/1977, Wengen (SUI)
DOWNHILL

1.	**FRANZ KLAMMER**	**(AUT)**
2.	Sepp Ferstl	(FRG)
3.	Bernhard Russi	(SUI)

23/01/1977, Wengen (SUI)
SLALOM

1.	**INGEMAR STENMARK**	**(SWE)**
2.	Paul Frommelt	(LIE)
3.	Klaus Heidegger	(AUT)

23/01/1977, Wengen (SUI)
COMBINED

1.	**WALTER TRESCH**	**(SUI)**
2.	Gustav Thöni	(ITA)
3.	Sepp Ferstl	(FRG)

24/01/1977, Adelboden (SUI)
GIANT SLALOM

1.	**HEINI HEMMI**	**(SUI)**
2.	Ingemar Stenmark	(SWE)
3.	Klaus Heidegger	(AUT)

30/01/1977, Morzine (FRA)
DOWNHILL

1.	**BERNHARD RUSSI**	**(SUI)**
2.	Josef Walcher	(AUT)
3.	Ernst Winkler	(AUT)

31/01/1977, Morzine (FRA)
DOWNHILL

1.	**JOSEF WALCHER**	**(AUT)**
2.	Herbert Plank	(ITA)
3.	Bernhard Russi	(SUI)

06/02/1977, Sankt Anton am Arlberg (AUT)
SLALOM

1.	**INGEMAR STENMARK**	**(SWE)**
2.	Klaus Heidegger	(AUT)
3.	Paul Frommelt	(LIE)

18/02/1977, Laax (SUI)
DOWNHILL

1.	**FRANZ KLAMMER**	**(AUT)**
2.	Sepp Ferstl	(FRG)
3.	Bernhard Russi	(SUI)

06-18/02/1977, Sankt Anton am Arlberg (AUT)/Laax (SUI)
COMBINED

1.	**SEPP FERSTL**	**(FRG)**
2.	Peter Lüscher	(SUI)
3.	Franz Klammer	(AUT)

25/02/1977, Furano (JPN)
GIANT SLALOM

1.	**HANSI HINTERSEER**	**(AUT)**
2.	Manfred Brunner	(AUT)
3.	Ernst Good	(SUI)

27/02/1977, Furano (JPN)
SLALOM

1.	**KLAUS HEIDEGGER**	**(AUT)**
2.	Ingemar Stenmark	(SWE)
3.	Bruno Nöckler	(ITA)

05/03/1977, Sun Valley (USA)
SLALOM

1.	**PHIL MAHRE**	**(USA)**
2.	Ingemar Stenmark	(SWE)
3.	Steve Mahre	(USA)

06/03/1977, Sun Valley (USA)
GIANT SLALOM

1.	**INGEMAR STENMARK**	**(SWE)**
2.	Christian Hemmi	(SUI)
3.	Heini Hemmi	(SUI)

12/03/1977, Heavenly Valley (USA)
DOWNHILL

1.	**JOSEF WALCHER**	**(AUT)**
2.	Werner Grissmann	(AUT)
3.	Bernhard Russi	(SUI)

13/03/1977, Heavenly Valley (USA)
DOWNHILL

1.	**BARTL GENSBICHLER**	**(AUT)**
2.	Ernst Winkler	(AUT)
3.	Peter Fischer	(FRG)

17/03/1977, Voss (NOR)
GIANT SLALOM

1.	**KLAUS HEIDEGGER**	**(AUT)**
2.	Piero Gros	(ITA)
3.	Phil Mahre	(USA)

18/03/1977, Voss (NOR)
SLALOM

1.	**INGEMAR STENMARK**	**(SWE)**
2.	Piero Gros	(ITA)
3.	Christian Neureuther	(FRG)

20/03/1977, Åre (SWE)
SLALOM

1.	**INGEMAR STENMARK**	**(SWE)**
2.	Franco Bieler	(ITA)
3.	Gustav Thöni	(ITA)

22/03/1977, Åre (SWE)
GIANT SLALOM

1.	**INGEMAR STENMARK**	**(SWE)**
2.	Klaus Heidegger	(AUT)
3.	Miloslav Sochor	(TCH)

25/03/1977, Sierra Nevada (ESP)
GIANT SLALOM

1.	**INGEMAR STENMARK**	**(SWE)**
2.	Heini Hemmi	(SUI)
3.	Christian Hemmi	(SUI)

1977-78

CUPS

OVERALL
1.	**INGEMAR STENMARK**	**(SWE)**
2.	Phil Mahre	(USA)
3.	Andreas Wenzel	(LIE)

SLALOM
1.	**INGEMAR STENMARK**	**(SWE)**
2.	Klaus Heidegger	(AUT)
3.	Phil Mahre	(USA)

GIANT SLALOM
1.	**INGEMAR STENMARK**	**(SWE)**
2.	Andreas Wenzel	(LIE)
3.	Phil Mahre	(USA)

DOWNHILL
1.	**FRANZ KLAMMER**	**(AUT)**
2.	Josef Walcher	(AUT)
3.	Herbert Plank	(ITA)

RACES

10/12/1977, Val-d'Isère (FRA)
GIANT SLALOM
1.	**INGEMAR STENMARK**	**(SWE)**
2.	Heini Hemmi	(SUI)
3.	Jean-Luc Fournier	(SUI)

11/12/1977, Val-d'Isère (FRA)
DOWNHILL
1.	**FRANZ KLAMMER**	**(AUT)**
2.	Herbert Plank	(ITA)
3.	Josef Walcher	(AUT)

13/12/1977, Madonna di Campiglio (ITA)
SLALOM
1.	**INGEMAR STENMARK**	**(SWE)**
2.	Klaus Heidegger	(AUT)
3.	Bojan Križaj	(YUG)

14/12/1977, Madonna di Campiglio (ITA)
GIANT SLALOM
1.	**INGEMAR STENMARK**	**(SWE)**
2.	Heini Hemmi	(SUI)
3.	Andreas Wenzel	(LIE)

18/12/1977, Val Gardena (ITA)
DOWNHILL
1.	**HERBERT PLANK**	**(ITA)**
2.	Peter Wirnsberger	(AUT)
3.	Franz Klammer	(AUT)

22/12/1977, Cortina d'Ampezzo (ITA)
DOWNHILL
1.	**HERBERT PLANK**	**(ITA)**
2.	Bernhard Russi	(SUI)
3.	Peter Wirnsberger	(AUT)

05/01/1978, Oberstaufen (FRG)
SLALOM
1.	**INGEMAR STENMARK**	**(SWE)**
2.	Klaus Heidegger	(AUT)
3.	Piero Gros	(ITA)

08/01/1978, Zwiesel (FRG)
GIANT SLALOM
1.	**INGEMAR STENMARK**	**(SWE)**
2.	Phil Mahre	(USA)
3.	Andreas Wenzel	(LIE)

09/01/1978, Zwiesel (FRG)
SLALOM
1.	**INGEMAR STENMARK**	**(SWE)**
2.	Mauro Bernardi	(ITA)
3.	Phil Mahre	(USA)

15/01/1978, Wengen (SUI)
SLALOM
1.	**KLAUS HEIDEGGER**	**(AUT)**
2.	Petăr Popangelov	(BUL)
3.	Mauro Bernardi	(ITA)

17/01/1978, Adelboden (SUI)
GIANT SLALOM
1.	**ANDREAS WENZEL**	**(LIE)**
2.	Ingemar Stenmark	(SWE)
3.	Piero Gros	(ITA)

20/01/1978, Kitzbühel (AUT)
DOWNHILL
1.	**JOSEF WALCHER**	**(AUT)**
2.	Walter Vesti	(SUI)
3.	Renato Antonioli	(ITA)

21/01/1978, Kitzbühel (AUT)
DOWNHILL
1.	**SEPP FERSTL**	**(FRG)**

=	**JOSEF WALCHER**	**(AUT)**
3.	Michael Veith	(FRG)

22/01/1978, Kitzbühel (AUT)
SLALOM

1.	**KLAUS HEIDEGGER**	**(AUT)**
2.	Petăr Popangelov	(BUL)
3.	Andreas Wenzel	(LIE)

11/02/1978, Les Houches (FRA)
DOWNHILL

1.	**KEN READ**	**(CAN)**
2.	Dave Murray	(CAN)
3.	Michael Veith	(FRG)

11/02/1978, Chamonix (FRA)
SLALOM

1.	**PHIL MAHRE**	**(USA)**
2.	Ingemar Stenmark	(SWE)
3.	Paolo De Chiesa	(ITA)

03/03/1978, Stratton Mountain (USA)
GIANT SLALOM

1.	**PHIL MAHRE**	**(USA)**
2.	Heini Hemmi	(SUI)
3.	Ingemar Stenmark	(SWE)

04/03/1978, Stratton Mountain (USA)
SLALOM

1.	**STEVE MAHRE**	**(USA)**
2.	Ingemar Stenmark	(SWE)
3.	Peter Lüscher	(SUI)

06/03/1978, Waterville Valley (USA)
GIANT SLALOM

1.	**ANDREAS WENZEL**	**(LIE)**
2.	Phil Mahre	(USA)
3.	Ingemar Stenmark	(SWE)

10/03/1978, Laax (SUI)
DOWNHILL

1.	**ULI SPIESS**	**(AUT)**
2.	Franz Klammer	(AUT)
3.	Erik Håker	(NOR)

11/03/1978, Laax (SUI)
DOWNHILL

1.	**FRANZ KLAMMER**	**(AUT)**
2.	Erik Håker	(NOR)
3.	Uli Spieß	(AUT)

18/03/1978, Arosa (SUI)
GIANT SLALOM

1.	**INGEMAR STENMARK**	**(SWE)**
2.	Andreas Wenzel	(LIE)
3.	Peter Lüscher	(SUI)

1978-79

CUPS

OVERALL
1.	**PETER LÜSCHER**	**(SUI)**
2.	Leonhard Stock	(AUT)
3.	Phil Mahre	(USA)

SLALOM
1.	**INGEMAR STENMARK**	**(SWE)**
2.	Phil Mahre	(USA)
3.	Christian Neureuther	(FRG)

GIANT SLALOM
1.	**INGEMAR STENMARK**	**(SWE)**
2.	Peter Lüscher	(SUI)
3.	Bojan Križaj	(YUG)

DOWNHILL
1.	**PETER MÜLLER**	**(SUI)**
2.	Peter Wirnsberger	(AUT)
3.	Toni Bürgler	(SUI)

RACES

09/12/1978, Schladming (AUT)
GIANT SLALOM
1.	**INGEMAR STENMARK**	**(SWE)**
2.	Peter Lüscher	(SUI)
3.	Leonardo David	(ITA)

10/12/1978, Schladming (AUT)
DOWNHILL
1.	**KEN READ**	**(CAN)**
2.	Dave Murray	(CAN)
3.	Vladimir Makeev	(URS)

10/12/1978, Schladming (AUT)
COMBINED
1.	**PETER LÜSCHER**	**(SUI)**
2.	Leonhard Stock	(AUT)
3.	Andreas Wenzel	(LIE)

13/12/1978, Madonna di Campiglio (ITA)
SLALOM
1.	**MARTIAL DONNET**	**(SUI)**
2.	Peter Lüscher	(SUI)
3.	Christian Neureuther	(FRG)

16/12/1978, Val Gardena (ITA)
DOWNHILL
1.	**JOSEF WALCHER**	**(AUT)**
2.	Peter Müller	(SUI)
3.	Walter Vesti	(SUI)

17/12/1978, Val Gardena (ITA)
DOWNHILL
1.	**ERIK HÅKER**	**(NOR)**
2.	Peter Müller	(SUI)
3.	Ken Read	(CAN)

21/12/1978, Kranjska Gora (YUG)
SLALOM
1.	**INGEMAR STENMARK**	**(SWE)**
2.	Paul Frommelt	(LIE)
3.	Leonardo David	(ITA)

22/12/1978, Kranjska Gora (YUG)
GIANT SLALOM
1.	**INGEMAR STENMARK**	**(SWE)**
2.	Peter Lüscher	(SUI)
3.	Bojan Križaj	(YUG)

06/01/1979, Morzine (FRA)
DOWNHILL
1.	**STEVE PODBORSKI**	**(CAN)**
2.	Herbert Plank	(ITA)
3.	Uli Spieß	(AUT)

07/01/1979, Courchevel (FRA)
GIANT SLALOM
1.	**INGEMAR STENMARK**	**(SWE)**
2.	Peter Lüscher	(SUI)
3.	Bojan Križaj	(YUG)

09/01/1979, Crans-Montana (SUI)
SLALOM
1.	**CHRISTIAN NEUREUTHER**	**(FRG)**
2.	Petăr Popangelov	(BUL)
3.	Karl Trojer	(ITA)

14/01/1979, Crans-Montana (SUI)
DOWNHILL
1.	**TONI BÜRGLER**	**(SUI)**
2.	Peter Müller	(SUI)
3.	Ken Read	(CAN)

15/01/1979, Crans-Montana (SUI)
SLALOM
1.	**PAUL FROMMELT**	**(LIE)**

| 2. | Andreas Wenzel | (LIE) |
| 3. | Ingemar Stenmark | (SWE) |

15/01/1979, Crans-Montana (SUI)
COMBINED

1.	**PHIL MAHRE**	**(USA)**
2.	Andreas Wenzel	(LIE)
3.	Piero Gros	(ITA)

16/01/1979, Adelboden (SUI)
GIANT SLALOM

1.	**INGEMAR STENMARK**	**(SWE)**
2.	Andreas Wenzel	(LIE)
3.	Jacques Lüthy	(SUI)

20/01/1979, Kitzbühel (AUT)
DOWNHILL

1.	**SEPP FERSTL**	**(FRG)**
2.	Peter Wirnsberger	(AUT)
3.	Uli Spieß	(AUT)

21/01/1979, Kitzbühel (AUT)
SLALOM

1.	**CHRISTIAN NEUREUTHER**	**(FRG)**
2.	Ingemar Stenmark	(SWE)
3.	Phil Mahre	(USA)

21/01/1979, Kitzbühel (AUT)
COMBINED

1.	**ANTON STEINER**	**(AUT)**
2.	Andreas Wenzel	(LIE)
3.	Peter Lüscher	(SUI)

23/01/1979, Steinach (AUT)
GIANT SLALOM

1.	**INGEMAR STENMARK**	**(SWE)**
2.	Peter Lüscher	(SUI)
3.	Andreas Wenzel	(LIE)

27/01/1979, Garmisch-Partenkirchen (FRG)
DOWNHILL

1.	**PETER WIRNSBERGER**	**(AUT)**
2.	Uli Spieß	(AUT)
3.	Herbert Plank	(ITA)

28/01/1979, Garmisch-Partenkirchen (FRG)
SLALOM

1.	**PETER LÜSCHER**	**(SUI)**
2.	Phil Mahre	(USA)
3.	Petăr Popangelov	(BUL)

28/01/1979, Garmisch-Partenkirchen (FRG)
COMBINED

1.	**PETER LÜSCHER**	**(SUI)**
2.	Phil Mahre	(USA)
3.	Andreas Wenzel	(LIE)

01/02/1979, Villars-sur-Ollon (SUI)
DOWNHILL

1.	**PETER MÜLLER**	**(SUI)**
2.	Leonhard Stock	(AUT)
3.	Werner Grissmann	(AUT)

04/02/1979, Jasná (TCH)
GIANT SLALOM

1.	**INGEMAR STENMARK**	**(SWE)**
2.	Bojan Križaj	(YUG)
3.	Heini Hemmi	(SUI)

05/02/1979, Jasná (TCH)
SLALOM

1.	**PHIL MAHRE**	**(USA)**
2.	Leonardo David	(ITA)
3.	Ingemar Stenmark	(SWE)

07/02/1979, Oslo (NOR)
SLALOM

1.	**LEONARDO DAVID**	**(ITA)**
2.	Ingemar Stenmark	(SWE)
3.	Phil Mahre	(USA)

10/02/1979, Åre (SWE)
GIANT SLALOM

1.	**INGEMAR STENMARK**	**(SWE)**
2.	Phil Mahre	(USA)
3.	Jacques Lüthy	(SUI)

11/02/1979, Åre (SWE)
SLALOM

1.	**INGEMAR STENMARK**	**(SWE)**
2.	Phil Mahre	(USA)
3.	Gustav Thöni	(ITA)

03/03/1979, Lake Placid (USA)
DOWNHILL

1.	**PETER WIRNSBERGER**	**(AUT)**
2.	Peter Müller	(SUI)
3.	Dave Murray	(CAN)

04/03/1979, Lake Placid (USA)
GIANT SLALOM

| 1. | **INGEMAR STENMARK** | **(SWE)** |

2.	Hans Enn	(AUT)
3.	Peter Lüscher	(SUI)

12/03/1979, Heavenly Valley (USA)
GIANT SLALOM

1.	**INGEMAR STENMARK**	**(SWE)**
2.	Bojan Križaj	(YUG)
3.	Hans Enn	(AUT)

17/03/1979, Furano (JPN)
SLALOM

1.	**INGEMAR STENMARK**	**(SWE)**
2.	Christian Neureuther	(FRG)
3.	Paul Frommelt	(LIE)

19/03/1979, Furano (JPN)
GIANT SLALOM

1.	**INGEMAR STENMARK**	**(SWE)**
2.	Heini Hemmi	(SUI)
3.	Jean-Luc Fournier	(SUI)

1979-80

CUPS

OVERALL

1.	**ANDREAS WENZEL**	**(LIE)**
2.	Ingemar Stenmark	(SWE)
3.	Phil Mahre	(USA)

SLALOM

1.	**INGEMAR STENMARK**	**(SWE)**
2.	Bojan Križaj	(YUG)
3.	Christian Neureuther	(FRG)

GIANT SLALOM

1.	**INGEMAR STENMARK**	**(SWE)**
2.	Hans Enn	(AUT)
3.	Jacques Lüthy	(SUI)

DOWNHILL

1.	**PETER MÜLLER**	**(SUI)**
2.	Ken Read	(CAN)
3.	Herbert Plank	(ITA)

COMBINED

1.	**PHIL MAHRE**	**(USA)**
2.	Andreas Wenzel	(LIE)
3.	Anton Steiner	(AUT)

RACES

07/12/1979, Val-d'Isère (FRA)
DOWNHILL

1.	**PETER WIRNSBERGER**	**(AUT)**
2.	Herbert Plank	(ITA)
3.	Erik Håker	(NOR)

08/12/1979, Val-d'Isère (FRA)
GIANT SLALOM

1.	**INGEMAR STENMARK**	**(SWE)**
2.	Bojan Križaj	(YUG)
3.	Hans Enn	(AUT)

08/12/1979, Val-d'Isère (FRA)
COMBINED

1.	**PHIL MAHRE**	**(USA)**
2.	Steve Mahre	(USA)
3.	Michel Vion	(FRA)

11/12/1979, Madonna di Campiglio (ITA)

SLALOM
1. **INGEMAR STENMARK** **(SWE)**
2. Bojan Križaj (YUG)
3. Paul Frommelt (LIE)

12/12/1979, Madonna di Campiglio (ITA)
GIANT SLALOM
1. **INGEMAR STENMARK** **(SWE)**
2. Jacques Lüthy (SUI)
3. Bojan Križaj (YUG)

16/12/1979, Val Gardena (ITA)
DOWNHILL
1. **PETER MÜLLER** **(SUI)**
2. Erik Håker (NOR)
3. Werner Grissmann (AUT)

11-16/12/1979, Madonna di Campiglio/Val Gardena (ITA)
COMBINED
1. **PETER LÜSCHER** **(SUI)**
2. Andreas Wenzel (LIE)
3. Anton Steiner (AUT)

06/01/1980, Pra Loup (FRA)
DOWNHILL
1. **PETER MÜLLER** **(SUI)**
2. Herbert Plank (ITA)
3. Erik Håker (NOR)

08/01/1980, Lenggries (FRG)
SLALOM
1. **PETAR POPANGELOV** **(BUL)**
2. Aleksandr Žirov (URS)
3. Ingemar Stenmark (SWE)

12/01/1980, Kitzbühel (AUT)
DOWNHILL
1. **KEN READ** **(CAN)**
2. Harti Weirather (AUT)
3. Herbert Plank (ITA)

08-12/01/1980, Lenggries (FRG)/Kitzbühel (AUT)
COMBINED
1. **ANDREAS WENZEL** **(LIE)**
2. Anton Steiner (AUT)
3. Phil Mahre (USA)

13/01/1980, Kitzbühel (AUT)
SLALOM
1. **ANDREAS WENZEL** **(LIE)**

2. Christian Neureuther (FRG)
3. Jacques Lüthy (SUI)

18/01/1980, Wengen (SUI)
DOWNHILL
1. **KEN READ** **(CAN)**
2. Josef Walcher (AUT)
3. Peter Wirnsberger (AUT)

19/01/1980, Wengen (SUI)
DOWNHILL
1. **PETER MÜLLER** **(SUI)**
2. Ken Read (CAN)
3. Steve Podborski (CAN)

20/01/1980, Wengen (SUI)
SLALOM
1. **BOJAN KRIŽAJ** **(YUG)**
2. Ingemar Stenmark (SWE)
3. Paul Frommelt (LIE)

21/01/1980, Adelboden (SUI)
GIANT SLALOM
1. **INGEMAR STENMARK** **(SWE)**
2. Jacques Lüthy (SUI)
3. Joël Gaspoz (SUI)

27/01/1980, Chamonix (FRA)
SLALOM
1. **INGEMAR STENMARK** **(SWE)**
2. Bojan Križaj (YUG)
3. Christian Orlainsky (AUT)

26/02/1980, Waterville Valley (USA)
GIANT SLALOM
1. **HANS ENN** **(AUT)**
2. Andreas Wenzel (LIE)
3. Jarle Halsnes (NOR)

27/02/1980, Waterville Valley (USA)
SLALOM
1. **INGEMAR STENMARK** **(SWE)**
2. Christian Neureuther (FRG)
3. Klaus Heidegger (AUT)

01/03/1980, Mont-Sainte-Anne (CAN)
GIANT SLALOM
1. **INGEMAR STENMARK** **(SWE)**
2. Phil Mahre (USA)
3. Bohumír Zeman (TCH)

04/03/1980, Lake Louise (CAN)
DOWNHILL

1.	**HERBERT PLANK**	**(ITA)**
2.	Harti Weirather	(AUT)
3.	Werner Grissmann	(AUT)

27/01-04/03/1980, Chamonix (FRA)/Lake Louise (CAN)
COMBINED

1.	**ANTON STEINER**	**(AUT)**
2.	Andreas Wenzel	(LIE)
3.	Phil Mahre	(USA)

08/03/1980, Oberstaufen (FRG)
GIANT SLALOM

1.	**ANDREAS WENZEL**	**(LIE)**
2.	Jacques Lüthy	(SUI)
3.	Ingemar Stenmark	(SWE)

10/03/1980, Cortina d'Ampezzo (ITA)
SLALOM

1.	**INGEMAR STENMARK**	**(SWE)**
2.	Aleksandr Žirov	(URS)
3.	Christian Orlainsky	(AUT)

11/03/1980, Cortina d'Ampezzo (ITA)
GIANT SLALOM

1.	**INGEMAR STENMARK**	**(SWE)**
2.	Hans Enn	(AUT)
3.	Joël Gaspoz	(SUI)

13/03/1980, Saalbach (AUT)
GIANT SLALOM

1.	**INGEMAR STENMARK**	**(SWE)**
2.	Joël Gaspoz	(SUI)
3.	Hans Enn	(AUT)

15/03/1980, Saalbach (AUT)
SLALOM

1.	**INGEMAR STENMARK**	**(SWE)**
2.	Steve Mahre	(USA)
3.	Petăr Popangelov	(BUL)

1980-81

CUPS

OVERALL

1.	**PHIL MAHRE**	**(USA)**
2.	Ingemar Stenmark	(SWE)
3.	Alexander Zhirov	(URS)

SLALOM

1.	**INGEMAR STENMARK**	**(SWE)**
2.	Phil Mahre	(USA)
3.	Bojan Križaj	(YUG)
=	Steve Mahre	(USA)

GIANT SLALOM

1.	**INGEMAR STENMARK**	**(SWE)**
2.	Alexander Zhirov	(URS)
3.	Phil Mahre	(USA)

DOWNHILL

1.	**HARTI WEIRATHER**	**(AUT)**
2.	Steve Podborski	(CAN)
3.	Peter Müller	(SUI)

COMBINED

1.	**PHIL MAHRE**	**(USA)**
2.	Andreas Wenzel	(LIE)
3.	Peter Müller	(SUI)

RACES

07/12/1980, Val-d'Isère (FRA)
DOWNHILL

1.	**ULI SPIESS**	**(AUT)**
2.	Ken Read	(CAN)
3.	Steve Podborski	(CAN)

09/12/1980, Madonna di Campiglio (ITA)
SLALOM

1.	**INGEMAR STENMARK**	**(SWE)**
2.	Paul Frommelt	(LIE)
3.	Bojan Križaj	(YUG)

10/12/1980, Madonna di Campiglio (ITA)
GIANT SLALOM

1.	**INGEMAR STENMARK**	**(SWE)**
2.	Aleksandr Žirov	(URS)
3.	Gerhard Jäger	(AUT)

14/12/1980, Val Gardena (ITA)
DOWNHILL

1.	PETER MÜLLER	(SUI)
2.	Harti Weirather	(AUT)
3.	Steve Podborski	(CAN)

09-14/12/1980, Madonna di Campiglio/Val Gardena (ITA)
COMBINED

1.	PETER MÜLLER	(SUI)
2.	Leonhard Stock	(AUT)
3.	Andreas Wenzel	(LIE)

15/12/1980, Val Gardena (ITA)
DOWNHILL

1.	HARTI WEIRATHER	(AUT)
2.	Uli Spieß	(AUT)
3.	Peter Müller	(SUI)

21/12/1980, Sankt Moritz (SUI)
DOWNHILL

1.	STEVE PODBORSKI	(CAN)
2.	Peter Wirnsberger	(AUT)
3.	Peter Müller	(SUI)

04/01/1981, Ebnat-Kappel (SUI)
GIANT SLALOM

1.	CHRISTIAN ORLAINSKY	(AUT)
2.	Hans Enn	(AUT)
3.	Jean-Luc Fournier	(SUI)

07/12-04/01/1981, St. Moritz/Ebnat-Kappel (SUI)
COMBINED

1.	ANDREAS WENZEL	(LIE)
2.	Hans Enn	(AUT)
3.	Phil Mahre	(USA)

06/01/1981, Morzine (FRA)
GIANT SLALOM

1.	INGEMAR STENMARK	(SWE)
2.	Joël Gaspoz	(SUI)
3.	Bojan Križaj	(YUG)

10/01/1981, Garmisch-Partenkirchen (FRG)
DOWNHILL

1.	STEVE PODBORSKI	(CAN)
2.	Peter Müller	(SUI)
3.	Harti Weirather	(AUT)

06-10/01/1981, Morzine (FRA)/Garmisch-Partenkirchen (FRG)

COMBINED

1.	PHIL MAHRE	(USA)
2.	Peter Müller	(SUI)
3.	Andreas Wenzel	(LIE)

11/01/1981, Garmisch-Partenkirchen (FRG)
SLALOM

1.	STEVE MAHRE	(USA)
2.	Petăr Popangelov	(BUL)
3.	Paul Frommelt	(LIE)

13/01/1981, Oberstaufen (FRG)
SLALOM

1.	PAUL FROMMELT	(LIE)
2.	Ingemar Stenmark	(SWE)
3.	Steve Mahre	(USA)

17/01/1981, Kitzbühel (AUT)
DOWNHILL

1.	STEVE PODBORSKI	(CAN)
2.	Peter Müller	(SUI)
3.	Peter Wirnsberger	(AUT)

13-17/01/1981, Oberstaufen (FRG)/Kitzbühel (AUT)
COMBINED

1.	PHIL MAHRE	(USA)
2.	Steve Mahre	(USA)
3.	Ingemar Stenmark	(SWE)

18/01/1981, Kitzbühel (AUT)
SLALOM

1.	INGEMAR STENMARK	(SWE)
2.	Vladimir Andreev	(URS)
3.	Christian Orlainsky	(AUT)

24/01/1981, Wengen (SUI)
DOWNHILL

1.	TONI BÜRGLER	(SUI)
2.	Harti Weirather	(AUT)
3.	Steve Podborski	(CAN)

25/01/1981, Wengen (SUI)
SLALOM

1.	BOJAN KRIŽAJ	(YUG)
2.	Marc Girardelli	(LUX)
3.	Ingemar Stenmark	(SWE)

26/01/1981, Adelboden (SUI)
GIANT SLALOM

1.	INGEMAR STENMARK	(SWE)

2.	Christian Orlainsky	(AUT)
=	Boris Strel	(YUG)

31/01/1981, Sankt Anton am Arlberg (AUT)
DOWNHILL

1.	**HARTI WEIRATHER**	**(AUT)**
2.	Peter Wirnsberger	(AUT)
3.	Steve Podborski	(CAN)

01/02/1981, Sankt Anton am Arlberg (AUT)
SLALOM

1.	**INGEMAR STENMARK**	**(SWE)**
2.	Phil Mahre	(USA)
3.	Jarle Halsnes	(NOR)

01/02/1981, Sankt Anton am Arlberg (AUT)
COMBINED

1.	**PHIL MAHRE**	**(USA)**
2.	Herbert Plank	(ITA)
3.	Herbert Renoth	(FRG)

02/02/1981, Schladming (AUT)
GIANT SLALOM

1.	**INGEMAR STENMARK**	**(SWE)**
2.	Hans Enn	(AUT)
3.	Jean-Luc Fournier	(SUI)

08/02/1981, Oslo (NOR)
SLALOM

1.	**INGEMAR STENMARK**	**(SWE)**
2.	Bengt Fjällberg	(SWE)
3.	Vladimir Andreev	(URS)

11/02/1981, Voss (NOR)
SLALOM

1.	**INGEMAR STENMARK**	**(SWE)**
2.	Aleksandr Žirov	(URS)
3.	Bruno Nöckler	(ITA)

14/02/1981, Åre (SWE)
GIANT SLALOM

1.	**INGEMAR STENMARK**	**(SWE)**
2.	Aleksandr Žirov	(URS)
3.	Phil Mahre	(USA)

15/02/1981, Åre (SWE)
SLALOM

1.	**PHIL MAHRE**	**(USA)**
2.	Ingemar Stenmark	(SWE)
3.	Franz Gruber	(AUT)

05/03/1981, Aspen (USA)
DOWNHILL

1.	**VALERIJ CYGANOV**	**(URS)**
2.	Harti Weirather	(AUT)
3.	Gerhard Pfaffenbichler	(AUT)

06/03/1981, Aspen (USA)
DOWNHILL

1.	**HARTI WEIRATHER**	**(AUT)**
2.	Steve Podborski	(CAN)
3.	Franz Heinzer	(SUI)

07/03/1981, Aspen (USA)
GIANT SLALOM

1.	**PHIL MAHRE**	**(USA)**
2.	Ingemar Stenmark	(SWE)
3.	Steve Mahre	(USA)

14/03/1981, Furano (JPN)
GIANT SLALOM

1.	**ALEKSANDR ŽIROV**	**(URS)**
2.	Gerhard Jäger	(AUT)
3.	Ingemar Stenmark	(SWE)

15/03/1981, Furano (JPN)
SLALOM

1.	**PHIL MAHRE**	**(USA)**
2.	Bojan Križaj	(YUG)
3.	Ingemar Stenmark	(SWE)

24/03/1981, Borovec (BUL)
GIANT SLALOM

1.	**ALEKSANDR ŽIROV**	**(URS)**
2.	Ingemar Stenmark	(SWE)
3.	Joël Gaspoz	(SUI)

25/03/1981, Borovec (BUL)
SLALOM

1.	**ALEKSANDR ŽIROV**	**(URS)**
2.	Steve Mahre	(USA)
3.	Phil Mahre	(USA)

28/03/1981, Laax (SUI)
GIANT SLALOM

1.	**ALEKSANDR ŽIROV**	**(URS)**
2.	Phil Mahre	(USA)
3.	Ingemar Stenmark	(SWE)

1981-82

CUPS

OVERALL
1. **PHIL MAHRE** **(USA)**
2. Ingemar Stenmark (SWE)
3. Steve Mahre (USA)

SLALOM
1. **PHIL MAHRE** **(USA)**
2. Ingemar Stenmark (SWE)
3. Steve Mahre (USA)

GIANT SLALOM
1. **PHIL MAHRE** **(USA)**
2. Ingemar Stenmark (SWE)
3. Marc Girardelli (LUX)

DOWNHILL
1. **STEVE PODBORSKI** **(CAN)**
2. Peter Müller (SUI)
3. Harti Weirather (AUT)

COMBINED
1. **PHIL MAHRE** **(USA)**
2. Andreas Wenzel (LIE)
3. Even Hole (NOR)

RACES

06/12/1981, Val-d'Isère (FRA)
DOWNHILL
1. **FRANZ KLAMMER** **(AUT)**
2. Peter Müller (SUI)
3. Toni Bürgler (SUI)

08/12/1981, Aprica (ITA)
GIANT SLALOM
1. **JOËL GASPOZ** **(SUI)**
2. Phil Mahre (USA)
3. Ingemar Stenmark (SWE)

06-08/12/1981, Val-d'Isère (FRA)/Aprica (ITA)
COMBINED
1. **PHIL MAHRE** **(USA)**
2. Andreas Wenzel (LIE)
3. Leonhard Stock (AUT)

09/12/1981, Madonna di Campiglio (ITA)

SLALOM
1. **PHIL MAHRE** **(USA)**
2. Ingemar Stenmark (SWE)
3. Paolo De Chiesa (ITA)

13/12/1981, Val Gardena (ITA)
DOWNHILL
1. **ERWIN RESCH** **(AUT)**
2. Konrad Bartelski (GBR)
3. Leonhard Stock (AUT)

09-13/12/1981, Madonna di Campiglio/Val Gardena (ITA)
COMBINED
1. **PHIL MAHRE** **(USA)**
2. Andreas Wenzel (LIE)
3. Even Hole (NOR)

14/12/1981, Cortina d'Ampezzo (ITA)
SLALOM
1. **STEVE MAHRE** **(USA)**
2. Phil Mahre (USA)
3. Ingemar Stenmark (SWE)

15/12/1981, Cortina d'Ampezzo (ITA)
GIANT SLALOM
1. **BORIS STREL** **(YUG)**
2. Phil Mahre (USA)
3. Joël Gaspoz (SUI)

21/12/1981, Crans-Montana (SUI)
DOWNHILL
1. **STEVE PODBORSKI** **(CAN)**
2. Peter Müller (SUI)
3. Ken Read (CAN)

09/01/1982, Morzine (FRA)
GIANT SLALOM
1. **INGEMAR STENMARK** **(SWE)**
2. Phil Mahre (USA)
3. Marc Girardelli (LUX)

12/01/1982, Bad Wiessee (FRG)
SLALOM
1. **INGEMAR STENMARK** **(SWE)**
2. Franz Gruber (AUT)
3. Phil Mahre (USA)

15/01/1982, Kitzbühel (AUT)
DOWNHILL
1. **HARTI WEIRATHER** **(AUT)**

2. Steve Podborski (CAN)
3. Ken Read (CAN)

12-15/01/1982, Bad Wiessee (FRG)/Kitzbühel (AUT)
COMBINED

1. **PHIL MAHRE** **(USA)**
2. Andreas Wenzel (LIE)
3. Peter Roth (SUI)

16/01/1982, Kitzbühel (AUT)
DOWNHILL

1. **STEVE PODBORSKI** **(CAN)**
2. Franz Klammer (AUT)
3. Ken Read (CAN)

17/01/1982, Kitzbühel (AUT)
SLALOM

1. **INGEMAR STENMARK** **(SWE)**
2. Phil Mahre (USA)
3. Paolo De Chiesa (ITA)
= Steve Mahre (USA)

19/01/1982, Adelboden (SUI)
GIANT SLALOM

1. **INGEMAR STENMARK** **(SWE)**
2. Phil Mahre (USA)
3. Max Julen (SUI)

23/01/1982, Wengen (SUI)
DOWNHILL

1. **HARTI WEIRATHER** **(AUT)**
2. Erwin Resch (AUT)
3. Peter Wirnsberger (AUT)

24/01/1982, Wengen (SUI)
SLALOM

1. **PHIL MAHRE** **(USA)**
2. Ingemar Stenmark (SWE)
3. Paul Frommelt (LIE)

24/01/1982, Wengen (SUI)
COMBINED

1. **PIRMIN ZURBRIGGEN** **(SUI)**
2. Ivan Pacák (TCH)
3. Thomas Kemenater (ITA)

09/02/1982, Kirchberg in Tirol (AUT)
GIANT SLALOM

1. **INGEMAR STENMARK** **(SWE)**
2. Phil Mahre (USA)

3. Marc Girardelli (LUX)

13/02/1982, Garmisch-Partenkirchen (FRG)
DOWNHILL

1. **STEVE PODBORSKI** **(CAN)**
2. Conradin Cathomen (SUI)
3. Harti Weirather (AUT)

14/02/1982, Garmisch-Partenkirchen (FRG)
SLALOM

1. **STEVE MAHRE** **(USA)**
2. Phil Mahre (USA)
3. Paolo De Chiesa (ITA)

14/02/1982, Garmisch-Partenkirchen (FRG)
COMBINED

1. **STEVE MAHRE** **(USA)**
2. Michel Vion (FRA)
3. Peter Lüscher (SUI)

17/02/1982, Whistler (CAN)
DOWNHILL

1. **PETER MÜLLER** **(SUI)**
2. Steve Podborski (CAN)
3. Dave Irwin (CAN)

05/03/1982, Aspen (USA)
DOWNHILL

1. **PETER MÜLLER** **(SUI)**
2. Harti Weirather (AUT)
3. Conradin Cathomen (SUI)

06/03/1982, Aspen (USA)
DOWNHILL

1. **PETER MÜLLER** **(SUI)**
2. Todd Brooker (CAN)
3. Helmut Höflehner (AUT)

13/03/1982, Jasná (TCH)
GIANT SLALOM

1. **STEVE MAHRE** **(USA)**
2. Hans Enn (AUT)
3. Phil Mahre (USA)

14/03/1982, Jasná (TCH)
SLALOM

1. **PHIL MAHRE** **(USA)**
2. Ingemar Stenmark (SWE)
3. Steve Mahre (USA)
= Anton Steiner (AUT)

17/03/1982, Bad Kleinkirchheim (AUT)
GIANT SLALOM
1. **STEVE MAHRE** **(USA)**
2. Phil Mahre (USA)
3. Pirmin Zurbriggen (SUI)

19/03/1982, Kranjska Gora (YUG)
GIANT SLALOM
1. **PHIL MAHRE** **(USA)**
2. Hans Enn (AUT)
3. Marc Girardelli (LUX)

20/03/1982, Kranjska Gora (YUG)
SLALOM
1. **BOJAN KRIŽAJ** **(YUG)**
2. Ingemar Stenmark (SWE)
3. Franz Gruber (AUT)

24/03/1982, San Sicario (ITA)
GIANT SLALOM
1. **PIRMIN ZURBRIGGEN** **(SUI)**
2. Marc Girardelli (LUX)
3. Phil Mahre (USA)

26/03/1982, Monginevro (FRA)
SLALOM
1. **PHIL MAHRE** **(USA)**
2. Ingemar Stenmark (SWE)
3. Joël Gaspoz (SUI)

1982-83

CUPS

OVERALL
1. **PHIL MAHRE** **(USA)**
2. Ingemar Stenmark (SWE)
3. Andreas Wenzel (LIE)

SLALOM
1. **INGEMAR STENMARK** **(SWE)**
2. Stig Strand (SWE)
3. Andreas Wenzel (LIE)

GIANT SLALOM
1. **PHIL MAHRE** **(USA)**
2. Max Julen (SUI)
= Ingemar Stenmark (SWE)

DOWNHILL
1. **FRANZ KLAMMER** **(AUT)**
2. Conradin Cathomen (SUI)
3. Harti Weirather (AUT)

COMBINED
1. **PHIL MAHRE** **(USA)**
2. Peter Lüscher (SUI)
3. Marc Girardelli (LUX)
= Pirmin Zurbriggen (SUI)

RACES

05/12/1982, Pontresina (SUI)
DOWNHILL
1. **HARTI WEIRATHER** **(AUT)**
2. Franz Klammer (AUT)
3. Peter Müller (SUI)

12/12/1982, Val-d'Isère (FRA)
SUPER-G
1. **PETER MÜLLER** **(SUI)**
2. Peter Lüscher (SUI)
3. Pirmin Zurbriggen (SUI)

14/12/1982, Courmayeur (ITA)
SLALOM
1. **INGEMAR STENMARK** **(SWE)**
2. Stig Strand (SWE)
3. Phil Mahre (USA)

19/12/1982, Val Gardena (ITA)
DOWNHILL

1.	**CONRADIN CATHOMEN**	**(SUI)**
2.	Erwin Resch	(AUT)
3.	Franz Klammer	(AUT)

12-19/12/1982, Val-d'Isère (FRA)/Val Gardena (ITA)
COMBINED

1.	**FRANZ HEINZER**	**(SUI)**
2.	Peter Müller	(SUI)
3.	Peter Lüscher	(SUI)

20/12/1982, Val Gardena (ITA)
DOWNHILL

1.	**FRANZ KLAMMER**	**(AUT)**
2.	Peter Müller	(SUI)
3.	Urs Räber	(SUI)

21/12/1982, Madonna di Campiglio (ITA)
SLALOM

1.	**STIG STRAND**	**(SWE)**
2.	Ingemar Stenmark	(SWE)
3.	Phil Mahre	(USA)

22/12/1982, Madonna di Campiglio (ITA)
SUPER-G

1.	**MICHAEL MAIR**	**(ITA)**
2.	Hans Enn	(AUT)
3.	Pirmin Zurbriggen	(SUI)

22/12/1982, Madonna di Campiglio (ITA)
COMBINED

1.	**PIRMIN ZURBRIGGEN**	**(SUI)**
2.	Christian Orlainsky	(AUT)
3.	Franz Gruber	(AUT)

04/01/1983, Parpan (SUI)
SLALOM

1.	**STEVE MAHRE**	**(USA)**
2.	Jacques Lüthy	(SUI)
3.	Andreas Wenzel	(LIE)

09/01/1983, Val-d'Isère (FRA)
DOWNHILL

1.	**ERWIN RESCH**	**(AUT)**
2.	Peter Lüscher	(SUI)
3.	Conradin Cathomen	(SUI)

10/01/1983, Val-d'Isère (FRA)
DOWNHILL

1.	**CONRADIN CATHOMEN**	**(SUI)**
2.	Ken Read	(CAN)
3.	Danilo Sbardellotto	(ITA)

11/01/1983, Adelboden (SUI)
GIANT SLALOM

1.	**PIRMIN ZURBRIGGEN**	**(SUI)**
2.	Max Julen	(SUI)
3.	Jacques Lüthy	(SUI)

21/01/1983, Kitzbühel (AUT)
DOWNHILL

1.	**BRUNO KERNEN**	**(SUI)**
2.	Steve Podborski	(CAN)
3.	Urs Räber	(SUI)

22/01/1983, Kitzbühel (AUT)
DOWNHILL

1.	**TODD BROOKER**	**(CAN)**
2.	Urs Räber	(SUI)
3.	Ken Read	(CAN)

23/01/1983, Kitzbühel (AUT)
SLALOM

1.	**INGEMAR STENMARK**	**(SWE)**
2.	Christian Orlainsky	(AUT)
3.	Phil Mahre	(USA)

23/01/1983, Kitzbühel (AUT)
COMBINED

1.	**PHIL MAHRE**	**(USA)**
2.	Marc Girardelli	(LUX)
3.	Peter Lüscher	(SUI)

28/01/1983, Sarajevo (YUG)
DOWNHILL

1.	**GERHARD PFAFFENBICHLER**	**(AUT)**
2.	Steve Podborski	(CAN)
3.	Franz Klammer	(AUT)

29/01/1983, Kranjska Gora (YUG)
GIANT SLALOM

1.	**HANS ENN**	**(AUT)**
2.	Max Julen	(SUI)
3.	Ingemar Stenmark	(SWE)

30/01/1983, Kranjska Gora (YUG)
SLALOM

1.	**FRANZ GRUBER**	**(AUT)**
2.	Stig Strand	(SWE)
3.	Michel Canac	(FRA)

05/02/1983, Sankt Anton am Arlberg (AUT)
DOWNHILL
1. **PETER LÜSCHER** **(SUI)**
2. Silvano Meli (SUI)
3. Harti Weirather (AUT)

06/02/1983, Sankt Anton am Arlberg (AUT)
SLALOM
1. **STEVE MAHRE** **(USA)**
2. Andreas Wenzel (LIE)
3. Phil Mahre (USA)

06/02/1983, Sankt Anton am Arlberg (AUT)
COMBINED
1. **PHIL MAHRE** **(USA)**
2. Andreas Wenzel (LIE)
3. Steve Mahre (USA)

09/02/1983, Garmisch-Partenkirchen (FRG)
SUPER-G
1. **PETER LÜSCHER** **(SUI)**
2. Pirmin Zurbriggen (SUI)
3. Hans Enn (AUT)

11/02/1983, Le Markstein (FRA)
SLALOM
1. **INGEMAR STENMARK** **(SWE)**
2. Paolo De Chiesa (ITA)
3. Phil Mahre (USA)

21/01-11/02/1983, Kitzbühel (AUT)/Le Markstein (FRA)
COMBINED
1. **PHIL MAHRE** **(USA)**
2. Andreas Wenzel (LIE)
3. Marc Girardelli (LUX)

12/02/1983, Le Markstein (FRA)
SLALOM
1. **BOJAN KRIŽAJ** **(YUG)**
2. Bengt Fjällberg (SWE)
3. Christian Orlainsky (AUT)

13/02/1983, Todtnau (FRG)
GIANT SLALOM
1. **INGEMAR STENMARK** **(SWE)**
2. Max Julen (SUI)
3. Pirmin Zurbriggen (SUI)

23/02/1983, Tärnaby (SWE)

SLALOM
1. **ANDREAS WENZEL** **(LIE)**
2. Stig Strand (SWE)
3. Bojan Križaj (YUG)

26/02/1983, Gällivare (SWE)
GIANT SLALOM
1. **INGEMAR STENMARK** **(SWE)**
2. Max Julen (SUI)
= Phil Mahre (USA)

27/02/1983, Gällivare (SWE)
SLALOM
1. **MARC GIRARDELLI** **(LUX)**
2. Stig Strand (SWE)
3. Ingemar Stenmark (SWE)

06/03/1983, Aspen (USA)
DOWNHILL
1. **TODD BROOKER** **(CAN)**
2. Michael Mair (ITA)
3. Helmut Höflehner (AUT)

07/03/1983, Aspen (USA)
GIANT SLALOM
1. **PHIL MAHRE** **(USA)**
2. Marc Girardelli (LUX)
3. Ingemar Stenmark (SWE)

08/03/1983, Vail (USA)
GIANT SLALOM
1. **PHIL MAHRE** **(USA)**
2. Ingemar Stenmark (SWE)
3. Max Julen (SUI)

12/03/1983, Lake Louise (CAN)
DOWNHILL
1. **HELMUT HÖFLEHNER** **(AUT)**
2. Franz Klammer (AUT)
3. Conradin Cathomen (SUI)

19/03/1983, Furano (JPN)
GIANT SLALOM
1. **PHIL MAHRE** **(USA)**
2. Max Julen (SUI)
3. Ingemar Stenmark (SWE)

20/03/1983, Furano (JPN)
SLALOM
1. **STIG STRAND** **(SWE)**
2. Andreas Wenzel (LIE)

3.   Bojan Križaj   (YUG)

| | 1983-84 | |

CUPS

OVERALL
1.	**PIRMIN ZURBRIGGEN**	**(SUI)**
2.	Ingemar Stenmark	(SWE)
3.	Marc Girardelli	(LUX)

SLALOM
1.	**MARC GIRARDELLI**	**(LUX)**
2.	Ingemar Stenmark	(SWE)
3.	Franz Gruber	(AUT)

GIANT SLALOM
1.	**INGEMAR STENMARK**	**(SWE)**
2.	Pirmin Zurbriggen	(SUI)
3.	Hans Enn	(AUT)

DOWNHILL
1.	**URS RÄBER**	**(SUI)**
2.	Erwin Resch	(AUT)
3.	Bill Johnson	(USA)

COMBINED
1.	**ANDREAS WENZEL**	**(LIE)**
2.	Pirmin Zurbriggen	(SUI)
3.	Anton Steiner	(AUT)

RACES

02/12/1983, Kranjska Gora (YUG)
SLALOM
1.	**ANDREAS WENZEL**	**(LIE)**
2.	Petăr Popangelov	(BUL)
3.	Paul Frommelt	(LIE)

04/12/1983, Schladming (AUT)
DOWNHILL
1.	**ERWIN RESCH**	**(AUT)**
2.	Harti Weirather	(AUT)
3.	Steve Podborski	(CAN)

09/12/1983, Val-d'Isère (FRA)
DOWNHILL
1.	**FRANZ HEINZER**	**(SUI)**
2.	Todd Brooker	(CAN)
3.	Harti Weirather	(AUT)

10/12/1983, Val-d'Isère (FRA)

SUPER-G
1. **HANS ENN** **(AUT)**
2. Pirmin Zurbriggen (SUI)
3. Jure Franko (YUG)

10/12/1983, Val-d'Isère (FRA)
COMBINED
1. **FRANZ HEINZER** **(SUI)**
2. Pirmin Zurbriggen (SUI)
3. Leonhard Stock (AUT)

12/12/1983, Les Diablerets (SUI)
GIANT SLALOM
1. **MAX JULEN** **(SUI)**
2. Pirmin Zurbriggen (SUI)
3. Jure Franko (YUG)

13/12/1983, Courmayeur (ITA)
SLALOM
1. **INGEMAR STENMARK** **(SWE)**
2. Bojan Križaj (YUG)
3. Steve Mahre (USA)

18/12/1983, Val Gardena (ITA)
DOWNHILL
1. **URS RÄBER** **(SUI)**
2. Todd Brooker (CAN)
3. Steve Podborski (CAN)

19/12/1983, Val Gardena (ITA)
SUPER-G
1. **PIRMIN ZURBRIGGEN** **(SUI)**
2. Martin Hangl (SUI)
3. Leonhard Stock (AUT)

20/12/1983, Madonna di Campiglio (ITA)
SLALOM
1. **INGEMAR STENMARK** **(SWE)**
2. Robert Zoller (AUT)
3. Petăr Popangelov (BUL)

19-20/12/1983, Val Gardena/Madonna di Campiglio (ITA)
COMBINED
1. **ANDREAS WENZEL** **(LIE)**
2. Thomas Bürgler (SUI)
3. Alex Giorgi (ITA)

07/01/1984, Laax (SUI)
DOWNHILL
1. **URS RÄBER** **(SUI)**

2. Franz Klammer (AUT)
3. Michael Mair (ITA)

10/01/1984, Adelboden (SUI)
GIANT SLALOM
1. **INGEMAR STENMARK** **(SWE)**
2. Hubert Strolz (AUT)
3. Pirmin Zurbriggen (SUI)

15/01/1984, Wengen (SUI)
DOWNHILL
1. **BILL JOHNSON** **(USA)**
2. Anton Steiner (AUT)
3. Erwin Resch (AUT)

16/01/1984, Parpan (SUI)
SLALOM
1. **MARC GIRARDELLI** **(LUX)**
2. Paolo De Chiesa (ITA)
3. Andreas Wenzel (LIE)

17/01/1984, Parpan (SUI)
SLALOM
1. **INGEMAR STENMARK** **(SWE)**
2. Marc Girardelli (LUX)
3. Franz Gruber (AUT)

15-17/01/1984, Wengen/Parpan (SUI)
COMBINED
1. **ANDREAS WENZEL** **(LIE)**
2. Anton Steiner (AUT)
3. Peter Lüscher (SUI)

21/01/1984, Kitzbühel (AUT)
DOWNHILL
1. **FRANZ KLAMMER** **(AUT)**
2. Erwin Resch (AUT)
3. Anton Steiner (AUT)

22/01/1984, Kitzbühel (AUT)
SLALOM
1. **MARC GIRARDELLI** **(LUX)**
2. Franz Gruber (AUT)
3. Bojan Križaj (YUG)

22/01/1984, Kitzbühel (AUT)
COMBINED
1. **ANTON STEINER** **(AUT)**
2. Pirmin Zurbriggen (SUI)
3. Phil Mahre (USA)

23/01/1984, Kirchberg in Tirol (AUT)
GIANT SLALOM

1.	**INGEMAR STENMARK**	**(SWE)**
2.	Marc Girardelli	(LUX)
3.	Jörgen Sundqvist	(SWE)

28/01/1984, Garmisch-Partenkirchen (FRG)
DOWNHILL

1.	**STEVE PODBORSKI**	**(CAN)**
2.	Erwin Resch	(AUT)
3.	Franz Klammer	(AUT)

29/01/1984, Garmisch-Partenkirchen (FRG)
SUPER-G

1.	**ANDREAS WENZEL**	**(LIE)**
2.	Pirmin Zurbriggen	(SUI)
3.	Hans Enn	(AUT)

29/01/1984, Garmisch-Partenkirchen (FRG)
COMBINED

1.	**PIRMIN ZURBRIGGEN**	**(SUI)**
2.	Andreas Wenzel	(LIE)
3.	Peter Müller	(SUI)

02/02/1984, Cortina d'Ampezzo (ITA)
DOWNHILL

1.	**HELMUT HÖFLEHNER**	**(AUT)**
2.	Urs Räber	(SUI)
3.	Conradin Cathomen	(SUI)

04/02/1984, Borovec (BUL)
GIANT SLALOM

1.	**INGEMAR STENMARK**	**(SWE)**
2.	Marc Girardelli	(LUX)
3.	Roberto Erlacher	(ITA)

05/02/1984, Borovec (BUL)
SLALOM

1.	**MARC GIRARDELLI**	**(LUX)**
2.	Ingemar Stenmark	(SWE)
3.	Franz Gruber	(AUT)

04/03/1984, Aspen (USA)
DOWNHILL

1.	**BILL JOHNSON**	**(USA)**
2.	Helmut Höflehner	(AUT)
=	Anton Steiner (AUT)	

05/03/1984, Aspen (USA)
GIANT SLALOM

1.	**PIRMIN ZURBRIGGEN**	**(SUI)**

2.	Marc Girardelli	(LUX)
3.	Phil Mahre	(USA)

06/03/1984, Vail (USA)
SLALOM

1.	**ROBERT ZOLLER**	**(AUT)**
2.	Petăr Popangelov	(BUL)
3.	Lars-Göran Halvarsson	(SWE)
=	Phil Mahre	(USA)

07/03/1984, Vail (USA)
GIANT SLALOM

1.	**INGEMAR STENMARK**	**(SWE)**
2.	Pirmin Zurbriggen	(SUI)
3.	Hans Enn	(AUT)

11/03/1984, Whistler (CAN)
DOWNHILL

1.	**BILL JOHNSON**	**(USA)**
2.	Helmut Höflehner	(AUT)
3.	Pirmin Zurbriggen	(SUI)

17/03/1984, Åre (SWE)
GIANT SLALOM

1.	**HANS ENN**	**(AUT)**
2.	Hubert Strolz	(AUT)
3.	Ingemar Stenmark	(SWE)

18/03/1984, Åre (SWE)
SLALOM

1.	**MARC GIRARDELLI**	**(LUX)**
2.	Franz Gruber	(AUT)
3.	Lars-Göran Halvarsson	(SWE)

20/03/1984, Oppdal (NOR)
SUPER-G

1.	**PIRMIN ZURBRIGGEN**	**(SUI)**
2.	Marc Girardelli	(LUX)
3.	Jure Franko	(YUG)

23/03/1984, Oslo (NOR)
GIANT SLALOM

1.	**HANS ENN**	**(AUT)**
2.	Alex Giorgi	(ITA)
3.	Thomas Bürgler	(SUI)

24/03/1984, Oslo (NOR)
SLALOM

1.	**MARC GIRARDELLI**	**(LUX)**
2.	Ingemar Stenmark	(SWE)
3.	Paolo De Chiesa	(ITA)

1984-85

CUPS

OVERALL
1.	**MARC GIRARDELLI**	**(LUX)**
2.	Pirmin Zurbriggen	(SUI)
3.	Andreas Wenzel	(LIE)

SLALOM
1.	**MARC GIRARDELLI**	**(LUX)**
2.	Paul Frommelt	(LIE)
3.	Ingemar Stenmark	(SWE)

GIANT SLALOM
1.	**MARC GIRARDELLI**	**(LUX)**
2.	Pirmin Zurbriggen	(SUI)
3.	Thomas Bürgler	(SUI)

DOWNHILL
1.	**HELMUT HÖFLEHNER**	**(AUT)**
2.	Peter Müller	(SUI)
3.	Karl Alpiger	(SUI)
=	Peter Wirnsberger	(AUT)

COMBINED
1.	**ANDREAS WENZEL**	**(LIE)**
2.	Franz Heinzer	(SUI)
3.	Peter Müller	(SUI)

RACES

02/12/1984, Sestriere (ITA)
SLALOM
1.	**MARC GIRARDELLI**	**(LUX)**
2.	Jonas Nilsson	(SWE)
3.	Paolo De Chiesa	(ITA)

07/12/1984, Puy-Saint-Vincent (FRA)
SUPER-G
1.	**PIRMIN ZURBRIGGEN**	**(SUI)**
2.	Marc Girardelli	(LUX)
3.	Thomas Bürgler	(SUI)

08/12/1984, Puy-Saint-Vincent (FRA)
GIANT SLALOM
1.	**ROBERTO ERLACHER**	**(ITA)**
2.	Martin Hangl	(SUI)
3.	Richard Pramotton	(ITA)

10/12/1984, Sestriere (ITA)
SLALOM
1.	**PIRMIN ZURBRIGGEN**	**(SUI)**
2.	Paolo De Chiesa	(ITA)
3.	Ivano Edalini	(ITA)

11/12/1984, Sestriere (ITA)
GIANT SLALOM
1.	**MARC GIRARDELLI**	**(LUX)**
2.	Markus Wasmeier	(FRG)
3.	Max Julen	(SUI)

15/12/1984, Val Gardena (ITA)
DOWNHILL
1.	**HELMUT HÖFLEHNER**	**(AUT)**
2.	Conradin Cathomen	(SUI)
3.	Peter Wirnsberger	(AUT)

16/12/1984, Madonna di Campiglio (ITA)
SLALOM
1.	**BOJAN KRIŽAJ**	**(YUG)**
2.	Andreas Wenzel	(LIE)
3.	Petăr Popangelov	(BUL)

17/12/1984, Madonna di Campiglio (ITA)
SUPER-G
1.	**MARC GIRARDELLI**	**(LUX)**
2.	Pirmin Zurbriggen	(SUI)
3.	Martin Hangl	(SUI)

17/12/1984, Madonna di Campiglio (ITA)
COMBINED
1.	**ANDREAS WENZEL**	**(LIE)**
2.	Thomas Stangassinger	(AUT)
3.	Max Julen	(SUI)

04/01/1985, Bad Wiessee (FRG)
SLALOM
1.	**MARC GIRARDELLI**	**(LUX)**
2.	Florian Beck	(FRG)
3.	Ingemar Stenmark	(SWE)

06/01/1985, La Mongie (FRA)
SLALOM
1.	**ANDREAS WENZEL**	**(LIE)**
2.	Jonas Nilsson	(SWE)
3.	Paul Frommelt	(LIE)

08/01/1985, Schladming (AUT)
GIANT SLALOM
1.	**THOMAS BÜRGLER**	**(SUI)**

2. Marc Girardelli (LUX)
3. Martin Hangl (SUI)

11/01/1985, Kitzbühel (AUT)
DOWNHILL
1. **PIRMIN ZURBRIGGEN** **(SUI)**
2. Franz Heinzer (SUI)
3. Peter Wirnsberger (AUT)

08/12/1984-11/01/1985, Puy-Saint-Vincent
(FRA)/Kitzbühel (AUT)
COMBINED
1. **PIRMIN ZURBRIGGEN** **(SUI)**
2. Franz Heinzer (SUI)
3. Andreas Wenzel (LIE)

12/01/1985, Kitzbühel (AUT)
DOWNHILL
1. **PIRMIN ZURBRIGGEN** **(SUI)**
2. Helmut Höflehner (AUT)
3. Todd Brooker (CAN)

13/01/1985, Kitzbühel (AUT)
SLALOM
1. **MARC GIRARDELLI** **(LUX)**
2. Oswald Tötsch (ITA)
3. Bojan Križaj (YUG)

13/01/1985, Kitzbühel (AUT)
COMBINED
1. **ANDREAS WENZEL** **(LIE)**
2. Franz Heinzer (SUI)
3. Gérard Rambaud (FRA)

15/01/1985, Adelboden (SUI)
GIANT SLALOM
1. **HANS ENN** **(AUT)**
2. Hubert Strolz (AUT)
3. Richard Pramotton (ITA)

19/01/1985, Wengen (SUI)
DOWNHILL
1. **HELMUT HÖFLEHNER** **(AUT)**
2. Franz Heinzer (SUI)
3. Peter Wirnsberger (AUT)

20/01/1985, Wengen (SUI)
DOWNHILL
1. **PETER WIRNSBERGER** **(AUT)**
2. Peter Lüscher (SUI)
3. Peter Müller (SUI)

21/01/1985, Wengen (SUI)
SLALOM
1. **MARC GIRARDELLI** **(LUX)**
2. Ingemar Stenmark (SWE)
3. Paul Frommelt (LIE)

21/01/1985, Wengen (SUI)
COMBINED
1. **MICHEL VION** **(FRA)**
2. Peter Roth (FRG)
3. Peter Lüscher (SUI)

26/01/1985, Garmisch-Partenkirchen (FRG)
DOWNHILL
1. **HELMUT HÖFLEHNER** **(AUT)**
2. Peter Müller (SUI)
3. Anton Steiner (AUT)

27/01/1985, Garmisch-Partenkirchen (FRG)
SUPER-G
1. **MARC GIRARDELLI** **(LUX)**
2. Andreas Wenzel (LIE)
3. Hans Stuffer (FRG)

27/01/1985, Garmisch-Partenkirchen (FRG)
COMBINED
1. **PETER MÜLLER** **(SUI)**
2. Peter Lüscher (SUI)
3. Franz Heinzer (SUI)

14/02/1985, Bad Kleinkirchheim (AUT)
DOWNHILL
1. **KARL ALPIGER** **(SUI)**
2. Peter Müller (SUI)
3. Stefan Niederseer (AUT)

15/02/1985, Kranjska Gora (YUG)
GIANT SLALOM
1. **THOMAS BÜRGLER** **(SUI)**
2. Pirmin Zurbriggen (SUI)
3. Marc Girardelli (LUX)

16/02/1985, Kranjska Gora (YUG)
SLALOM
1. **MARC GIRARDELLI** **(LUX)**
2. Ingemar Stenmark (SWE)
3. Paul Frommelt (LIE)
= Jonas Nilsson (SWE)

02/03/1985, Furano (JPN)

DOWNHILL

1.	**TODD BROOKER**	**(CAN)**
2.	Sepp Wildgruber	(FRG)
3.	Bruno Kernen	(SUI)

03/03/1985, Furano (JPN)
SUPER-G

1.	**STEVEN LEE**	**(AUS)**
=	**DANIEL MAHRER**	**(SUI)**
3.	Brian Stemmle	(CAN)

09/03/1985, Aspen (USA)
DOWNHILL

1.	**PETER MÜLLER**	**(SUI)**
2.	Karl Alpiger	(SUI)
3.	Sepp Wildgruber	(FRG)

10/03/1985, Aspen (USA)
GIANT SLALOM

1.	**MARC GIRARDELLI**	**(LUX)**
2.	Ingemar Stenmark	(SWE)
3.	Max Julen	(SUI)

16/03/1985, Panorama (CAN)
DOWNHILL

1.	**PETER MÜLLER**	**(SUI)**
2.	Daniel Mahrer	(SUI)
3.	Helmut Höflehner	(AUT)

17/03/1985, Panorama (CAN)
SUPER-G

1.	**PIRMIN ZURBRIGGEN**	**(SUI)**
2.	Roberto Erlacher	(ITA)
3.	Thomas Bürgler	(SUI)

20/03/1985, Park City (USA)
SLALOM

1.	**MARC GIRARDELLI**	**(LUX)**
2.	Rok Petrovič	(YUG)
3.	Paul Frommelt	(LIE)

23/03/1985, Heavenly Valley (USA)
SLALOM

1.	**MARC GIRARDELLI**	**(LUX)**
2.	Paul Frommelt	(LIE)
3.	Robert Zoller	(AUT)

1985-86

CUPS

OVERALL

1.	**MARC GIRARDELLI**	**(LUX)**
2.	Pirmin Zurbriggen	(SUI)
3.	Markus Wasmeier	(FRG)

SLALOM

1.	**ROK PETROVIČ**	**(YUG)**
2.	Bojan Križaj	(YUG)
=	Ingemar Stenmark	(SWE)
=	Paul Frommelt	(LIE)

GIANT SLALOM

1.	**JOËL GASPOZ**	**(SUI)**
2.	Ingemar Stenmark	(SWE)
3.	Hubert Strolz	(AUT)

SUPER-G

1.	**MARKUS WASMEIER**	**(FRG)**
2.	Pirmin Zurbriggen	(SUI)
3.	Marc Girardelli	(LUX)

DOWNHILL

1.	**PETER WIRNSBERGER**	**(AUT)**
2.	Peter Müller	(SUI)
3.	Michael Mair	(ITA)

COMBINED

1.	**PIRMIN ZURBRIGGEN**	**(SUI)**
2.	Marc Girardelli	(LUX)
=	Markus Wasmeier	(FRG)

RACES

16/08/1985, Las Leñas (ARG)
DOWNHILL

1.	**KARL ALPIGER**	**(SUI)**
2.	Doug Lewis	(USA)
3.	Helmut Höflehner	(AUT)

18/08/1985, Las Leñas (ARG)
DOWNHILL

1.	**KARL ALPIGER**	**(SUI)**
2.	Peter Müller	(SUI)
3.	Markus Wasmeier	(FRG)

01/12/1985, Sestriere (ITA)

SLALOM
1. **ROK PETROVIČ** **(YUG)**
2. Bojan Križaj (YUG)
3. Ivano Edalini (ITA)

07/12/1985, Val-d'Isère (FRA)
DOWNHILL
1. **MICHAEL MAIR** **(ITA)**
2. Marc Girardelli (LUX)
3. Peter Wirnsberger (AUT)

14/12/1985, Val Gardena (ITA)
DOWNHILL
1. **PETER WIRNSBERGER** **(AUT)**
2. Peter Müller (SUI)
3. Sepp Wildgruber (FRG)

15/12/1985, Alta Badia (ITA)
GIANT SLALOM
1. **INGEMAR STENMARK** **(SWE)**
2. Hubert Strolz (AUT)
3. Roberto Erlacher (ITA)

14-15/12/1985, Val Gardena/Alta Badia (ITA)
COMBINED
1. **MARC GIRARDELLI** **(LUX)**
2. Niklas Henning (SWE)
3. Pirmin Zurbriggen (SUI)

16/12/1985, Madonna di Campiglio (ITA)
SLALOM
1. **JONAS NILSSON** **(SWE)**
2. Bojan Križaj (YUG)
3. Paul Frommelt (LIE)

20/12/1985, Kranjska Gora (YUG)
GIANT SLALOM
1. **JOËL GASPOZ** **(SUI)**
2. Roberto Erlacher (ITA)
3. Hubert Strolz (AUT)

21/12/1985, Kranjska Gora (YUG)
SLALOM
1. **ROK PETROVIČ** **(YUG)**
2. Jonas Nilsson (SWE)
3. Thomas Stangassinger (AUT)

31/12/1985, Schladming (AUT)
DOWNHILL
1. **PETER WIRNSBERGER** **(AUT)**
2. Peter Müller (SUI)

3. Erwin Resch (AUT)

03/01/1986, Kranjska Gora (YUG)
GIANT SLALOM
1. **JOËL GASPOZ** **(SUI)**
2. Hubert Strolz (AUT)
3. Markus Wasmeier (FRG)

14/01/1986, Berchtesgaden (FRG)
SLALOM
1. **JOHAN WALLNER** **(SWE)**
2. Bojan Križaj (YUG)
3. Daniel Mougel (FRA)

17/01/1986, Kitzbühel (AUT)
DOWNHILL
1. **PETER WIRNSBERGER** **(AUT)**
2. Erwin Resch (AUT)
3. Pirmin Zurbriggen (SUI)

18/01/1986, Kitzbühel (AUT)
DOWNHILL
1. **PETER WIRNSBERGER** **(AUT)**
2. Erwin Resch (AUT)
3. Michael Mair (ITA)

19/01/1986, Kitzbühel (AUT)
SLALOM
1. **PAUL FROMMELT** **(LIE)**
2. Ingemar Stenmark (SWE)
3. Dietmar Köhlbichler (AUT)
= Andreas Wenzel (LIE)

19/01/1986, Kitzbühel (AUT)
COMBINED
1. **PIRMIN ZURBRIGGEN** **(SUI)**
2. Andreas Wenzel (LIE)
3. Markus Wasmeier (FRG)

21/01/1986, Parpan (SUI)
SLALOM
1. **DIDIER BOUVET** **(FRA)**
2. Ingemar Stenmark (SWE)
3. Thomas Bürgler (SUI)

25/01/1986, Sankt Anton am Arlberg (AUT)
SLALOM
1. **INGEMAR STENMARK** **(SWE)**
2. Rok Petrovič (YUG)
3. Jonas Nilsson (SWE)

28/01/1986, Adelboden (SUI)
GIANT SLALOM

1.	**RICHARD PRAMOTTON**	**(ITA)**
2.	Marco Tonazzi	(ITA)
3.	Hubert Strolz	(AUT)

02/02/1986, Wengen (SUI)
SLALOM

1.	**ROK PETROVIČ**	**(YUG)**
2.	Didier Bouvet	(FRA)
3.	Bojan Križaj	(YUG)

03/02/1986, Crans-Montana (SUI)
SUPER-G

1.	**PETER MÜLLER**	**(SUI)**
2.	Pirmin Zurbriggen	(SUI)
3.	Markus Wasmeier	(FRG)

*07/12/1985-03/02/1986, Val d'Isère
(FRA)/Crans-Montana (SUI)*
COMBINED

1.	**PETER MÜLLER**	**(SUI)**
2.	Michael Mair	(ITA)
3.	Karl Alpiger	(SUI)

05/02/1986, Crans-Montana (SUI)
SUPER-G

1.	**MARC GIRARDELLI**	**(LUX)**
2.	Markus Wasmeier	(FRG)
3.	Peter Müller	(SUI)

07/02/1986, Morzine (FRA)
DOWNHILL

1.	**ANTON STEINER**	**(AUT)**
2.	Gustav Oehrli	(SUI)
3.	Peter Wirnsberger	(AUT)

*25/01-07/02/1986, Sankt Anton am Arlberg
(AUT)/Morzine (FRA)*
COMBINED

1.	**MARC GIRARDELLI**	**(LUX)**
2.	Leonhard Stock	(AUT)
3.	Gustav Oehrli	(SUI)

08/02/1986, Morzine (FRA)
DOWNHILL

1.	**PETER MÜLLER**	**(SUI)**
2.	Leonhard Stock	(AUT)
3.	Atle Skårdal	(NOR)

09/02/1986, Morzine (FRA)

SUPER-G

1.	**MARKUS WASMEIER**	**(FRG)**
2.	Marc Girardelli	(LUX)
3.	Hubert Strolz	(AUT)

09/02/1986, Morzine (FRA)
COMBINED

1.	**MARKUS WASMEIER**	**(FRG)**
2.	Leonhard Stock	(AUT)
3.	Peter Müller	(SUI)

21/02/1986, Åre (SWE)
DOWNHILL

1.	**PETER MÜLLER**	**(SUI)**
2.	Michael Mair	(ITA)
3.	Marc Girardelli	(LUX)

02-21/02/1986, Wengen (SUI)/Åre (SWE)
COMBINED

1.	**GÜNTHER MADER**	**(AUT)**
2.	Andreas Wenzel	(LIE)
3.	Gustav Oehrli	(SUI)

22/02/1986, Åre (SWE)
DOWNHILL

1.	**FRANZ HEINZER**	**(SUI)**
2.	Marc Girardelli	(LUX)
3.	Armin Assinger	(AUT)

23/02/1986, Åre (SWE)
SLALOM

1.	**PIRMIN ZURBRIGGEN**	**(SUI)**
2.	Paul Frommelt	(LIE)
3.	Jonas Nilsson	(SWE)

23/02/1986, Åre (SWE)
COMBINED

1.	**PIRMIN ZURBRIGGEN**	**(SUI)**
2.	Markus Wasmeier	(FRG)
3.	Leonhard Stock	(AUT)

25/02/1986, Lillehammer (NOR)
SLALOM

1.	**ROK PETROVIČ**	**(YUG)**
2.	Ingemar Stenmark	(SWE)
3.	Marc Girardelli	(LUX)

27/02/1986, Hemsedal (NOR)
GIANT SLALOM

1.	**INGEMAR STENMARK**	**(SWE)**
2.	Hans Stuffer	(FRG)

3. Hubert Strolz (AUT)

28/02/1986, Hemsedal (NOR)
SUPER-G

1.	**PIRMIN ZURBRIGGEN**	**(SUI)**
2.	Markus Wasmeier	(FRG)
3.	Leonhard Stock	(AUT)

02/03/1986, Geilo (NOR)
SLALOM

1.	**GÜNTHER MADER**	**(AUT)**
2.	Paul Frommelt	(LIE)
3.	Rok Petrovič	(YUG)

08/03/1986, Aspen (USA)
DOWNHILL

1.	**PETER MÜLLER**	**(SUI)**
2.	Peter Wirnsberger	(AUT)
3.	Leonhard Stock	(AUT)

11/03/1986, Heavenly Valley (USA)
SLALOM

1.	**ROK PETROVIČ**	**(YUG)**
2.	Pirmin Zurbriggen	(SUI)
3.	Ingemar Stenmark	(SWE)

15/03/1986, Whistler (CAN)
DOWNHILL

1.	**ANTON STEINER**	**(AUT)**
2.	Michael Mair	(ITA)
3.	Leonhard Stock	(AUT)

16/03/1986, Whistler (CAN)
SUPER-G

1.	**MARKUS WASMEIER**	**(FRG)**
2.	Martin Hangl	(SUI)
3.	Peter Roth	(SUI)

18/03/1986, Lake Placid (USA)
GIANT SLALOM

1.	**INGEMAR STENMARK**	**(SWE)**
2.	Hubert Strolz	(AUT)
3.	Roberto Erlacher	(ITA)

19/03/1986, Lake Placid (USA)
GIANT SLALOM

1.	**JOËL GASPOZ**	**(SUI)**
2.	Roberto Erlacher	(ITA)
3.	Hubert Strolz	(AUT)

21/03/1986, Bromont (CAN)

SLALOM

1.	**BOJAN KRIŽAJ**	**(YUG)**
2.	Paul Frommelt	(LIE)
3.	Pirmin Zurbriggen	(SUI)

1986-87

CUPS

OVERALL
1. **PIRMIN ZURBRIGGEN** **(SUI)**
2. Marc Girardelli (LUX)
3. Markus Wasmeier (FRG)

SLALOM
1. **BOJAN KRIŽAJ** **(YUG)**
2. Ingemar Stenmark (SWE)
3. Armin Bittner (FRG)

GIANT SLALOM
1. **PIRMIN ZURBRIGGEN** **(SUI)**
2. Joël Gaspoz (SUI)
3. Richard Pramotton (ITA)

SUPER-G
1. **PIRMIN ZURBRIGGEN** **(SUI)**
2. Marc Girardelli (LUX)
3. Markus Wasmeier (FRG)

DOWNHILL
1. **PIRMIN ZURBRIGGEN** **(SUI)**
2. Peter Müller (SUI)
3. Franz Heinzer (SUI)

COMBINED
1. **PIRMIN ZURBRIGGEN** **(SUI)**
2. Andreas Wenzel (LIE)
only two competitors ranked

RACES

15/08/1986, Las Leñas (ARG)
DOWNHILL
1. **PETER MÜLLER** **(SUI)**
2. Karl Alpiger (SUI)
3. Franz Heinzer (SUI)

16/08/1986, Las Leñas (ARG)
DOWNHILL
1. **PIRMIN ZURBRIGGEN** **(SUI)**
2. Leonhard Stock (AUT)
3. Franz Heinzer (SUI)
= Peter Müller (SUI)

29/11/1986, Sestriere (ITA)

SLALOM
1. **INGEMAR STENMARK** **(SWE)**
2. Jonas Nilsson (SWE)
3. Richard Pramotton (ITA)

30/11/1986, Sestriere (ITA)
GIANT SLALOM
1. **RICHARD PRAMOTTON** **(ITA)**
2. Hubert Strolz (AUT)
3. Pirmin Zurbriggen (SUI)

05/12/1986, Val-d'Isère (FRA)
DOWNHILL
1. **PIRMIN ZURBRIGGEN** **(SUI)**
2. Markus Wasmeier (FRG)
3. Michael Mair (ITA)

06/12/1986, Val-d'Isère (FRA)
SUPER-G
1. **MARKUS WASMEIER** **(FRG)**
2. Roberto Erlacher (ITA)
3. Marc Girardelli (LUX)

13/12/1986, Val Gardena (ITA)
DOWNHILL
1. **ROB BOYD** **(CAN)**
2. Michael Mair (ITA)
3. Markus Wasmeier (FRG)

14/12/1986, Alta Badia (ITA)
GIANT SLALOM
1. **RICHARD PRAMOTTON** **(ITA)**
2. Alberto Tomba (ITA)
3. Oswald Tötsch (ITA)

15/12/1986, Alta Badia (ITA)
GIANT SLALOM
1. **JOËL GASPOZ** **(SUI)**
2. Richard Pramotton (ITA)
3. Markus Wasmeier (FRG)

16/12/1986, Madonna di Campiglio (ITA)
SLALOM
1. **IVANO EDALINI** **(ITA)**
2. Ingemar Stenmark (SWE)
3. Joël Gaspoz (SUI)

19/12/1986, Kranjska Gora (YUG)
GIANT SLALOM
1. **JOËL GASPOZ** **(SUI)**
2. Roberto Erlacher (ITA)

3. Richard Pramotton (ITA)

20/12/1986, Kranjska Gora (YUG)
SLALOM
1. **BOJAN KRIŽAJ** **(YUG)**
2. Rok Petrovič (YUG)
3. Ingemar Stenmark (SWE)

21/12/1986, Hinterstoder (AUT)
SLALOM
1. **ARMIN BITTNER** **(FRG)**
2. Bojan Križaj (YUG)
3. Oswald Tötsch (ITA)

04/01/1987, Laax (SUI)
DOWNHILL
1. **FRANZ HEINZER** **(SUI)**
2. Peter Wirnsberger (AUT)
3. Erwin Resch (AUT)

10/01/1987, Garmisch-Partenkirchen (FRG)
DOWNHILL
1. **PIRMIN ZURBRIGGEN** **(SUI)**
2. Michael Mair (ITA)
3. Peter Müller (SUI)

11/01/1987, Garmisch-Partenkirchen (FRG)
SUPER-G
1. **MARKUS WASMEIER** **(FRG)**
2. Pirmin Zurbriggen (SUI)
3. Alberto Ghidoni (ITA)

13/01/1987, Adelboden (SUI)
GIANT SLALOM
1. **PIRMIN ZURBRIGGEN** **(SUI)**
2. Marc Girardelli (LUX)
3. Hubert Strolz (AUT)

17/01/1987, Wengen (SUI)
DOWNHILL
1. **MARKUS WASMEIER** **(FRG)**
2. Karl Alpiger (SUI)
3. Franz Heinzer (SUI)

18/01/1987, Wengen (SUI)
SLALOM
1. **JOËL GASPOZ** **(SUI)**
2. Dietmar Köhlbichler (AUT)
3. Bojan Križaj (YUG)

18/01/1987, Wengen (SUI)
COMBINED
1. **PIRMIN ZURBRIGGEN** **(SUI)**
only one competitor ranked

20/01/1987, Adelboden (SUI)
GIANT SLALOM
1. **PIRMIN ZURBRIGGEN** **(SUI)**
2. Joël Gaspoz (SUI)
3. Ingemar Stenmark (SWE)

25/01/1987, Kitzbühel (AUT)
DOWNHILL
1. **PIRMIN ZURBRIGGEN** **(SUI)**
2. Erwin Resch (AUT)
3. Peter Müller (SUI)

25/01/1987, Kitzbühel (AUT)
SLALOM
1. **BOJAN KRIŽAJ** **(YUG)**
2. Mathias Berthold (AUT)
3. Armin Bittner (FRG)

25/01/1987, Kitzbühel (AUT)
COMBINED
1. **PIRMIN ZURBRIGGEN** **(SUI)**
2. Andreas Wenzel (LIE)
only two competitors ranked

14/02/1987, Le Markstein (FRA)
SLALOM
1. **INGEMAR STENMARK** **(SWE)**
2. Armin Bittner (FRG)
3. Günther Mader (AUT)

15/02/1987, Todtnau (FRG)
GIANT SLALOM
1. **PIRMIN ZURBRIGGEN** **(SUI)**
2. Marc Girardelli (LUX)
3. Markus Wasmeier (FRG)

28/02/1987, Furano (JPN)
DOWNHILL
1. **PETER MÜLLER** **(SUI)**
2. Marc Girardelli (LUX)
3. Michael Mair (ITA)

01/03/1987, Furano (JPN)
SUPER-G
1. **MARC GIRARDELLI** **(LUX)**
2. Pirmin Zurbriggen (SUI)
3. Leonhard Stock (AUT)

07/03/1987, Aspen (USA)
DOWNHILL

1.	**PIRMIN ZURBRIGGEN**	**(SUI)**
2.	Daniel Mahrer	(SUI)
3.	Karl Alpiger	(SUI)

08/03/1987, Aspen (USA)
SUPER-G

1.	**PIRMIN ZURBRIGGEN**	**(SUI)**
2.	Richard Pramotton	(ITA)
3.	Peter Roth	(SUI)

14/03/1987, Calgary (CAN)
DOWNHILL

1.	**PETER MÜLLER**	**(SUI)**
2.	Franz Heinzer	(SUI)
3.	Daniel Mahrer	(SUI)

15/03/1987, Calgary (CAN)
SUPER-G

1.	**MARC GIRARDELLI**	**(LUX)**
2.	Pirmin Zurbriggen	(SUI)
3.	Leonhard Stock	(AUT)

21/03/1987, Sarajevo (YUG)
SLALOM

1.	**GREGA BENEDIK**	**(YUG)**
2.	Bojan Križaj	(YUG)
3.	Didier Bouvet	(FRA)

22/03/1987, Sarajevo (YUG)
GIANT SLALOM

1.	**MARC GIRARDELLI**	**(LUX)**
2.	Joël Gaspoz	(SUI)
3.	Rudolf Nierlich	(AUT)

1987-88

CUPS

OVERALL

1.	**PIRMIN ZURBRIGGEN**	**(SUI)**
2.	Alberto Tomba	(ITA)
3.	Hubert Strolz	(AUT)

SLALOM

1.	**ALBERTO TOMBA**	**(ITA)**
2.	Günther Mader	(AUT)
3.	Felix McGrath	(USA)

GIANT SLALOM

1.	**ALBERTO TOMBA**	**(ITA)**
2.	Hubert Strolz	(AUT)
3.	Helmut Mayer	(AUT)

SUPER-G

1.	**PIRMIN ZURBRIGGEN**	**(SUI)**
2.	Markus Wasmeier	(FRG)
3.	Franck Piccard	(FRA)

DOWNHILL

1.	**PIRMIN ZURBRIGGEN**	**(SUI)**
2.	Michael Mair	(ITA)
3.	Rob Boyd	(CAN)
=	Franz Heinzer	(SUI)

COMBINED

1.	**HUBERT STROLZ**	**(AUT)**
2.	Günther Mader	(AUT)
3.	Franck Piccard	(FRA)

RACES

27/11/1987, Sestriere (ITA)
SLALOM

1.	**ALBERTO TOMBA**	**(ITA)**
2.	Jonas Nilsson	(SWE)
3.	Günther Mader	(AUT)

29/11/1987, Sestriere (ITA)
GIANT SLALOM

1.	**ALBERTO TOMBA**	**(ITA)**
2.	Ingemar Stenmark	(SWE)
3.	Joël Gaspoz	(SUI)

07/12/1987, Val-d'Isère (FRA)

DOWNHILL
1. **DANIEL MAHRER** (SUI)
2. Pirmin Zurbriggen (SUI)
3. Michael Mair (ITA)

12/12/1987, Val Gardena (ITA)
DOWNHILL
1. **ROB BOYD** (CAN)
2. Pirmin Zurbriggen (SUI)
3. Brian Stemmle (CAN)

13/12/1987, Alta Badia (ITA)
GIANT SLALOM
1. **ALBERTO TOMBA** (ITA)
2. Rudolf Nierlich (AUT)
3. Joël Gaspoz (SUI)
= Hans Pieren (SUI)

16/12/1987, Madonna di Campiglio (ITA)
SLALOM
1. **ALBERTO TOMBA** (ITA)
2. Rudolf Nierlich (AUT)
3. Bojan Križaj (YUG)

19/12/1987, Kranjska Gora (YUG)
GIANT SLALOM
1. **HELMUT MAYER** (AUT)
2. Pirmin Zurbriggen (SUI)
3. Hubert Strolz (AUT)

20/12/1987, Kranjska Gora (YUG)
SLALOM
1. **ALBERTO TOMBA** (ITA)
2. Richard Pramotton (ITA)
3. Günther Mader (AUT)

09/01/1988, Val-d'Isère (FRA)
DOWNHILL
1. **PIRMIN ZURBRIGGEN** (SUI)
2. Anton Steiner (AUT)
3. Marc Girardelli (LUX)

10/01/1988, Val-d'Isère (FRA)
SUPER-G
1. **MARKUS WASMEIER** (FRG)
2. Franck Piccard (FRA)
3. Pirmin Zurbriggen (SUI)

12/01/1988, Lienz (AUT)
SLALOM
1. **BERNHARD GSTREIN** (AUT)

2. Alberto Tomba (ITA)
3. Jonas Nilsson (SWE)

16/01/1988, Bad Kleinkirchheim (AUT)
DOWNHILL
1. **PETER MÜLLER** (SUI)
2. Pirmin Zurbriggen (SUI)
3. Franck Piccard (FRA)

17/01/1988, Bad Kleinkirchheim (AUT)
SLALOM
1. **ALBERTO TOMBA** (ITA)
2. Thomas Stangassinger (AUT)
3. Bernhard Gstrein (AUT)

17/01/1988, Bad Kleinkirchheim (AUT)
COMBINED
1. **HUBERT STROLZ** (AUT)
2. Markus Wasmeier (FRG)
3. Franck Piccard (FRA)

19/01/1988, Saas-Fee (SUI)
GIANT SLALOM
1. **ALBERTO TOMBA** (ITA)
2. Günther Mader (AUT)
3. Helmut Mayer (AUT)

23/01/1988, Leukerbad (SUI)
DOWNHILL
1. **MICHAEL MAIR** (ITA)
2. Giorgio Piantanida (ITA)
3. Werner Perathoner (ITA)

24/01/1988, Leukerbad (SUI)
DOWNHILL
1. **DANIEL MAHRER** (SUI)
2. Franz Heinzer (SUI)
3. Igor Cigolla (ITA)

25/01/1988, Leukerbad (SUI)
SUPER-G
1. **FELIX BELCZYK** (CAN)
2. Pirmin Zurbriggen (SUI)
3. Heinz Holzer (ITA)

29/01/1988, Schladming (AUT)
DOWNHILL
1. **PIRMIN ZURBRIGGEN** (SUI)
2. Franz Heinzer (SUI)
3. Peter Dürr (FRG)

30/01/1988, Schladming (AUT)
GIANT SLALOM

1.	**RUDOLF NIERLICH**	**(AUT)**
2.	Hubert Strolz	(AUT)
3.	Helmut Mayer	(AUT)

11/03/1988, Beaver Creek (USA)
DOWNHILL

1.	**FRANZ HEINZER**	**(SUI)**
2.	Christophe Plé	(FRA)
3.	Marc Girardelli	(LUX)

12/03/1988, Beaver Creek (USA)
DOWNHILL

1.	**PETER MÜLLER**	**(SUI)**
2.	Donald Stevens	(CAN)
3.	Marc Girardelli	(LUX)

13/03/1988, Beaver Creek (USA)
SUPER-G

1.	**FRANCK PICCARD**	**(FRA)**
2.	Markus Wasmeier	(FRG)
3.	Marc Girardelli	(LUX)

19/03/1988, Åre (SWE)
SLALOM

1.	**ALBERTO TOMBA**	**(ITA)**
2.	Felix McGrath	(USA)
3.	Günther Mader	(AUT)

20/03/1988, Åre (SWE)
DOWNHILL

1.	**KARL ALPIGER**	**(SUI)**
2.	Danilo Sbardellotto	(ITA)
3.	Franz Heinzer	(SUI)

20/03/1988, Åre (SWE)
COMBINED

1.	**GÜNTHER MADER**	**(AUT)**
2.	Pirmin Zurbriggen	(SUI)
3.	Hubert Strolz	(AUT)

22/03/1988, Oppdal (NOR)
SLALOM

1.	**ALBERTO TOMBA**	**(ITA)**
2.	Tetsuya Okabe	(JPN)
3.	Paul Frommelt	(LIE)

24/03/1988, Saalbach-Hinterglemm (AUT)
SUPER-G

1.	**MARTIN HANGL**	**(SUI)**
2.	Hubert Strolz	(AUT)
3.	Marc Girardelli	(LUX)

25/03/1988, Saalbach-Hinterglemm (AUT)
GIANT SLALOM

1.	**MARTIN HANGL**	**(SUI)**
2.	Marc Girardelli	(LUX)
3.	Pirmin Zurbriggen	(SUI)

26/03/1988, Saalbach-Hinterglemm (AUT)
SLALOM

1.	**PAUL FROMMELT**	**(LIE)**
2.	Armin Bittner	(FRG)
3.	Hubert Strolz	(AUT)

1988-89

CUPS

OVERALL
1.	**MARC GIRARDELLI**	**(LUX)**
2.	Pirmin Zurbriggen	(SUI)
3.	Alberto Tomba	(ITA)

SLALOM
1.	**ARMIN BITTNER**	**(FRG)**
2.	Alberto Tomba	(ITA)
3.	Ole Kristian Furuseth	(NOR)

GIANT SLALOM
1.	**OLE KRISTIAN FURUSETH**	**(NOR)**
2.	Pirmin Zurbriggen	(SUI)
3.	Rudolf Nierlich	(AUT)

SUPER-G
1.	**PIRMIN ZURBRIGGEN**	**(SUI)**
2.	Lars-Börje Eriksson	(SWE)
3.	Franck Piccard	(FRA)

DOWNHILL
1.	**MARC GIRARDELLI**	**(LUX)**
2.	Helmut Höflehner	(AUT)
3.	Daniel Mahrer	(SUI)

COMBINED
1.	**MARC GIRARDELLI**	**(LUX)**
2.	Markus Wasmeier	(FRG)
3.	Pirmin Zurbriggen	(SUI)

RACES

27/11/1988, Schladming (AUT)
SUPER-G
1.	**PIRMIN ZURBRIGGEN**	**(SUI)**
2.	Franck Piccard	(FRA)
3.	Leonhard Stock	(AUT)

19/11/1988, Val Thorens (FRA)
GIANT SLALOM
1.	**PIRMIN ZURBRIGGEN**	**(SUI)**
2.	Rudolf Nierlich	(AUT)
3.	Hans Enn	(AUT)

06/12/1988, Sestriere (ITA)
SLALOM
1.	**MARC GIRARDELLI**	**(LUX)**
2.	Jonas Nilsson	(SWE)
3.	Paul Accola	(SUI)

09/12/1988, Val Gardena (ITA)
DOWNHILL
1.	**PETER MÜLLER**	**(SUI)**
2.	Armin Assinger	(AUT)
3.	Rob Boyd	(CAN)

10/12/1988, Val Gardena (ITA)
DOWNHILL
1.	**HELMUT HÖFLEHNER**	**(AUT)**
2.	Patrick Ortlieb	(AUT)
3.	Peter Müller	(SUI)

11/12/1988, Madonna di Campiglio (ITA)
SLALOM
1.	**ALBERTO TOMBA**	**(ITA)**
2.	Marc Girardelli	(LUX)
3.	Michael Tritscher	(AUT)

17/12/1988, Kranjska Gora (YUG)
SLALOM
1.	**MARC GIRARDELLI**	**(LUX)**
2.	Armin Bittner	(FRG)
3.	Alberto Tomba	(ITA)

21/12/1988, Sankt Anton am Arlberg (AUT)
SLALOM
1.	**ARMIN BITTNER**	**(FRG)**
2.	Bernhard Gstrein	(AUT)
3.	Pirmin Zurbriggen	(SUI)

22/12/1988, Sankt Anton am Arlberg (AUT)
DOWNHILL
1.	**HELMUT HÖFLEHNER**	**(AUT)**
2.	Pirmin Zurbriggen	(SUI)
3.	Leonhard Stock	(AUT)

22/12/1988, Sankt Anton am Arlberg (AUT)
COMBINED
1.	**PIRMIN ZURBRIGGEN**	**(SUI)**
2.	Markus Wasmeier	(FRG)
3.	Hubert Strolz	(AUT)

06/01/1989, Laax (SUI)
DOWNHILL
1.	**LEONHARD STOCK**	**(AUT)**
2.	Peter Wirnsberger	(AUT)
3.	Helmut Höflehner	(AUT)

08/01/1989, Laax (SUI)
SUPER-G

1. **MARTIN HANGL** **(SUI)**
2. Hans Enn (AUT)
3. Helmut Mayer (AUT)

10/01/1989, Kirchberg in Tirol (AUT)
GIANT SLALOM

1. **RUDOLF NIERLICH** **(AUT)**
2. Pirmin Zurbriggen (SUI)
3. Alberto Tomba (ITA)

13/01/1989, Kitzbühel (AUT)
DOWNHILL

1. **MARC GIRARDELLI** **(LUX)**
2. Michael Mair (ITA)
3. Roman Rupp (AUT)

14/01/1989, Kitzbühel (AUT)
DOWNHILL

1. **DANIEL MAHRER** **(SUI)**
2. Marc Girardelli (LUX)
3. Peter Wirnsberger (AUT)

15/01/1989, Kitzbühel (AUT)
SLALOM

1. **ARMIN BITTNER** **(FRG)**
2. Alberto Tomba (ITA)
3. Rudolf Nierlich (AUT)

15/01/1989, Kitzbühel (AUT)
COMBINED

1. **MARC GIRARDELLI** **(LUX)**
2. Paul Accola (SUI)
3. Michael Mair (ITA)

17/01/1989, Adelboden (SUI)
GIANT SLALOM

1. **MARC GIRARDELLI** **(LUX)**
2. Ole Kristian Furuseth (NOR)
3. Alberto Tomba (ITA)

20/01/1989, Wengen (SUI)
DOWNHILL

1. **MARC GIRARDELLI** **(LUX)**
2. Markus Wasmeier (FRG)
3. Daniel Mahrer (SUI)

21/01/1989, Wengen (SUI)
DOWNHILL

1. **MARC GIRARDELLI** **(LUX)**
2. Pirmin Zurbriggen (SUI)
3. Daniel Mahrer (SUI)

22/01/1989, Wengen (SUI)
SLALOM

1. **RUDOLF NIERLICH** **(AUT)**
2. Alberto Tomba (ITA)
3. Hubert Strolz (AUT)

22/01/1989, Wengen (SUI)
COMBINED

1. **MARC GIRARDELLI** **(LUX)**
2. Pirmin Zurbriggen (SUI)
3. Markus Wasmeier (FRG)

17/02/1989, Aspen (USA)
DOWNHILL

1. **KARL ALPIGER** **(SUI)**
2. Marc Girardelli (LUX)
3. Daniel Mahrer (SUI)

18/02/1989, Aspen (USA)
SUPER-G

1. **LARS-BÖRJE ERIKSSON** **(SWE)**
2. Markus Wasmeier (FRG)
3. Helmut Mayer (AUT)

19/02/1989, Aspen (USA)
GIANT SLALOM

1. **INGEMAR STENMARK** **(SWE)**
2. Marc Girardelli (LUX)
3. Lars-Börje Eriksson (SWE)

25/02/1989, Whistler (CAN)
DOWNHILL

1. **ROB BOYD** **(CAN)**
2. Daniel Mahrer (SUI)
3. Pirmin Zurbriggen (SUI)

26/02/1989, Whistler (CAN)
SUPER-G

1. **MARC GIRARDELLI** **(LUX)**
2. Lars-Börje Eriksson (SWE)
3. Pirmin Zurbriggen (SUI)

03/03/1989, Furano (JPN)
GIANT SLALOM

1. **RUDOLF NIERLICH** **(AUT)**
2. Ole Kristian Furuseth (NOR)
3. Pirmin Zurbriggen (SUI)

05/03/1989, Furano (JPN)
SLALOM

1.	**OLE KRISTIAN FURUSETH**	**(NOR)**
2.	Alberto Tomba	(ITA)
3.	Jonas Nilsson	(SWE)

09/03/1989, Shigakōgen (JPN)
GIANT SLALOM

1.	**OLE KRISTIAN FURUSETH**	**(NOR)**
2.	Hubert Strolz	(AUT)
3.	Johan Wallner	(SWE)

10/03/1989, Shigakōgen (JPN)
SLALOM

1.	**RUDOLF NIERLICH**	**(AUT)**
2.	Ole Kristian Furuseth	(NOR)
3.	Armin Bittner	(FRG)

1989-90

CUPS

OVERALL

1.	**PIRMIN ZURBRIGGEN**	**(SUI)**
2.	Ole Kristian Furuseth	(NOR)
3.	Günther Mader	(AUT)

SLALOM

1.	**ARMIN BITTNER**	**(FRG)**
2.	Ole Kristian Furuseth	(NOR)
=	Alberto Tomba	(ITA)

GIANT SLALOM

1.	**OLE KRISTIAN FURUSETH**	**(NOR)**
2.	Günther Mader	(AUT)
3.	Hubert Strolz	(AUT)

SUPER-G

1.	**PIRMIN ZURBRIGGEN**	**(SUI)**
2.	Günther Mader	(AUT)
3.	Lars-Börje Eriksson	(SWE)

DOWNHILL

1.	**HELMUT HÖFLEHNER**	**(AUT)**
2.	Atle Skårdal	(NOR)
3.	Pirmin Zurbriggen	(SUI)

COMBINED

1.	**PIRMIN ZURBRIGGEN**	**(SUI)**
2.	Paul Accola	(SUI)
3.	Markus Wasmeier	(FRG)

RACES

11/08/1989, Thredbo (AUS)
GIANT SLALOM

1.	**LARS-BÖRJE ERIKSSON**	**(SWE)**
2.	Ole Kristian Furuseth	(NOR)
3.	Günther Mader	(AUT)

12/08/1989, Thredbo (AUS)
SLALOM

1.	**ARMIN BITTNER**	**(FRG)**
2.	Ole Kristian Furuseth	(NOR)
3.	Bernhard Gstrein	(AUT)

23/11/1989, Park City (USA)
GIANT SLALOM

1.	OLE KRISTIAN FURUSETH	(NOR)
2.	Pirmin Zurbriggen	(SUI)
3.	Ivano Camozzi	(ITA)

29/11/1989, Waterville Valley (USA)
SLALOM

1.	ALBERTO TOMBA	(ITA)
2.	Pirmin Zurbriggen	(SUI)
3.	Marc Girardelli	(LUX)

30/11/1989, Waterville Valley (USA)
GIANT SLALOM

1.	URS KÄLIN	(SUI)
2.	Lars-Börje Eriksson	(SWE)
3.	Günther Mader	(AUT)

02/12/1989, Mont-Sainte-Anne (CAN)
GIANT SLALOM

1.	GÜNTHER MADER	(AUT)
2.	Ole Kristian Furuseth	(NOR)
3.	Armin Bittner	(FRG)

03/12/1989, Mont-Sainte-Anne (CAN)
SLALOM

1.	THOMAS STANGASSINGER	(AUT)
2.	Bernhard Gstrein	(AUT)
3.	Marc Girardelli	(LUX)

10/12/1989, Val-d'Isère (FRA)
SUPER-G

1.	NIKLAS HENNING	(SWE)
2.	Franck Piccard	(FRA)
3.	Peter Runggaldier	(ITA)

12/12/1989, Sestriere (ITA)
SUPER-G

1.	PIRMIN ZURBRIGGEN	(SUI)
2.	Lars-Börje Eriksson	(SWE)
3.	Franck Piccard	(FRA)

16/12/1989, Val Gardena (ITA)
DOWNHILL

1.	PIRMIN ZURBRIGGEN	(SUI)
2.	Franz Heinzer	(SUI)
3.	Kristian Ghedina	(ITA)

06/01/1990, Kranjska Gora (YUG)
SLALOM

1.	JONAS NILSSON	(SWE)
2.	Hubert Strolz	(AUT)
3.	Michael Tritscher	(AUT)

07/01/1990, Kranjska Gora (YUG)
SLALOM

1.	ARMIN BITTNER	(FRG)
2.	Bernhard Gstrein	(AUT)
3.	Paul Accola	(SUI)

11/01/1990, Schladming (AUT)
DOWNHILL

1.	FRANCK PICCARD	(FRA)
2.	Kristian Ghedina	(ITA)
3.	Daniel Mahrer	(SUI)

12/01/1990, Schladming (AUT)
SLALOM

1.	ARMIN BITTNER	(FRG)
2.	Michael Tritscher	(AUT)
3.	Konrad Kurt Ladstätter	(ITA)
=	Tetsuya Okabe	(JPN)

12/01/1990, Schladming (AUT)
COMBINED

1.	PIRMIN ZURBRIGGEN	(SUI)
2.	Paul Accola	(SUI)
3.	Günther Mader	(AUT)

14/01/1990, Alta Badia (ITA)
GIANT SLALOM

1.	RICHARD KRÖLL	(AUT)
2.	Günther Mader	(AUT)
3.	Rudolf Nierlich	(AUT)
=	Hubert Strolz	(AUT)

20/01/1990, Kitzbühel (AUT)
DOWNHILL

1.	ATLE SKÅRDAL	(NOR)
2.	Helmut Höflehner	(AUT)
3.	Pirmin Zurbriggen	(SUI)

21/01/1990, Kitzbühel (AUT)
SLALOM

1.	RUDOLF NIERLICH	(AUT)
2.	Ole Kristian Furuseth	(NOR)
3.	Armin Bittner	(FRG)

21/01/1990, Kitzbühel (AUT)
COMBINED

1.	PIRMIN ZURBRIGGEN	(SUI)
2.	Paul Accola	(SUI)
3.	Markus Wasmeier	(FRG)

23/01/1990, Veysonnaz (SUI)
GIANT SLALOM

1. **RICHARD KRÖLL** **(AUT)**
2. Hubert Strolz (AUT)
3. Rudolf Nierlich (AUT)

27/01/1990, Val-d'Isère (FRA)
DOWNHILL

1. **HELMUT HÖFLEHNER** **(AUT)**
2. Atle Skårdal (NOR)
3. William Besse (SUI)

29/01/1990, Val-d'Isère (FRA)
DOWNHILL

1. **HELMUT HÖFLEHNER** **(AUT)**
2. William Besse (SUI)
3. Franz Heinzer (SUI)

29/01/1990, Val-d'Isère (FRA)
SUPER-G

1. **STEVE LOCHER** **(SUI)**
2. Armand Schiele (FRA)
3. Günther Mader (AUT)

30/01/1990, Les Menuires (FRA)
SUPER-G

1. **GÜNTHER MADER** **(AUT)**
2. Ole Kristian Furuseth (NOR)
3. Atle Skårdal (NOR)

03/02/1990, Cortina d'Ampezzo (ITA)
DOWNHILL

1. **KRISTIAN GHEDINA** **(ITA)**
2. Daniel Mahrer (SUI)
3. Helmut Höflehner (AUT)

04/02/1990, Cortina d'Ampezzo (ITA)
DOWNHILL

1. **HELMUT HÖFLEHNER** **(AUT)**
2. Franz Heinzer (SUI)
= Atle Skårdal (NOR)

06/02/1990, Courmayeur (ITA)
SUPER-G

1. **PIRMIN ZURBRIGGEN** **(SUI)**
2. Günther Mader (AUT)
3. Peter Runggaldier (ITA)

03/03/1990, Veysonnaz (SUI)
GIANT SLALOM

1. **FREDRIK NYBERG** **(SWE)**

2. Hubert Strolz (AUT)
3. Richard Kröll (AUT)

04/03/1990, Veysonnaz (SUI)
SLALOM

1. **ARMIN BITTNER** **(FRG)**
2. Alberto Tomba (ITA)
3. Hubert Strolz (AUT)

08/03/1990, Geilo (NOR)
SLALOM

1. **ALBERTO TOMBA** **(ITA)**
2. Michael Tritscher (AUT)
3. Jonas Nilsson (SWE)

10/03/1990, Hemsedal (NOR)
SUPER-G

1. **PIRMIN ZURBRIGGEN** **(SUI)**
2. Karl Alpiger (SUI)
3. Hans Stuffer (FRG)

12/03/1990, Sälen (SWE)
SLALOM

1. **ALBERTO TOMBA** **(ITA)**
2. Rudolf Nierlich (AUT)
3. Armin Bittner (FRG)

15/03/1990, Åre (SWE)
DOWNHILL

1. **KRISTIAN GHEDINA** **(ITA)**
2. Franz Heinzer (SUI)
3. Helmut Höflehner (AUT)

17/03/1990, Åre (SWE)
DOWNHILL

1. **ATLE SKÅRDAL** **(NOR)**
2. Helmut Höflehner (AUT)
3. Felix Belczyk (CAN)

1990-91

CUPS

OVERALL

1. **MARC GIRARDELLI** **(LUX)**
2. Alberto Tomba (ITA)
3. Rudolf Nierlich (AUT)

SLALOM

1. **MARC GIRARDELLI** **(LUX)**
2. Ole Kristian Furuseth (NOR)
3. Rudolf Nierlich (AUT)

GIANT SLALOM

1. **ALBERTO TOMBA** **(ITA)**
2. Rudolf Nierlich (AUT)
3. Marc Girardelli (LUX)

SUPER-G

1. **FRANZ HEINZER** **(SUI)**
2. Stephan Eberharter (AUT)
3. Atle Skårdal (NOR)

DOWNHILL

1. **FRANZ HEINZER** **(SUI)**
2. Atle Skårdal (NOR)
3. Daniel Mahrer (SUI)

COMBINED

1. **MARC GIRARDELLI** **(LUX)**
2. Lasse Kjus (NOR)
3. Günther Mader (AUT)

RACES

08/08/1990, Mount Hutt (NZL)
SLALOM

1. **PETER ROTH** **(FRG)**
2. Michael Tritscher (AUT)
3. Alberto Tomba (ITA)

09/08/1990, Mount Hutt (NZL)
GIANT SLALOM

1. **FREDRIK NYBERG** **(SWE)**
2. Lasse Kjus (NOR)
3. Franck Piccard (FRA)

02/12/1990, Valloire (FRA)
SUPER-G

1. **FRANCK PICCARD** **(FRA)**
2. Franz Heinzer (SUI)
3. Stephan Eberharter (AUT)

08/12/1990, Val-d'Isère (FRA)
DOWNHILL

1. **LEONHARD STOCK** **(AUT)**
2. Franz Heinzer (SUI)
3. Peter Wirnsberger (AUT)

11/12/1990, Sestriere (ITA)
SLALOM

1. **ALBERTO TOMBA** **(ITA)**
2. Ole Kristian Furuseth (NOR)
3. Rudolf Nierlich (AUT)

14/12/1990, Val Gardena (ITA)
DOWNHILL

1. **FRANZ HEINZER** **(SUI)**
2. Berni Huber (GER)
3. Atle Skårdal (NOR)

15/12/1990, Val Gardena (ITA)
DOWNHILL

1. **ATLE SKÅRDAL** **(NOR)**
2. Rob Boyd (CAN)
3. Luc Alphand (FRA)

16/12/1990, Alta Badia (ITA)
GIANT SLALOM

1. **ALBERTO TOMBA** **(ITA)**
2. Urs Kälin (SUI)
3. Marc Girardelli (LUX)

18/12/1990, Madonna di Campiglio (ITA)
SLALOM

1. **OLE KRISTIAN FURUSETH** **(NOR)**
2. Thomas Fogdö (SWE)
3. Marc Girardelli (LUX)

21/12/1990, Kranjska Gora (YUG)
GIANT SLALOM

1. **ALBERTO TOMBA** **(ITA)**
2. Urs Kälin (SUI)
3. Marc Girardelli (LUX)

22/12/1990, Kranjska Gora (YUG)
SLALOM

1. **OLE KRISTIAN FURUSETH** **(NOR)**
2. Thomas Fogdö (SWE)
3. Thomas Stangassinger (AUT)

05/01/1991, Garmisch-Partenkirchen (GER)
DOWNHILL

1.	**DANIEL MAHRER**	**(SUI)**
2.	Atle Skårdal	(NOR)
=	Hannes Zehentner	(GER)

06/01/1991, Garmisch-Partenkirchen (GER)
SUPER-G

1.	**GÜNTHER MADER**	**(AUT)**
2.	Franz Heinzer	(SUI)
3.	Marc Girardelli	(LUX)

12/01/1991, Kitzbühel (AUT)
DOWNHILL

1.	**FRANZ HEINZER**	**(SUI)**
2.	Peter Runggaldier	(ITA)
3.	Rob Boyd	(CAN)

13/01/1991, Kitzbühel (AUT)
SLALOM

1.	**MARC GIRARDELLI**	**(LUX)**
2.	Ole Kristian Furuseth	(NOR)
3.	Rudolf Nierlich	(AUT)

13/01/1991, Kitzbühel (AUT)
COMBINED

1.	**MARC GIRARDELLI**	**(LUX)**
2.	Lasse Kjus	(NOR)
3.	Günther Mader	(AUT)

15/01/1991, Adelboden (SUI)
GIANT SLALOM

1.	**MARC GIRARDELLI**	**(LUX)**
2.	Alberto Tomba	(ITA)
3.	Rudolf Nierlich	(AUT)

26/02/1991, Oppdal (NOR)
SLALOM

1.	**RUDOLF NIERLICH**	**(AUT)**
2.	Paul Accola	(SUI)
3.	Marc Girardelli	(LUX)

01/03/1991, Lillehammer (NOR)
GIANT SLALOM

1.	**ALBERTO TOMBA**	**(ITA)**
2.	Rudolf Nierlich	(AUT)
3.	Stephan Eberharter	(AUT)

02/03/1991, Lillehammer (NOR)
SLALOM

1.	**MICHAEL TRITSCHER**	**(AUT)**
2.	Thomas Stangassinger	(AUT)
3.	Paul Accola	(SUI)

08/03/1991, Aspen (USA)
DOWNHILL

1.	**FRANZ HEINZER**	**(SUI)**
2.	Atle Skårdal	(NOR)
3.	Helmut Höflehner	(AUT)

09/03/1991, Aspen (USA)
GIANT SLALOM

1.	**ALBERTO TOMBA**	**(ITA)**
2.	Rudolf Nierlich	(AUT)
3.	Marc Girardelli	(LUX)

10/03/1991, Aspen (USA)
SLALOM

1.	**RUDOLF NIERLICH**	**(AUT)**
2.	Thomas Fogdö	(SWE)
3.	Fabio De Crignis	(ITA)

15/03/1991, Lake Louise (CAN)
DOWNHILL

1.	**ATLE SKÅRDAL**	**(NOR)**
2.	Franz Heinzer	(SUI)
3.	Helmut Höflehner	(AUT)

16/03/1991, Lake Louise (CAN)
DOWNHILL

1.	**FRANZ HEINZER**	**(SUI)**
2.	Atle Skårdal	(NOR)
3.	Patrick Ortlieb	(AUT)

17/03/1991, Lake Louise (CAN)
SUPER-G

1.	**MARKUS WASMEIER**	**(GER)**
2.	Patrick Holzer	(ITA)
3.	Stephan Eberharter	(AUT)

21/03/1991, Waterville Valley (USA)
GIANT SLALOM

1.	**ALBERTO TOMBA**	**(ITA)**
2.	Ole Kristian Furuseth	(NOR)
3.	Rudolf Nierlich	(AUT)

23/03/1991, Waterville Valley (USA)
SLALOM

1.	**THOMAS FOGDÖ**	**(SWE)**
2.	Rudolf Nierlich	(AUT)
=	Alberto Tomba	(ITA)

1991-92

CUPS

OVERALL

1.	**PAUL ACCOLA**	**(SUI)**
2.	Alberto Tomba	(ITA)
3.	Marc Girardelli	(LUX)

SLALOM

1.	**ALBERTO TOMBA**	**(ITA)**
2.	Paul Accola	(SUI)
3.	Finn Christian Jagge	(NOR)

GIANT SLALOM

1.	**ALBERTO TOMBA**	**(ITA)**
2.	Hans Pieren	(SUI)
3.	Paul Accola	(SUI)

SUPER-G

1.	**PAUL ACCOLA**	**(SUI)**
2.	Marc Girardelli	(LUX)
3.	Günther Mader	(AUT)

DOWNHILL

1.	**FRANZ HEINZER**	**(SUI)**
2.	Daniel Mahrer	(SUI)
3.	AJ Kitt	(USA)

COMBINED

1.	**PAUL ACCOLA**	**(SUI)**
2.	Hubert Strolz	(AUT)
3.	Markus Wasmeier	(GER)

RACES

23/11/1991, Park City (USA)
GIANT SLALOM

1.	**ALBERTO TOMBA**	**(ITA)**
2.	Paul Accola	(SUI)
3.	Roberto Spampatti	(ITA)

24/11/1991, Park City (USA)
SLALOM

1.	**ALBERTO TOMBA**	**(ITA)**
2.	Paul Accola	(SUI)
3.	Konrad Kurt Ladstätter	(ITA)

29/11/1991, Breckenridge (USA)
GIANT SLALOM

1.	**PAUL ACCOLA**	**(SUI)**
2.	Alberto Tomba	(ITA)
3.	Fredrik Nyberg	(SWE)

30/11/1991, Breckenridge (USA)
SLALOM

1.	**PAUL ACCOLA**	**(SUI)**
2.	Thomas Fogdö	(SWE)
=	Alberto Tomba	(ITA)

07/12/1991, Val-d'Isère (FRA)
DOWNHILL

1.	**A J KITT**	**(USA)**
2.	Leonhard Stock	(AUT)
3.	Franz Heinzer	(SUI)

08/12/1991, Val-d'Isère (FRA)
SUPER-G

1.	**MARC GIRARDELLI**	**(LUX)**
2.	Atle Skårdal	(NOR)
3.	Urs Kälin	(SUI)

10/12/1991, Sestriere (ITA)
SLALOM

1.	**ALBERTO TOMBA**	**(ITA)**
2.	Finn Christian Jagge	(NOR)
3.	Ole Kristian Furuseth	(NOR)

14/12/1991, Val Gardena (ITA)
DOWNHILL

1.	**FRANZ HEINZER**	**(SUI)**
2.	Leonhard Stock	(AUT)
3.	Atle Skårdal	(NOR)

15/12/1991, Alta Badia (ITA)
GIANT SLALOM

1.	**ALBERTO TOMBA**	**(ITA)**
2.	Steve Locher	(SUI)
3.	Paul Accola	(SUI)

17/12/1991, Madonna di Campiglio (ITA)
SLALOM

1.	**FINN CHRISTIAN JAGGE**	**(NOR)**
2.	Alberto Tomba	(ITA)
3.	Thomas Fogdö	(SWE)

04/01/1992, Kranjska Gora (SLO)
GIANT SLALOM

1.	**SERGIO BERGAMELLI**	**(ITA)**
2.	Hans Pieren	(SUI)
3.	Alberto Tomba	(ITA)

05/01/1992, Kranjska Gora (SLO)
SLALOM

1.	**ALBERTO TOMBA**	**(ITA)**
2.	Armin Bittner	(GER)
3.	Finn Christian Jagge	(NOR)

11/01/1992, Garmisch-Partenkirchen (GER)
DOWNHILL

1.	**MARKUS WASMEIER**	**(GER)**
2.	Patrick Ortlieb	(AUT)
3.	Hansjörg Tauscher	(GER)

12/01/1992, Garmisch-Partenkirchen (GER)
SUPER-G

1.	**PATRICK HOLZER**	**(ITA)**
2.	Paul Accola	(SUI)
3.	Peter Rzehak	(AUT)

13/01/1992, Garmisch-Partenkirchen (GER)
SLALOM

1.	**PATRICE BIANCHI**	**(FRA)**
2.	Hubert Strolz	(AUT)
3.	Alberto Tomba	(ITA)

13/01/1992, Garmisch-Partenkirchen (GER)
COMBINED

1.	**PAUL ACCOLA**	**(SUI)**
2.	Ole Kristian Furuseth	(NOR)
3.	Hubert Strolz	(AUT)

17/01/1992, Kitzbühel (AUT)
DOWNHILL

1.	**FRANZ HEINZER**	**(SUI)**
2.	Daniel Mahrer	(SUI)
3.	Xavier Gigandet	(SUI)

18/01/1992, Kitzbühel (AUT)
DOWNHILL

1.	**FRANZ HEINZER**	**(SUI)**
2.	A J Kitt	(USA)
3.	Patrick Ortlieb	(AUT)

19/01/1992, Kitzbühel (AUT)
SLALOM

1.	**ALBERTO TOMBA**	**(ITA)**
2.	Patrice Bianchi	(FRA)
3.	Armin Bittner	(GER)

19/01/1992, Kitzbühel (AUT)
COMBINED

1.	**PAUL ACCOLA**	**(SUI)**
2.	Marc Girardelli	(LUX)
3.	Hubert Strolz	(AUT)

22/01/1992, Adelboden (SUI)
GIANT SLALOM

1.	**OLE KRISTIAN FURUSETH**	**(NOR)**
2.	Hans Pieren	(SUI)
3.	Marc Girardelli	(LUX)

25/01/1992, Wengen (SUI)
DOWNHILL

1.	**FRANZ HEINZER**	**(SUI)**
2.	Markus Wasmeier	(GER)
3.	Helmut Höflehner	(AUT)

26/01/1992, Wengen (SUI)
SLALOM

1.	**ALBERTO TOMBA**	**(ITA)**
2.	Paul Accola	(SUI)
3.	Armin Bittner	(GER)

26/01/1992, Wengen (SUI)
COMBINED

1.	**PAUL ACCOLA**	**(SUI)**
2.	Günther Mader	(AUT)
3.	Hubert Strolz	(AUT)

01/02/1992, Megève (FRA)
SUPER-G

1.	**PAUL ACCOLA**	**(SUI)**
2.	Marco Hangl	(SUI)
3.	Franz Heinzer	(SUI)

02/02/1992, Saint-Gervais-les-Bains (FRA)
GIANT SLALOM

1.	**DIDRIK MARKSTEN**	**(NOR)**
2.	Alberto Tomba	(ITA)
3.	Markus Wasmeier	(GER)

01/03/1992, Morioka (JPN)
SUPER-G

1.	**PAUL ACCOLA**	**(SUI)**
2.	Urs Kälin	(SUI)
3.	Jan Einar Thorsen	(NOR)

06/03/1992, Panorama (CAN)
DOWNHILL

1.	**WILLIAM BESSE**	**(SUI)**
2.	Günther Mader	(AUT)
=	Daniel Mahrer	(SUI)

07/03/1992, Panorama (CAN)
DOWNHILL

1.	**DANIEL MAHRER**	**(SUI)**
2.	Jan Einar Thorsen	(NOR)
3.	A J Kitt	(USA)

08/03/1992, Panorama (CAN)
SUPER-G

1.	**GÜNTHER MADER**	**(AUT)**
2.	Kjetil André Aamodt	(NOR)
3.	Marc Girardelli	(LUX)

14/03/1992, Aspen (USA)
DOWNHILL

1.	**DANIEL MAHRER**	**(SUI)**
2.	William Besse	(SUI)
3.	Patrick Ortlieb	(AUT)

15/03/1992, Aspen (USA)
SUPER-G

1.	**KJETIL ANDRÉ AAMODT**	**(NOR)**
2.	Günther Mader	(AUT)
3.	Paul Accola	(SUI)

20/03/1992, Crans-Montana (SUI)
GIANT SLALOM

1.	**ALBERTO TOMBA**	**(ITA)**
2.	Kjetil André Aamodt	(NOR)
3.	Didrik Marksten	(NOR)

22/03/1992, Crans-Montana (SUI)
SLALOM

1.	**ALBERTO TOMBA**	**(ITA)**
2.	Paul Accola	(SUI)
3.	Finn Christian Jagge	(NOR)

1992-93

CUPS

OVERALL

1.	**MARC GIRARDELLI**	**(LUX)**
2.	Kjetil André Aamodt	(NOR)
3.	Franz Heinzer	(SUI)

SLALOM

1.	**THOMAS FOGDÖ**	**(SWE)**
2.	Alberto Tomba	(ITA)
3.	Thomas Stangassinger	(AUT)

GIANT SLALOM

1.	**KJETIL ANDRÉ AAMODT**	**(NOR)**
2.	Alberto Tomba	(ITA)
3.	Marc Girardelli	(LUX)

SUPER-G

1.	**KJETIL ANDRÉ AAMODT**	**(NOR)**
2.	Günther Mader	(AUT)
3.	Franz Heinzer	(SUI)

DOWNHILL

1.	**FRANZ HEINZER**	**(SUI)**
2.	Atle Skårdal	(NOR)
3.	William Besse	(SUI)

COMBINED

1.	**MARC GIRARDELLI**	**(LUX)**
2.	Günther Mader	(AUT)
3.	Kjetil André Aamodt	(NOR)

RACES

28/11/1992, Sestriere (ITA)
GIANT SLALOM

1.	**KJETIL ANDRÉ AAMODT**	**(NOR)**
2.	Alberto Tomba	(ITA)
3.	Johan Wallner	(SWE)

29/11/1992, Sestriere (ITA)
SLALOM

1.	**FABRIZIO TESCARI**	**(ITA)**
2.	Michael Tritscher	(AUT)
3.	Armin Bittner	(GER)
=	Hubert Strolz	(AUT)

05/12/1992, Val-d'Isère (FRA)

SUPER-G

1.	**JAN EINAR THORSEN**	**(NOR)**
2.	Franz Heinzer	(SUI)
3.	Luigi Colturi	(ITA)

06/12/1992, Val-d'Isère (FRA)
SLALOM

1.	**THOMAS FOGDÖ**	**(SWE)**
2.	Thomas Sykora	(AUT)
3.	Hubert Strolz	(AUT)

11/12/1992, Val Gardena (ITA)
DOWNHILL

1.	**WILLIAM BESSE**	**(SUI)**
2.	Jan Einar Thorsen	(NOR)
3.	Patrick Ortlieb	(AUT)

12/12/1992, Val Gardena (ITA)
DOWNHILL

1.	**LEONHARD STOCK**	**(AUT)**
2.	William Besse	(SUI)
3.	A J Kitt	(USA)

13/12/1992, Alta Badia (ITA)
GIANT SLALOM

1.	**MARC GIRARDELLI**	**(LUX)**
2.	Alain Feutrier	(FRA)
3.	Alberto Tomba	(ITA)

15/12/1992, Madonna di Campiglio (ITA)
SLALOM

1.	**PATRICE BIANCHI**	**(FRA)**
2.	Alberto Tomba	(ITA)
3.	Thomas Sykora	(AUT)

19/12/1992, Kranjska Gora (SLO)
SLALOM

1.	**THOMAS FOGDÖ**	**(SWE)**
2.	Alberto Tomba	(ITA)
3.	Peter Roth	(SUI)

20/12/1992, Kranjska Gora (SLO)
GIANT SLALOM

1.	**MARC GIRARDELLI**	**(LUX)**
2.	Lasse Kjus	(NOR)
3.	Fredrik Nyberg	(SWE)

22/12/1992, Bad Kleinkirchheim (AUT)
SUPER-G

1.	**ARMIN ASSINGER**	**(AUT)**
2.	Leonhard Stock	(AUT)

3.	Kjetil André Aamodt	(NOR)

09/01/1993, Garmisch-Partenkirchen (GER)
SLALOM

1.	**ALBERTO TOMBA**	**(ITA)**
2.	Kjetil André Aamodt	(NOR)
=	Thomas Stangassinger	(AUT)

10/01/1993, Garmisch-Partenkirchen (GER)
DOWNHILL

1.	**FRANZ HEINZER**	**(SUI)**
2.	Pietro Vitalini	(ITA)
3.	Günther Mader	(AUT)

10/01/1993, Garmisch-Partenkirchen (GER)
COMBINED

1.	**MARC GIRARDELLI**	**(LUX)**
2.	Kjetil André Aamodt	(NOR)
3.	Günther Mader	(AUT)

11/01/1993, Garmisch-Partenkirchen (GER)
DOWNHILL

1.	**DANIEL MAHRER**	**(SUI)**
2.	Peter Rzehak	(AUT)
3.	Franz Heinzer	(SUI)

12/01/1993, Sankt Anton am Arlberg (AUT)
SUPER-G

1.	**MARC GIRARDELLI**	**(LUX)**
2.	Jan Einar Thorsen	(NOR)
3.	Günther Mader	(AUT)

16/01/1993, Sankt Anton am Arlberg (AUT)
DOWNHILL

1.	**FRANZ HEINZER**	**(SUI)**
2.	Peter Runggaldier	(ITA)
3.	Günther Mader	(AUT)

17/01/1993, Lech (AUT)
SLALOM

1.	**THOMAS FOGDÖ**	**(SWE)**
2.	Jure Košir	(SLO)
3.	Alberto Tomba	(ITA)

16-17/01/1993, Sankt Anton am Arlberg/Lech (AUT)
COMBINED

1.	**MARC GIRARDELLI**	**(LUX)**
2.	Günther Mader	(AUT)
3.	Hubert Strolz	(AUT)

19/01/1993, Veysonnaz (SUI)
GIANT SLALOM

1. **MICHAEL VON GRÜNIGEN** **(SUI)**
2. Alberto Tomba (ITA)
3. Lasse Kjus (NOR)

23/01/1993, Veysonnaz (SUI)
DOWNHILL

1. **FRANZ HEINZER** **(SUI)**
2. Patrick Ortlieb (AUT)
3. William Besse (SUI)

24/01/1993, Veysonnaz (SUI)
SLALOM

1. **THOMAS STANGASSINGER** **(AUT)**
2. Alberto Tomba (ITA)
3. Thomas Fogdö (SWE)

24/01/1993, Veysonnaz (SUI)
COMBINED

1. **MARC GIRARDELLI** **(LUX)**
2. Kjetil André Aamodt (NOR)
3. Günther Mader (AUT)

27/02/1993, Whistler (CAN)
DOWNHILL

1. **ATLE SKÅRDAL** **(NOR)**
2. Tommy Moe (USA)
3. Franz Heinzer (SUI)

28/02/1993, Whistler (CAN)
SUPER-G

1. **GÜNTHER MADER** **(AUT)**
2. Franz Heinzer (SUI)
3. Patrick Ortlieb (AUT)

07/03/1993, Aspen (USA)
SUPER-G

1. **KJETIL ANDRÉ AAMODT** **(NOR)**
2. Stephan Eberharter (AUT)
3. Daniel Mahrer (SUI)

15/03/1993, Sierra Nevada (ESP)
DOWNHILL

1. **ARMIN ASSINGER** **(AUT)**
2. Daniel Mahrer (SUI)
3. Hannes Trinkl (AUT)

19/03/1993, Kvitfjell (NOR)
DOWNHILL

1. **ADRIEN DUVILLARD** **(FRA)**

2. Werner Perathoner (ITA)
3. Atle Skårdal (NOR)

20/03/1993, Kvitfjell (NOR)
DOWNHILL

1. **ARMIN ASSINGER** **(AUT)**
2. Werner Perathoner (ITA)
3. Hannes Trinkl (AUT)

21/03/1993, Kvitfjell (NOR)
SUPER-G

1. **KJETIL ANDRÉ AAMODT** **(NOR)**
2. Daniel Mahrer (SUI)
3. Dietmar Thöni (AUT)

23/03/1993, Oppdal (NOR)
GIANT SLALOM

1. **KJETIL ANDRÉ AAMODT** **(NOR)**
2. Johan Wallner (SWE)
3. Fredrik Nyberg (SWE)

26/03/1993, Åre (SWE)
SUPER-G

1. **KJETIL ANDRÉ AAMODT** **(NOR)**
2. Günther Mader (AUT)
3. Franz Heinzer (SUI)

27/03/1993, Åre (SWE)
GIANT SLALOM

1. **KJETIL ANDRÉ AAMODT** **(NOR)**
2. Alberto Tomba (ITA)
3. Marc Girardelli (LUX)

28/03/1993, Åre (SWE)
SLALOM

1. **THOMAS FOGDÖ** **(SWE)**
2. Kjetil André Aamodt (NOR)
3. Thomas Stangassinger (AUT)

1993-94

CUPS

OVERALL
1. **KJETIL ANDRÉ AAMODT** **(NOR)**
2. Marc Girardelli (LUX)
3. Alberto Tomba (ITA)

SLALOM
1. **ALBERTO TOMBA** **(ITA)**
2. Thomas Stangassinger (AUT)
3. Jure Košir (SLO)

GIANT SLALOM
1. **CHRISTIAN MAYER** **(AUT)**
2. Kjetil André Aamodt (NOR)
3. Franck Piccard (FRA)

SUPER-G
1. **JAN EINAR THORSEN** **(NOR)**
2. Marc Girardelli (LUX)
3. Tommy Moe (USA)

DOWNHILL
1. **MARC GIRARDELLI** **(LUX)**
2. Hannes Trinkl (AUT)
3. Patrick Ortlieb (AUT)

COMBINED
1. **LASSE KJUS** **(NOR)**
1. **KJETIL ANDRÉ AAMODT** **(NOR)**
3. H. C. Strand Nilsen (NOR)

RACES

30/10/1993, Sölden (AUT)
GIANT SLALOM
1. **FRANCK PICCARD** **(FRA)**
2. Fredrik Nyberg (SWE)
3. Kjetil André Aamodt (NOR)

27/11/1993, Park City (USA)
GIANT SLALOM
1. **GÜNTHER MADER** **(AUT)**
2. Alberto Tomba (ITA)
3. Kjetil André Aamodt (NOR)

28/11/1993, Park City (USA)
SLALOM
1. **THOMAS STANGASSINGER** **(AUT)**
2. Jure Košir (SLO)
3. Finn Christian Jagge (NOR)

05/12/1993, Stoneham (CAN)
SLALOM
1. **ALBERTO TOMBA** **(ITA)**
2. Thomas Stangassinger (AUT)
3. Jure Košir (SLO)

12/12/1993, Val-d'Isère (FRA)
SUPER-G
1. **GÜNTHER MADER** **(AUT)**
2. Kjetil André Aamodt (NOR)
3. Tommy Moe (USA)

13/12/1993, Val-d'Isère (FRA)
GIANT SLALOM
1. **CHRISTIAN MAYER** **(AUT)**
2. Tobias Barnerssoi (GER)
3. Michael von Grünigen (SUI)

14/12/1993, Sestriere (ITA)
SLALOM
1. **ALBERTO TOMBA** **(ITA)**
2. Thomas Stangassinger (AUT)
3. Ole Kristian Furuseth (NOR)

17/12/1993, Val Gardena (ITA)
DOWNHILL
1. **MARKUS FOSER** **(LIE)**
2. Werner Franz (AUT)
3. Marc Girardelli (LUX)

18/12/1993, Val Gardena (ITA)
DOWNHILL
1. **PATRICK ORTLIEB** **(AUT)**
2. Daniel Mahrer (SUI)
3. Jean-Luc Crétier (FRA)

19/12/1993, Alta Badia (ITA)
GIANT SLALOM
1. **STEVE LOCHER** **(SUI)**
2. Alberto Tomba (ITA)
3. Christian Mayer (AUT)

20/12/1993, Madonna di Campiglio (ITA)
SLALOM
1. **JURE KOŠIR** **(SLO)**
2. Alberto Tomba (ITA)
3. Finn Christian Jagge (NOR)

22/12/1993, Lech (AUT)
SUPER-G

1.	**HANNES TRINKL**	**(AUT)**
2.	Werner Perathoner	(ITA)
3.	Armin Assinger	(AUT)

29/12/1993, Bormio (ITA)
DOWNHILL

1.	**HANNES TRINKL**	**(AUT)**
2.	Marc Girardelli	(LUX)
3.	Tommy Moe	(USA)

06/01/1994, Saalbach-Hinterglemm (AUT)
DOWNHILL

1.	**ED PODIVINSKY**	**(CAN)**
2.	Cary Mullen	(CAN)
3.	Atle Skårdal	(NOR)

08/01/1994, Kranjska Gora (SLO)
GIANT SLALOM

1.	**FREDRIK NYBERG**	**(SWE)**
2.	Matteo Belfrond	(ITA)
3.	Tobias Barnerssoi	(GER)

09/01/1994, Kranjska Gora (SLO)
SLALOM

1.	**FINN CHRISTIAN JAGGE**	**(NOR)**
2.	Ole Kristian Furuseth	(NOR)
3.	Thomas Fogdö	(SWE)

11/01/1994, Hinterstoder (AUT)
GIANT SLALOM

1.	**KJETIL ANDRÉ AAMODT**	**(NOR)**
2.	Christian Mayer	(AUT)
3.	Richard Kröll	(AUT)

15/01/1994, Kitzbühel (AUT)
DOWNHILL

1.	**PATRICK ORTLIEB**	**(AUT)**
2.	Marc Girardelli	(LUX)
3.	William Besse	(SUI)

16/01/1994, Kitzbühel (AUT)
SLALOM

1.	**THOMAS STANGASSINGER**	**(AUT)**
2.	Thomas Sykora	(AUT)
3.	Alberto Tomba	(ITA)

16/01/1994, Kitzbühel (AUT)
COMBINED

1.	**LASSE KJUS**	**(NOR)**
2.	Kjetil André Aamodt	(NOR)
3.	Günther Mader	(AUT)

18/01/1994, Crans-Montana (SUI)
GIANT SLALOM

1.	**JAN EINAR THORSEN**	**(NOR)**
2.	Mitja Kunc	(SLO)
3.	Rainer Salzgeber	(AUT)

22/01/1994, Wengen (SUI)
DOWNHILL

1.	**WILLIAM BESSE**	**(SUI)**
2.	Marc Girardelli	(LUX)
=	Peter Runggaldier	(ITA)

23/01/1994, Wengen (SUI)
SUPER-G

1.	**MARC GIRARDELLI**	**(LUX)**
2.	Jan Einar Thorsen	(NOR)
3.	Atle Skårdal	(NOR)

29/01/1994, Chamonix (FRA)
DOWNHILL

1.	**KJETIL ANDRÉ AAMODT**	**(NOR)**
2.	Jean-Luc Crétier	(FRA)
3.	Hannes Trinkl	(AUT)

30/01/1994, Chamonix (FRA)
SLALOM

1.	**ALBERTO TOMBA**	**(ITA)**
2.	Thomas Fogdö	(SWE)
3.	Thomas Sykora	(AUT)
=	Jure Košir	(SLO)

30/01/1994, Chamonix (FRA)
COMBINED

1.	**KJETIL ANDRÉ AAMODT**	**(NOR)**
2.	Lasse Kjus	(NOR)
3.	Harald Christian Strand Nilsen	(NOR)

06/02/1994, Garmisch-Partenkirchen (GER)
SLALOM

1.	**ALBERTO TOMBA**	**(ITA)**
2.	Thomas Fogdö	(SWE)
3.	Jure Košir	(SLO)

04/03/1994, Aspen (USA)
DOWNHILL

1.	**HANNES TRINKL**	**(AUT)**
2.	Cary Mullen	(CAN)

3. Marc Girardelli (LUX)

05/03/1994, Aspen (USA)
DOWNHILL
1. **CARY MULLEN** **(CAN)**
2. Atle Skårdal (NOR)
3. Pietro Vitalini (ITA)

06/03/1994, Aspen (USA)
GIANT SLALOM
1. **FREDRIK NYBERG** **(SWE)**
2. Christian Mayer (AUT)
3. Matteo Belfrond (ITA)

12/03/1994, Whistler (CAN)
DOWNHILL
1. **ATLE SKÅRDAL** **(NOR)**
2. Hannes Trinkl (AUT)
3. Tommy Moe (USA)

13/03/1994, Whistler (CAN)
SUPER-G
1. **TOMMY MOE** **(USA)**
2. Marc Girardelli (LUX)
3. Werner Perathoner (ITA)

16/03/1994, Vail (USA)
DOWNHILL
1. **WILLIAM BESSE** **(SUI)**
2. Hannes Trinkl (AUT)
3. Tommy Moe (USA)
= Patrick Ortlieb (AUT)

17/03/1994, Vail (USA)
SUPER-G
1. **JAN EINAR THORSEN** **(NOR)**
2. Lasse Kjus (NOR)
3. Hans Knauß (AUT)

19/03/1994, Vail (USA)
GIANT SLALOM
1. **KJETIL ANDRÉ AAMODT** **(NOR)**
2. Christian Mayer (AUT)
3. Steve Locher (SUI)

1994-95

CUPS

OVERALL
1. **ALBERTO TOMBA** **(ITA)**
2. Günther Mader (AUT)
3. Jure Košir (SLO)

SLALOM
1. **ALBERTO TOMBA** **(ITA)**
2. Michael Tritscher (AUT)
3. Jure Košir (SLO)

GIANT SLALOM
1. **ALBERTO TOMBA** **(ITA)**
2. Jure Košir (SLO)
3. H. C. Strand Nilsen (NOR)

SUPER-G
1. **PETER RUNGGALDIER** **(ITA)**
2. Günther Mader (AUT)
3. Werner Perathoner (ITA)

DOWNHILL
1. **LUC ALPHAND** **(FRA)**
2. Kristian Ghedina (ITA)
3. Patrick Ortlieb (AUT)

COMBINED
1. **MARC GIRARDELLI** **(LUX)**
2. H. C. Strand Nilsen (NOR)
3. Lasse Kjus (NOR)

RACES

03/12/1994, Tignes (FRA)
GIANT SLALOM
1. **ACHIM VOGT** **(LIE)**
2. Michael von Grünigen (SUI)
3. Kjetil André Aamodt (NOR)

04/12/1994, Tignes (FRA)
SLALOM
1. **ALBERTO TOMBA** **(ITA)**
2. Michael Tritscher (AUT)
3. Thomas Fogdö (SWE)

11/12/1994, Tignes (FRA)
SUPER-G

1.	**PATRICK ORTLIEB**	**(AUT)**
2.	Tommy Moe	(USA)
3.	Luc Alphand	(FRA)

12/12/1994, Sestriere (ITA)
SLALOM

1.	**ALBERTO TOMBA**	**(ITA)**
2.	Thomas Fogdö	(SWE)
3.	Michael Tritscher	(AUT)

16/12/1994, Val-d'Isère (FRA)
DOWNHILL

1.	**JOSEF STROBL**	**(AUT)**
2.	Luc Alphand	(FRA)
3.	Günther Mader	(AUT)

17/12/1994, Val-d'Isère (FRA)
DOWNHILL

1.	**ARMIN ASSINGER**	**(AUT)**
2.	Patrick Ortlieb	(AUT)
3.	Josef Strobl	(AUT)

18/12/1994, Val-d'Isère (FRA)
GIANT SLALOM

1.	**MICHAEL VON GRÜNIGEN**	**(SUI)**
2.	Kjetil André Aamodt	(NOR)
3.	Günther Mader	(AUT)

20/12/1994, Lech (AUT)
SLALOM

1.	**ALBERTO TOMBA**	**(ITA)**
2.	Thomas Sykora	(AUT)
3.	Jure Košir	(SLO)

21/12/1994, Lech (AUT)
SLALOM

1.	**ALBERTO TOMBA**	**(ITA)**
2.	Thomas Sykora	(AUT)
3.	Michael Tritscher	(AUT)

22/12/1994, Alta Badia (ITA)
GIANT SLALOM

1.	**ALBERTO TOMBA**	**(ITA)**
2.	Urs Kälin	(SUI)
3.	Christian Mayer	(AUT)

06/01/1995, Kranjska Gora (SLO)
GIANT SLALOM

1.	**ALBERTO TOMBA**	**(ITA)**
2.	Mitja Kunc	(SLO)
=	Harald Christian Strand Nilsen	(NOR)

08/01/1995, Garmisch-Partenkirchen (GER)
SLALOM

1.	**ALBERTO TOMBA**	**(ITA)**
2.	Marc Girardelli	(LUX)
3.	Yves Dimier	(FRA)

13/01/1995, Kitzbühel (AUT)
DOWNHILL

1.	**LUC ALPHAND**	**(FRA)**
2.	Patrick Ortlieb	(AUT)
3.	Kristian Ghedina	(ITA)

14/01/1995, Kitzbühel (AUT)
DOWNHILL

1.	**LUC ALPHAND**	**(FRA)**
2.	Armin Assinger	(AUT)
3.	Werner Perathoner	(ITA)

15/01/1995, Kitzbühel (AUT)
SLALOM

1.	**ALBERTO TOMBA**	**(ITA)**
2.	Jure Košir	(SLO)
3.	Ole Kristian Furuseth	(NOR)

15/01/1995, Kitzbühel (AUT)
COMBINED

1.	**MARC GIRARDELLI**	**(LUX)**
2.	Harald Christian Strand Nilsen	(NOR)
3.	Günther Mader	(AUT)

16/01/1995, Kitzbühel (AUT)
SUPER-G

1.	**GÜNTHER MADER**	**(AUT)**
2.	Peter Runggaldier	(ITA)
3.	Armin Assinger	(AUT)

20/01/1995, Wengen (SUI)
DOWNHILL

1.	**KRISTIAN GHEDINA**	**(ITA)**
2.	Peter Rzehak	(AUT)
3.	Hannes Trinkl	(AUT)

21/01/1995, Wengen (SUI)
DOWNHILL

1.	**KYLE RASMUSSEN**	**(USA)**
2.	Werner Franz	(AUT)
3.	Armin Assinger	(AUT)

22/01/1995, Wengen (SUI)
SLALOM

1.	**ALBERTO TOMBA**	**(ITA)**

2. Michael von Grünigen (SUI)
3. Jure Košir (SLO)

22/01/1995, Wengen (SUI)
COMBINED

1. **MARC GIRARDELLI** **(LUX)**
2. Lasse Kjus (NOR)
3. Harald Christian Strand Nilsen (NOR)

04/02/1995, Adelboden (SUI)
GIANT SLALOM

1. **ALBERTO TOMBA** **(ITA)**
2. Jure Košir (SLO)
3. Harald Christian Strand Nilsen (NOR)

19/02/1995, Furano (JPN)
SLALOM

1. **MICHAEL TRITSCHER** **(AUT)**
2. Mario Reiter (AUT)
3. Ole Kristian Furuseth (NOR)

20/02/1995, Furano (JPN)
GIANT SLALOM

1. **MARIO REITER** **(AUT)**
2. Jure Košir (SLO)
3. Harald Christian Strand Nilsen (NOR)

25/02/1995, Whistler (CAN)
DOWNHILL

1. **KRISTIAN GHEDINA** **(ITA)**
2. Lasse Kjus (NOR)
3. Patrick Ortlieb (AUT)

26/02/1995, Whistler (CAN)
SUPER-G

1. **PETER RUNGGALDIER** **(ITA)**
2. A J Kitt (USA)
3. Christian Greber (AUT)

10/03/1995, Kvitfjell (NOR)
SUPER-G

1. **WERNER PERATHONER** **(ITA)**
2. Kristian Ghedina (ITA)
3. Kyle Rasmussen (USA)

11/03/1995, Kvitfjell (NOR)
DOWNHILL

1. **KYLE RASMUSSEN** **(USA)**
2. Kristian Ghedina (ITA)
3. Patrick Ortlieb (AUT)

15/03/1995, Bormio (ITA)
DOWNHILL

1. **LUC ALPHAND** **(FRA)**
2. A J Kitt (USA)
3. Lasse Kjus (NOR)

16/03/1995, Bormio (ITA)
SUPER-G

1. **RICHARD KRÖLL** **(AUT)**
2. Peter Runggaldier (ITA)
3. Werner Perathoner (ITA)

18/03/1995, Bormio (ITA)
GIANT SLALOM

1. **ALBERTO TOMBA** **(ITA)**
2. Günther Mader (AUT)
3. Rainer Salzgeber (AUT)

19/03/1995, Bormio (ITA)
SLALOM

1. **OLE KRISTIAN FURUSETH** **(NOR)**
2. Thomas Stangassinger (AUT)
3. Yves Dimier (FRA)

1995-96

CUPS

OVERALL
1.	**LASSE KJUS**	**(NOR)**
2.	Günther Mader	(AUT)
3.	Michael von Grünigen	(SUI)

SLALOM
1.	**SÉBASTIEN AMIEZ**	**(FRA)**
2.	Alberto Tomba	(ITA)
3.	Thomas Sykora	(AUT)

GIANT SLALOM
1.	**MICHAEL VON GRÜNIGEN**	**(SUI)**
2.	Urs Kälin	(SUI)
3.	Lasse Kjus	(NOR)

SUPER-G
1.	**ATLE SKÅRDAL**	**(NOR)**
2.	Hans Knauß	(AUT)
3.	Lasse Kjus	(NOR)

DOWNHILL
1.	**LUC ALPHAND**	**(FRA)**
2.	Günther Mader	(AUT)
3.	Patrick Ortlieb	(AUT)

COMBINED
1.	**GÜNTHER MADER**	**(AUT)**
2.	Marc Girardelli	(LUX)
3.	Alessandro Fattori	(ITA)

RACES

12/11/1995, Tignes (FRA)
GIANT SLALOM
1.	**MICHAEL VON GRÜNIGEN**	**(SUI)**
2.	Lasse Kjus	(NOR)
3.	Urs Kälin	(SUI)

17/11/1995, Beaver Creek (USA)
GIANT SLALOM
1.	**MICHAEL VON GRÜNIGEN**	**(SUI)**
2.	Lasse Kjus	(NOR)
3.	Urs Kälin	(SUI)

19/11/1995, Beaver Creek (USA)
SLALOM
1.	**MICHAEL TRITSCHER**	**(AUT)**
2.	Sébastien Amiez	(FRA)
3.	Alberto Tomba	(ITA)

25/11/1995, Park City (USA)
GIANT SLALOM
1.	**MICHAEL VON GRÜNIGEN**	**(SUI)**
2.	Lasse Kjus	(NOR)
3.	Hans Knauß	(AUT)

26/11/1995, Park City (USA)
SLALOM
1.	**ANDREJ MIKLAVC**	**(SLO)**
2.	Christian Mayer	(AUT)
3.	Fabio De Crignis	(ITA)

01/12/1995, Vail (USA)
DOWNHILL
1.	**LUC ALPHAND**	**(FRA)**
2.	Lasse Kjus	(NOR)
3.	Patrick Ortlieb	(AUT)

02/12/1995, Vail (USA)
SUPER-G
1.	**LASSE KJUS**	**(NOR)**
2.	Richard Kröll	(AUT)
3.	Pietro Vitalini	(ITA)

09/12/1995, Val-d'Isère (FRA)
DOWNHILL
1.	**LUC ALPHAND**	**(FRA)**
2.	Roland Assinger	(AUT)
3.	Hannes Trinkl	(AUT)

10/12/1995, Val-d'Isère (FRA)
SUPER-G
1.	**ATLE SKÅRDAL**	**(NOR)**
2.	Lasse Kjus	(NOR)
3.	Hans Knauß	(AUT)

16/12/1995, Val Gardena (ITA)
DOWNHILL
1.	**PATRICK ORTLIEB**	**(AUT)**
2.	Xavier Gigandet	(SUI)
3.	Luc Alphand	(FRA)

17/12/1995, Alta Badia (ITA)
GIANT SLALOM
1.	**HANS KNAUSS**	**(AUT)**
2.	Michael von Grünigen	(SUI)
3.	Alberto Tomba	(ITA)

19/12/1995, Madonna di Campiglio (ITA)
SLALOM

1.	**ALBERTO TOMBA**	**(ITA)**
2.	Yves Dimier	(FRA)
3.	Konrad Kurt Ladstätter	(ITA)

21/12/1995, Kranjska Gora (SLO)
GIANT SLALOM

1.	**LASSE KJUS**	**(NOR)**
2.	Michael von Grünigen	(SUI)
3.	Mario Reiter	(AUT)

22/12/1995, Kranjska Gora (SLO)
SLALOM

1.	**ALBERTO TOMBA**	**(ITA)**
2.	Jure Košir	(SLO)
3.	Sébastien Amiez	(FRA)

29/12/1995, Bormio (ITA)
DOWNHILL

1.	**LASSE KJUS**	**(NOR)**
2.	Andreas Schifferer	(AUT)
3.	Ed Podivinsky	(CAN)

06/01/1996, Flachau (AUT)
GIANT SLALOM

1.	**URS KÄLIN**	**(SUI)**
2.	Alberto Tomba	(ITA)
3.	Michael von Grünigen	(SUI)

07/01/1996, Flachau (AUT)
SLALOM

1.	**ALBERTO TOMBA**	**(ITA)**
2.	Mario Reiter	(AUT)
3.	Jure Košir	(SLO)

13/01/1996, Kitzbühel (AUT)
DOWNHILL

1.	**GÜNTHER MADER**	**(AUT)**
2.	Luc Alphand	(FRA)
3.	Peter Runggaldier	(ITA)

14/01/1996, Kitzbühel (AUT)
SLALOM

1.	**THOMAS SYKORA**	**(AUT)**
2.	Alberto Tomba	(ITA)
3.	Jure Košir	(SLO)

14/01/1996, Kitzbühel (AUT)
COMBINED

1.	**GÜNTHER MADER**	**(AUT)**
2.	Hans Knauß	(AUT)
3.	Bruno Kernen	(SUI)

16/01/1996, Adelboden (SUI)
GIANT SLALOM

1.	**MICHAEL VON GRÜNIGEN**	**(SUI)**
2.	Urs Kälin	(SUI)
3.	Tom Stiansen	(NOR)

19/01/1996, Veysonnaz (SUI)
DOWNHILL

1.	**BRUNO KERNEN**	**(SUI)**
2.	William Besse	(SUI)
3.	Daniel Mahrer	(SUI)

20/01/1996, Veysonnaz (SUI)
DOWNHILL

1.	**BRUNO KERNEN**	**(SUI)**
2.	Luc Alphand	(FRA)
=	Patrick Ortlieb	(AUT)

21/01/1996, Veysonnaz (SUI)
SLALOM

1.	**SÉBASTIEN AMIEZ**	**(FRA)**
2.	Rene Mlekuž	(SLO)
3.	Thomas Sykora	(AUT)

21/01/1996, Veysonnaz (SUI)
COMBINED

1.	**MARC GIRARDELLI**	**(LUX)**
2.	Günther Mader	(AUT)
3.	Kjetil André Aamodt	(NOR)

23/01/1996, Valloire (FRA)
SUPER-G

1.	**HANS KNAUSS**	**(AUT)**
2.	Atle Skårdal	(NOR)
3.	Fredrik Nyberg	(SWE)

27/01/1996, Sestriere (ITA)
SLALOM

1.	**MARIO REITER**	**(AUT)**
2.	Thomas Sykora	(AUT)
3.	Thomas Stangassinger	(AUT)

02/02/1996, Garmisch-Partenkirchen (GER)
DOWNHILL

1.	**LUC ALPHAND**	**(FRA)**
2.	Brian Stemmle	(CAN)
3.	Peter Runggaldier	(ITA)

05/02/1996, Garmisch-Partenkirchen (GER)
SUPER-G

1.	**WERNER PERATHONER**	**(ITA)**
2.	Luc Alphand	(FRA)
3.	Patrick Wirth	(AUT)

10/02/1996, Hinterstoder (AUT)
GIANT SLALOM

1.	**MICHAEL VON GRÜNIGEN**	**(SUI)**
2.	Urs Kälin	(SUI)
3.	Mario Reiter	(AUT)

03/03/1996, Hakuba (JPN)
SUPER-G

1.	**PETER RUNGGALDIER**	**(ITA)**
2.	Atle Skårdal	(NOR)
3.	Hans Knauß	(AUT)

06/03/1996, Kvitfjell (NOR)
DOWNHILL

1.	**LASSE KJUS**	**(NOR)**
2.	Günther Mader	(AUT)
3.	Kristian Ghedina	(ITA)

07/03/1996, Kvitfjell (NOR)
SUPER-G

1.	**KJETIL ANDRÉ AAMODT**	**(NOR)**
2.	Luc Alphand	(FRA)
3.	Lasse Kjus	(NOR)

09/03/1996, Hafjell (NOR)
GIANT SLALOM

1.	**URS KÄLIN**	**(SUI)**
2.	Tom Stiansen	(NOR)
3.	Christophe Saioni	(FRA)

10/03/1996, Hafjell (NOR)
SLALOM

1.	**THOMAS SYKORA**	**(AUT)**
2.	Sébastien Amiez	(FRA)
3.	Jure Košir	(SLO)

1996-97

CUPS

OVERALL

1.	**LUC ALPHAND**	**(FRA)**
2.	Kjetil André Aamodt	(NOR)
3.	Josef Strobl	(AUT)

SLALOM

1.	**THOMAS SYKORA**	**(AUT)**
2.	Thomas Stangassinger	(AUT)
3.	Finn Christian Jagge	(NOR)

GIANT SLALOM

1.	**MICHAEL VON GRÜNIGEN**	**(SUI)**
2.	Kjetil André Aamodt	(NOR)
3.	Hans Knauß	(AUT)

SUPER-G

1.	**LUC ALPHAND**	**(FRA)**
2.	Josef Strobl	(AUT)
3.	Andreas Schifferer	(AUT)

DOWNHILL

1.	**LUC ALPHAND**	**(FRA)**
2.	Kristian Ghedina	(ITA)
3.	Fritz Strobl	(AUT)

COMBINED

1.	**KJETIL ANDRÉ AAMODT**	**(NOR)**
2.	Lasse Kjus	(NOR)
=	Günther Mader	(AUT)

RACES

27/10/1996, Sölden (AUT)
GIANT SLALOM

1.	**STEVE LOCHER**	**(SUI)**
2.	Michael von Grünigen	(SUI)
3.	Kjetil André Aamodt	(NOR)

24/11/1996, Park City (USA)
SLALOM

1.	**THOMAS SYKORA**	**(AUT)**
2.	Thomas Stangassinger	(AUT)
3.	Kjetil André Aamodt	(NOR)

25/11/1996, Park City (USA)
GIANT SLALOM

1. **JOSEF STROBL** **(AUT)**
2. Hans Knauß (AUT)
3. Michael von Grünigen (SUI)

30/11/1996, Breckenridge (USA)
GIANT SLALOM
1. **FREDRIK NYBERG** **(SWE)**
2. Urs Kälin (SUI)
3. Hans Knauß (AUT)

01/12/1996, Breckenridge (USA)
SLALOM
1. **TOM STIANSEN** **(NOR)**
2. Thomas Sykora (AUT)
3. Thomas Stangassinger (AUT)

15/12/1996, Val-d'Isère (FRA)
DOWNHILL
1. **FRITZ STROBL** **(AUT)**
2. Werner Franz (AUT)
3. Patrick Ortlieb (AUT)

16/12/1996, Val-d'Isère (FRA)
SUPER-G
1. **HANS KNAUSS** **(AUT)**
2. Günther Mader (AUT)
3. Steve Locher (SUI)

17/12/1996, Madonna di Campiglio (ITA)
SLALOM
1. **THOMAS SYKORA** **(AUT)**
2. Alberto Tomba (ITA)
3. Sébastien Amiez (FRA)

20/12/1996, Val Gardena (ITA)
DOWNHILL
1. **LUC ALPHAND** **(FRA)**
2. Atle Skårdal (NOR)
3. Kristian Ghedina (ITA)

21/12/1996, Val Gardena (ITA)
DOWNHILL
1. **KRISTIAN GHEDINA** **(ITA)**
2. Luc Alphand (FRA)
3. Josef Strobl (AUT)

22/12/1996, Alta Badia (ITA)
GIANT SLALOM
1. **MICHAEL VON GRÜNIGEN** **(SUI)**
2. Steve Locher (SUI)
3. Matteo Nana (ITA)

29/12/1996, Bormio (ITA)
DOWNHILL
1. **LUC ALPHAND** **(FRA)**
2. William Besse (SUI)
3. Kristian Ghedina (ITA)

05/01/1997, Kranjska Gora (SLO)
GIANT SLALOM
1. **MICHAEL VON GRÜNIGEN** **(SUI)**
2. Siegfried Voglreiter (AUT)
3. Kjetil André Aamodt (NOR)

06/01/1997, Kranjska Gora (SLO)
SLALOM
1. **THOMAS SYKORA** **(AUT)**
2. Sébastien Amiez (FRA)
3. Thomas Stangassinger (AUT)

11/01/1997, Chamonix (FRA)
DOWNHILL
1. **KRISTIAN GHEDINA** **(ITA)**
2. Atle Skårdal (NOR)
3. Werner Franz (AUT)

12/01/1997, Chamonix (FRA)
SLALOM
1. **THOMAS SYKORA** **(AUT)**
2. Thomas Stangassinger (AUT)
3. Martin Hansson (SWE)

12/01/1997, Chamonix (FRA)
COMBINED
1. **GÜNTHER MADER** **(AUT)**
2. Kjetil André Aamodt (NOR)
3. Bruno Kernen (SUI)

14/01/1997, Adelboden (SUI)
GIANT SLALOM
1. **KJETIL ANDRÉ AAMODT** **(NOR)**
2. Michael von Grünigen (SUI)
3. Andreas Schifferer (AUT)

18/01/1997, Wengen (SUI)
DOWNHILL
1. **KRISTIAN GHEDINA** **(ITA)**
2. Luc Alphand (FRA)
3. Fritz Strobl (AUT)

19/01/1997, Wengen (SUI)
SLALOM

1. **THOMAS SYKORA** **(AUT)**
2. Thomas Stangassinger (AUT)
3. Sébastien Amiez (FRA)

24/01/1997, Kitzbühel (AUT)
DOWNHILL
1. **LUC ALPHAND** **(FRA)**
2. Werner Franz (AUT)
3. William Besse (SUI)

25/01/1997, Kitzbühel (AUT)
DOWNHILL
1. **FRITZ STROBL** **(AUT)**
2. Werner Franz (AUT)
3. Luc Alphand (FRA)

26/01/1997, Kitzbühel (AUT)
SLALOM
1. **MARIO REITER** **(AUT)**
2. Alberto Tomba (ITA)
3. Finn Christian Jagge (NOR)

26/01/1997, Kitzbühel (AUT)
COMBINED
1. **LASSE KJUS** **(NOR)**
2. Kjetil André Aamodt (NOR)
3. Werner Franz (AUT)

29/01/1997, Laax (SUI)
SUPER-G
1. **LUC ALPHAND** **(FRA)**
2. Josef Strobl (AUT)
3. Peter Runggaldier (ITA)

30/01/1997, Schladming (AUT)
SLALOM
1. **ALBERTO TOMBA** **(ITA)**
2. Thomas Stangassinger (AUT)
3. Sébastien Amiez (FRA)

21/02/1997, Garmisch-Partenkirchen (GER)
SUPER-G
1. **LUC ALPHAND** **(FRA)**
2. Hermann Maier (AUT)
3. Werner Perathoner (ITA)

22/02/1997, Garmisch-Partenkirchen (GER)
DOWNHILL
1. **LUC ALPHAND** **(FRA)**
2. Pietro Vitalini (ITA)
3. Kristian Ghedina (ITA)

23/02/1997, Garmisch-Partenkirchen (GER)
SUPER-G
1. **HERMANN MAIER** **(AUT)**
2. Kristian Ghedina (ITA)
3. Lasse Kjus (NOR)
= Atle Skårdal (NOR)

02/03/1997, Kvitfjell (NOR)
DOWNHILL
1. **LASSE KJUS** **(NOR)**
2. Pietro Vitalini (ITA)
3. Ed Podivinsky (CAN)

02/03/1997, Kvitfjell (NOR)
SUPER-G
1. **JOSEF STROBL** **(AUT)**
2. Andreas Schifferer (AUT)
3. Lasse Kjus (NOR)

08/03/1997, Shigakōgen (JPN)
GIANT SLALOM
1. **MICHAEL VON GRÜNIGEN** **(SUI)**
2. Andreas Schifferer (AUT)
3. Paul Accola (SUI)

09/03/1997, Shigakōgen (JPN)
SLALOM
1. **THOMAS STANGASSINGER** **(AUT)**
2. Finn Christian Jagge (NOR)
3. Ole Kristian Furuseth (NOR)

12/03/1997, Vail (USA)
DOWNHILL
1. **FRITZ STROBL** **(AUT)**
2. Kristian Ghedina (ITA)
3. Hannes Trinkl (AUT)

13/03/1997, Vail (USA)
SUPER-G
1. **ANDREAS SCHIFFERER** **(AUT)**
2. Josef Strobl (AUT)
3. Kristian Ghedina (ITA)

15/03/1997, Vail (USA)
SLALOM
1. **FINN CHRISTIAN JAGGE** **(NOR)**
2. Thomas Stangassinger (AUT)
3. Alberto Tomba (ITA)

15/03/1997, Vail (USA)

GIANT SLALOM

1.	**MICHAEL VON GRÜNIGEN**	**(SUI)**
2.	Rainer Salzgeber	(AUT)
3.	Andreas Schifferer	(AUT)

1997-98

CUPS

OVERALL

1.	**HERMANN MAIER**	**(AUT)**
2.	Andreas Schifferer	(AUT)
3.	Stephan Eberharter	(AUT)

SLALOM

1.	**THOMAS SYKORA**	**(AUT)**
2.	Thomas Stangassinger	(AUT)
3.	Hans Petter Buraas	(NOR)

GIANT SLALOM

1.	**HERMANN MAIER**	**(AUT)**
2.	Michael von Grünigen	(SUI)
3.	Christian Mayer	(AUT)

SUPER-G

1.	**HERMANN MAIER**	**(AUT)**
2.	Hans Knauß	(AUT)
3.	Stephan Eberharter	(AUT)

DOWNHILL

1.	**ANDREAS SCHIFFERER**	**(AUT)**
2.	Hermann Maier	(AUT)
3.	Nicolas Burtin	(FRA)

COMBINED

1.	**WERNER FRANZ**	**(AUT)**
2.	Kjetil André Aamodt	(NOR)
=	Hermann Maier	(AUT)

RACES

24/10/1997, Tignes (FRA)
PARALLEL SLALOM

1.	**JOSEF STROBL**	**(AUT)**
2.	Kjetil André Aamodt	(NOR)
3.	Hermann Maier	(AUT)

26/10/1997, Tignes (FRA)
GIANT SLALOM

1.	**MICHAEL VON GRÜNIGEN**	**(SUI)**
2.	Steve Locher	(SUI)
3.	Hermann Maier	(AUT)

20/11/1997, Park City (USA)
GIANT SLALOM

1. **HERMANN MAIER** **(AUT)**
2. Kjetil André Aamodt (NOR)
3. Thomas Grandi (CAN)

22/11/1997, Park City (USA)
SLALOM

1. **THOMAS STANGASSINGER** **(AUT)**
2. Kristinn Björnsson (ISL)
3. Finn Christian Jagge (NOR)

04/12/1997, Beaver Creek (USA)
DOWNHILL

1. **KRISTIAN GHEDINA** **(ITA)**
2. Jean-Luc Crétier (FRA)
3. Lasse Kjus (NOR)

05/12/1997, Beaver Creek (USA)
DOWNHILL

1. **ANDREAS SCHIFFERER** **(AUT)**
2. Hermann Maier (AUT)
3. Stephan Eberharter (AUT)

06/12/1997, Beaver Creek (USA)
SUPER-G

1. **HERMANN MAIER** **(AUT)**
2. Stephan Eberharter (AUT)
3. Hans Knauß (AUT)

14/12/1997, Val-d'Isère (FRA)
GIANT SLALOM

1. **MICHAEL VON GRÜNIGEN** **(SUI)**
2. Stephan Eberharter (AUT)
3. Hans Knauß (AUT)

15/12/1997, Sestriere (ITA)
SLALOM

1. **FINN CHRISTIAN JAGGE** **(NOR)**
2. Thomas Sykora (AUT)
3. Hans Petter Buraas (NOR)

21/12/1997, Alta Badia (ITA)
GIANT SLALOM

1. **CHRISTIAN MAYER** **(AUT)**
2. Michael von Grünigen (SUI)
3. Hermann Maier (AUT)

29/12/1997, Bormio (ITA)
DOWNHILL

1. **HERMANN MAIER** **(AUT)**
2. Andreas Schifferer (AUT)
3. Werner Franz (AUT)

30/12/1997, Bormio (ITA)
DOWNHILL

1. **ANDREAS SCHIFFERER** **(AUT)**
2. Werner Franz (AUT)
3. Lasse Kjus (NOR)

03/01/1998, Kranjska Gora (SLO)
GIANT SLALOM

1. **CHRISTIAN MAYER** **(AUT)**
2. Hermann Maier (AUT)
3. Michael von Grünigen (SUI)

04/01/1998, Kranjska Gora (SLO)
SLALOM

1. **THOMAS SYKORA** **(AUT)**
2. Pierrick Bourgeat (FRA)
3. Thomas Stangassinger (AUT)

06/01/1998, Saalbach-Hinterglemm (AUT)
GIANT SLALOM

1. **HERMANN MAIER** **(AUT)**
2. Alberto Tomba (ITA)
3. Rainer Salzgeber (AUT)

08/01/1998, Schladming (AUT)
SLALOM

1. **ALBERTO TOMBA** **(ITA)**
2. Thomas Sykora (AUT)
3. Hans Petter Buraas (NOR)

10/01/1998, Schladming (AUT)
SUPER-G

1. **HERMANN MAIER** **(AUT)**
2. Stephan Eberharter (AUT)
3. Luca Cattaneo (ITA)

11/01/1998, Schladming (AUT)
SUPER-G

1. **HERMANN MAIER** **(AUT)**
2. Andreas Schifferer (AUT)
3. Stephan Eberharter (AUT)

13/01/1998, Adelboden (SUI)
GIANT SLALOM

1. **HERMANN MAIER** **(AUT)**
2. Michael von Grünigen (SUI)
3. Paul Accola (SUI)

16/01/1998, Wengen (SUI)
DOWNHILL

1. **HERMANN MAIER** **(AUT)**
2. Nicolas Burtin (FRA)
3. Andreas Schifferer (AUT)

17/01/1998, Wengen (SUI)
DOWNHILL
1. **ANDREAS SCHIFFERER** **(AUT)**
2. Jean-Luc Crétier (FRA)
3. Hermann Maier (AUT)

18/01/1998, Veysonnaz (SUI)
SLALOM
1. **THOMAS STANGASSINGER** **(AUT)**
2. Kristinn Björnsson (ISL)
3. Kiminobu Kimura (JPN)

16-18/01/1998, Wengen/Veysonnaz (SUI)
COMBINED
1. **HERMANN MAIER** **(AUT)**
2. Bruno Kernen (SUI)
3. Paul Accola (SUI)

23/01/1998, Kitzbühel (AUT)
DOWNHILL
1. **DIDIER CUCHE** **(SUI)**
2. Nicolas Burtin (FRA)
3. Jean-Luc Crétier (FRA)

24/01/1998, Kitzbühel (AUT)
DOWNHILL
1. **KRISTIAN GHEDINA** **(ITA)**
2. Didier Cuche (SUI)
3. Josef Strobl (AUT)

25/01/1998, Kitzbühel (AUT)
SLALOM
1. **THOMAS STANGASSINGER** **(AUT)**
2. Thomas Sykora (AUT)
3. Ole Kristian Furuseth (NOR)

25/01/1998, Kitzbühel (AUT)
COMBINED
1. **KJETIL ANDRÉ AAMODT** **(NOR)**
2. Werner Franz (AUT)
3. Ed Podivinsky (CAN)

26/01/1998, Kitzbühel (AUT)
SLALOM
1. **THOMAS SYKORA** **(AUT)**
2. Hans Petter Buraas (NOR)
3. Thomas Stangassinger (AUT)

31/01/1998, Garmisch-Partenkirchen (GER)
DOWNHILL
1. **ANDREAS SCHIFFERER** **(AUT)**
2. Nicolas Burtin (FRA)
3. Hermann Maier (AUT)

01/02/1998, Garmisch-Partenkirchen (GER)
SUPER-G
1. **HERMANN MAIER** **(AUT)**
2. Hans Knauß (AUT)
3. Lasse Kjus (NOR)

28/02/1998, Yongpyong (KOR)
GIANT SLALOM
1. **MICHAEL VON GRÜNIGEN** **(SUI)**
2. Christian Mayer (AUT)
3. Hermann Maier (AUT)

01/03/1998, Yongpyong (KOR)
SLALOM
1. **OLE KRISTIAN FURUSETH** **(NOR)**
2. Finn Christian Jagge (NOR)
3. Tom Stiansen (NOR)

07/03/1998, Kvitfjell (NOR)
DOWNHILL
1. **NICOLAS BURTIN** **(FRA)**
2. Werner Perathoner (ITA)
3. Lasse Kjus (NOR)
= Josef Strobl (AUT)

08/03/1998, Kvitfjell (NOR)
SUPER-G
1. **HANS KNAUSS** **(AUT)**
2. Patrik Järbyn (SWE)
3. Didier Cuche (SUI)

13/03/1998, Crans-Montana (SUI)
DOWNHILL
1. **JOSEF STROBL** **(AUT)**
2. Didier Cuche (SUI)
3. Fritz Strobl (AUT)

14/03/1998, Crans-Montana (SUI)
GIANT SLALOM
1. **STEPHAN EBERHARTER** **(AUT)**
2. Hans Knauß (AUT)
3. Hermann Maier (AUT)

15/03/1998, Crans-Montana (SUI)

SLALOM

1.	**ALBERTO TOMBA**	**(ITA)**
2.	Hans Petter Buraas	(NOR)
3.	Finn Christian Jagge	(NOR)

1998-99

CUPS

OVERALL

1.	**LASSE KJUS**	**(NOR)**
2.	Kjetil André Aamodt	(NOR)
3.	Hermann Maier	(AUT)

SLALOM

1.	**THOMAS STANGASSINGER**	**(AUT)**
2.	Jure Košir	(SLO)
3.	Finn Christian Jagge	(NOR)

GIANT SLALOM

1.	**MICHAEL VON GRÜNIGEN**	**(SUI)**
2.	Stephan Eberharter	(AUT)
3.	Hermann Maier	(AUT)

SUPER-G

1.	**HERMANN MAIER**	**(AUT)**
2.	Stephan Eberharter	(AUT)
3.	Andreas Schifferer	(AUT)

DOWNHILL

1.	**LASSE KJUS**	**(NOR)**
2.	Andreas Schifferer	(AUT)
3.	Werner Franz	(AUT)

COMBINED

1.	**LASSE KJUS**	**(NOR)**
=	**KJETIL ANDRÉ AAMODT**	**(NOR)**
3.	Werner Franz	(AUT)

RACES

25/10/1998, Sölden (AUT)
GIANT SLALOM

1.	**HERMANN MAIER**	**(AUT)**
2.	Stephan Eberharter	(AUT)
3.	Heinz Schilchegger	(AUT)

20/11/1998, Park City (USA)
GIANT SLALOM

1.	**STEPHAN EBERHARTER**	**(AUT)**
2.	Christian Mayer	(AUT)
3.	Marco Büchel	(LIE)

22/11/1998, Park City (USA)
SLALOM

1. **PIERRICK BOURGEAT** **(FRA)**
2. Hans Petter Buraas (NOR)
3. Christian Mayer (AUT)

27/11/1998, Aspen (USA)
SUPER-G

1. **STEPHAN EBERHARTER** **(AUT)**
2. Hermann Maier (AUT)
3. Christian Mayer (AUT)

28/11/1998, Aspen (USA)
SLALOM

1. **THOMAS STANGASSINGER** **(AUT)**
2. Sébastien Amiez (FRA)
3. Tom Stiansen (NOR)

12/12/1998, Val-d'Isère (FRA)
DOWNHILL

1. **LASSE KJUS** **(NOR)**
2. Luca Cattaneo (ITA)
3. Erik Seletto (ITA)

13/12/1998, Val-d'Isère (FRA)
SUPER-G

1. **HERMANN MAIER** **(AUT)**
2. Stephan Eberharter (AUT)
3. Lasse Kjus (NOR)

14/12/1998, Sestriere (ITA)
SLALOM

1. **FINN CHRISTIAN JAGGE** **(NOR)**
2. Thomas Stangassinger (AUT)
3. Jure Košir (SLO)

18/12/1998, Val Gardena (ITA)
DOWNHILL

1. **LASSE KJUS** **(NOR)**
2. Werner Franz (AUT)
3. Hermann Maier (AUT)

19/12/1998, Val Gardena (ITA)
DOWNHILL

1. **KRISTIAN GHEDINA** **(ITA)**
2. Lasse Kjus (NOR)
3. Werner Franz (AUT)

20/12/1998, Alta Badia (ITA)
GIANT SLALOM

1. **MICHAEL VON GRÜNIGEN** **(SUI)**
2. Patrick Holzer (ITA)
3. Andreas Schifferer (AUT)

21/12/1998, Innsbruck (AUT)
SUPER-G

1. **HERMANN MAIER** **(AUT)**
2. Christian Mayer (AUT)
3. Fritz Strobl (AUT)

29/12/1998, Bormio (ITA)
DOWNHILL

1. **HERMANN MAIER** **(AUT)**
2. Fritz Strobl (AUT)
3. Stephan Eberharter (AUT)

05/01/1999, Kranjska Gora (SLO)
GIANT SLALOM

1. **PATRICK HOLZER** **(ITA)**
2. Christian Mayer (AUT)
3. Hans Knauß (AUT)

06/01/1999, Kranjska Gora (SLO)
SLALOM

1. **JURE KOŠIR** **(SLO)**
2. Thomas Stangassinger (AUT)
3. Benjamin Raich (AUT)

07/01/1999, Schladming (AUT)
SLALOM

1. **BENJAMIN RAICH** **(AUT)**
2. Pierrick Bourgeat (FRA)
3. Kjetil André Aamodt (NOR)

09/01/1999, Schladming (AUT)
SUPER-G

1. **HERMANN MAIER** **(AUT)**
2. Rainer Salzgeber (AUT)
3. Hans Knauß (AUT)

10/01/1999, Flachau (AUT)
GIANT SLALOM

1. **BENJAMIN RAICH** **(AUT)**
2. Michael von Grünigen (SUI)
3. Hermann Maier (AUT)

12/01/1999, Adelboden (SUI)
GIANT SLALOM

1. **HERMANN MAIER** **(AUT)**
2. Kjetil André Aamodt (NOR)
3. Benjamin Raich (AUT)

16/01/1999, Wengen (SUI)
DOWNHILL

1.	LASSE KJUS	(NOR)
2.	Hannes Trinkl	(AUT)
3.	Hans Knauß	(AUT)

17/01/1999, Wengen (SUI)
SLALOM

1.	BENJAMIN RAICH	(AUT)
2.	Michael von Grünigen	(SUI)
3.	Lasse Kjus	(NOR)

17/01/1999, Wengen (SUI)
COMBINED

1.	LASSE KJUS	(NOR)
2.	Kjetil André Aamodt	(NOR)
3.	Hermann Maier	(AUT)

22/01/1999, Kitzbühel (AUT)
DOWNHILL

1.	LASSE KJUS	(NOR)
2.	Kjetil André Aamodt	(NOR)
3.	Werner Franz	(AUT)

23/01/1999, Kitzbühel (AUT)
DOWNHILL

1.	HANS KNAUSS	(AUT)
2.	Peter Rzehak	(AUT)
3.	Werner Franz	(AUT)

24/01/1999, Kitzbühel (AUT)
SLALOM

1.	JURE KOŠIR	(SLO)
2.	Didier Plaschy	(SUI)
3.	Giorgio Rocca	(ITA)

24/01/1999, Kitzbühel (AUT)
COMBINED

1.	KJETIL ANDRÉ AAMODT	(NOR)
2.	Lasse Kjus	(NOR)
3.	Paul Accola	(SUI)

27/02/1999, Ofterschwang (GER)
GIANT SLALOM

1.	STEPHAN EBERHARTER	(AUT)
2.	Hans Knauß	(AUT)
3.	Michael von Grünigen	(SUI)

28/02/1999, Ofterschwang (GER)
SLALOM

1.	FINN CHRISTIAN JAGGE	(NOR)
2.	Thomas Stangassinger	(AUT)
3.	Kjetil André Aamodt	(NOR)

05/03/1999, Kvitfjell (NOR)
DOWNHILL

1.	ANDREAS SCHIFFERER	(AUT)
2.	Stephan Eberharter	(AUT)
3.	Kjetil André Aamodt	(NOR)

06/03/1999, Kvitfjell (NOR)
DOWNHILL

1.	ANDREAS SCHIFFERER	(AUT)
2.	Lasse Kjus	(NOR)
3.	Stephan Eberharter	(AUT)

07/03/1999, Kvitfjell (NOR)
SUPER-G

1.	HERMANN MAIER	(AUT)
2.	Stephan Eberharter	(AUT)
3.	Andreas Schifferer	(AUT)

10/03/1999, Sierra Nevada (ESP)
DOWNHILL

1.	LASSE KJUS	(NOR)
2.	Chad Fleischer	(USA)
3.	Audun Grønvold	(NOR)

11/03/1999, Sierra Nevada (ESP)
SUPER-G

1.	CHRISTIAN MAYER	(AUT)
2.	Andreas Schifferer	(AUT)
3.	Josef Strobl	(AUT)

13/03/1999, Sierra Nevada (ESP)
SLALOM

1.	THOMAS STANGASSINGER	(AUT)
2.	Kjetil André Aamodt	(NOR)
3.	Marco Casanova	(SUI)

14/03/1999, Sierra Nevada (ESP)
GIANT SLALOM

1.	MICHAEL VON GRÜNIGEN	(SUI)
2.	Steve Locher	(SUI)
3.	Heinz Schilchegger	(AUT)

1999-2000

CUPS

OVERALL
1. **HERMANN MAIER** **(AUT)**
2. Kjetil André Aamodt (NOR)
3. Josef Strobl (AUT)

SLALOM
1. **KJETIL ANDRÉ AAMODT** **(NOR)**
2. Ole Kristian Furuseth (NOR)
3. Matjaž Vrhovnik (SLO)

GIANT SLALOM
1. **HERMANN MAIER** **(AUT)**
2. Christian Mayer (AUT)
3. Michael von Grünigen (SUI)

SUPER-G
1. **HERMANN MAIER** **(AUT)**
2. Werner Franz (AUT)
3. Fritz Strobl (AUT)

DOWNHILL
1. **HERMANN MAIER** **(AUT)**
2. Kristian Ghedina (ITA)
3. Josef Strobl (AUT)

COMBINED
1. **KJETIL ANDRÉ AAMODT** **(NOR)**
2. Hermann Maier (AUT)
3. Fredrik Nyberg (SWE)

RACES

31/10/1999, Tignes (FRA)
GIANT SLALOM
1. **HERMANN MAIER** **(AUT)**
2. Michael von Grünigen (SUI)
3. Kjetil André Aamodt (NOR)
= Stephan Eberharter (AUT)

23/11/1999, Vail (USA)
SLALOM
1. **DIDIER PLASCHY** **(SUI)**
2. Thomas Stangassinger (AUT)
3. Kjetil André Aamodt (NOR)
= Matteo Nana (ITA)

24/11/1999, Vail (USA)
GIANT SLALOM
1. **HERMANN MAIER** **(AUT)**
2. Michael von Grünigen (SUI)
3. Andreas Schifferer (AUT)

27/11/1999, Beaver Creek (USA)
DOWNHILL
1. **HERMANN MAIER** **(AUT)**
2. Stephan Eberharter (AUT)
3. Kristian Ghedina (ITA)

28/11/1999, Beaver Creek (USA)
SUPER-G
1. **HERMANN MAIER** **(AUT)**
2. Stephan Eberharter (AUT)
3. Lasse Kjus (NOR)

04/12/1999, Lake Louise (CAN)
DOWNHILL
1. **HANNES TRINKL** **(AUT)**
2. Hermann Maier (AUT)
3. Stephan Eberharter (AUT)

05/12/1999, Lake Louise (CAN)
SUPER-G
1. **HERMANN MAIER** **(AUT)**
2. Fredrik Nyberg (SWE)
3. Josef Strobl (AUT)

13/12/1999, Madonna di Campiglio (ITA)
SLALOM
1. **FINN CHRISTIAN JAGGE** **(NOR)**
2. Benjamin Raich (AUT)
3. Thomas Stangassinger (AUT)

17/12/1999, Val Gardena (ITA)
DOWNHILL
1. **KRISTIAN GHEDINA** **(ITA)**
2. Josef Strobl (AUT)
3. Ed Podivinsky (CAN)

18/12/1999, Val Gardena (ITA)
DOWNHILL
1. **ANDREAS SCHIFFERER** **(AUT)**
2. Kristian Ghedina (ITA)
3. Hermann Maier (AUT)

19/12/1999, Alta Badia (ITA)
GIANT SLALOM
1. **JOËL CHENAL** **(FRA)**

2.	Hermann Maier	(AUT)
3.	Rainer Salzgeber	(AUT)

21/12/1999, Kranjska Gora (SLO)
SLALOM

1.	**DIDIER PLASCHY**	**(SUI)**
2.	Benjamin Raich	(AUT)
3.	Thomas Stangassinger	(AUT)

22/12/1999, Saalbach-Hinterglemm (AUT)
GIANT SLALOM

1.	**CHRISTIAN MAYER**	**(AUT)**
2.	Hermann Maier	(AUT)
3.	Benjamin Raich	(AUT)

08/01/2000, Chamonix (FRA)
DOWNHILL

1.	**HERMANN MAIER**	**(AUT)**
2.	Stephan Eberharter	(AUT)
3.	Hannes Trinkl	(AUT)

09/01/2000, Chamonix (FRA)
SLALOM

1.	**ANGELO WEISS**	**(ITA)**
2.	Kjetil André Aamodt	(NOR)
3.	Matjaž Vrhovnik	(SLO)

09/01/2000, Chamonix (FRA)
COMBINED

1.	**KJETIL ANDRÉ AAMODT**	**(NOR)**
2.	Hermann Maier	(AUT)
3.	Paul Accola	(SUI)

15/01/2000, Wengen (SUI)
DOWNHILL

1.	**JOSEF STROBL**	**(AUT)**
2.	Hermann Maier	(AUT)
3.	Ed Podivinsky	(CAN)

16/01/2000, Wengen (SUI)
SLALOM

1.	**KJETIL ANDRÉ AAMODT**	**(NOR)**
2.	Ole Kristian Furuseth	(NOR)
3.	Drago Grubelnik	(SLO)

21/01/2000, Kitzbühel (AUT)
SUPER-G

1.	**HERMANN MAIER**	**(AUT)**
2.	Werner Franz	(AUT)
3.	Didier Cuche	(SUI)

22/01/2000, Kitzbühel (AUT)
DOWNHILL

1.	**FRITZ STROBL**	**(AUT)**
2.	Kristian Ghedina	(ITA)
=	Josef Strobl	(AUT)

23/01/2000, Kitzbühel (AUT)
SLALOM

1.	**MARIO MATT**	**(AUT)**
2.	Matjaž Vrhovnik	(SLO)
3.	Benjamin Raich	(AUT)

23/01/2000, Kitzbühel (AUT)
COMBINED

1.	**KJETIL ANDRÉ AAMODT**	**(NOR)**
2.	Fredrik Nyberg	(SWE)
3.	Hermann Maier	(AUT)

29/01/2000, Garmisch-Partenkirchen (GER)
DOWNHILL

1.	**HERMANN MAIER**	**(AUT)**
2.	Kristian Ghedina	(ITA)
3.	Hannes Trinkl	(AUT)

05/02/2000, Todtnau (GER)
GIANT SLALOM

1.	**HERMANN MAIER**	**(AUT)**
2.	Fredrik Nyberg	(SWE)
3.	Michael von Grünigen	(SUI)

06/02/2000, Todtnau (GER)
SLALOM

1.	**RAINER SCHÖNFELDER**	**(AUT)**
2.	Kjetil André Aamodt	(NOR)
3.	Ole Kristian Furuseth	(NOR)

12/02/2000, Sankt Anton am Arlberg (AUT)
SUPER-G

1.	**JOSEF STROBL**	**(AUT)**
2.	Didier Cuche	(SUI)
3.	Stephan Eberharter	(AUT)

13/02/2000, Sankt Anton am Arlberg (AUT)
SUPER-G

1.	**WERNER FRANZ**	**(AUT)**
=.	**FRITZ STROBL**	**(AUT)**
3.	Hermann Maier	(AUT)

20/02/2000, Adelboden (SUI)
SLALOM

1.	**MATJAŽ VRHOVNIK**	**(SLO)**

2.	Kjetil André Aamodt	(NOR)
3.	Mario Matt	(AUT)

26/02/2000, Yongpyong (KOR)
GIANT SLALOM

1.	**BENJAMIN RAICH**	**(AUT)**
2.	Michael von Grünigen	(SUI)
3.	Joël Chenal	(FRA)

27/02/2000, Yongpyong (KOR)
SLALOM

1.	**MITJA KUNC**	**(SLO)**
2.	Ole Kristian Furuseth	(NOR)
3.	Mario Matt	(AUT)

03/03/2000, Kvitfjell (NOR)
DOWNHILL

1.	**DARON RAHLVES**	**(USA)**
2.	Didier Cuche	(SUI)
3.	Hermann Maier	(AUT)

04/03/2000, Kvitfjell (NOR)
DOWNHILL

1.	**DARON RAHLVES**	**(USA)**
2.	Kristian Ghedina	(ITA)
3.	Max Rauffer	(GER)

05/03/2000, Kvitfjell (NOR)
SUPER-G

1.	**KRISTIAN GHEDINA**	**(ITA)**
2.	Hermann Maier	(AUT)
3.	Andreas Schifferer	(AUT)

08/03/2000, Kranjska Gora (SLO)
GIANT SLALOM

1.	**CHRISTIAN MAYER**	**(AUT)**
2.	Joël Chenal	(FRA)
3.	Marco Büchel	(LIE)

09/03/2000, Schladming (AUT)
SLALOM

1.	**MARIO MATT**	**(AUT)**
2.	Ole Kristian Furuseth	(NOR)
3.	Thomas Stangassinger	(AUT)

11/03/2000, Hinterstoder (AUT)
GIANT SLALOM

1.	**CHRISTIAN MAYER**	**(AUT)**
2.	Marco Büchel	(LIE)
3.	Hermann Maier	(AUT)

15/03/2000, Bormio (ITA)
DOWNHILL

1.	**HANNES TRINKL**	**(AUT)**
2.	Hermann Maier	(AUT)
3.	Christian Greber	(AUT)

16/03/2000, Bormio (ITA)
SUPER-G

1.	**HERMANN MAIER**	**(AUT)**
2.	Fritz Strobl	(AUT)
3.	Werner Franz	(AUT)
=	Andreas Schifferer	(AUT)

18/03/2000, Bormio (ITA)
GIANT SLALOM

1.	**BENJAMIN RAICH**	**(AUT)**
2.	Christian Mayer	(AUT)
3.	Heinz Schilchegger	(AUT)

19/03/2000, Bormio (ITA)
SLALOM

1.	**OLE KRISTIAN FURUSETH**	**(NOR)**
2.	Benjamin Raich	(AUT)
3.	Matjaž Vrhovnik	(SLO)

2000-01

CUPS

OVERALL
1.	**HERMANN MAIER**	**(AUT)**
2.	Stephan Eberharter	(AUT)
3.	Lasse Kjus	(NOR)

SLALOM
1.	**BENJAMIN RAICH**	**(AUT)**
2.	Heinz Schilchegger	(AUT)
3.	Mario Matt	(AUT)

GIANT SLALOM
1.	**HERMANN MAIER**	**(AUT)**
2.	Michael von Grünigen	(SUI)
3.	Erik Schlopy	(USA)

SUPER-G
1.	**HERMANN MAIER**	**(AUT)**
2.	Christoph Gruber	(AUT)
3.	Josef Strobl	(AUT)

DOWNHILL
1.	**HERMANN MAIER**	**(AUT)**
2.	Stephan Eberharter	(AUT)
3.	Fritz Strobl	(AUT)

COMBINED
1.	**LASSE KJUS**	**(NOR)**
2.	Michael Walchhofer	(AUT)
3.	Kjetil André Aamodt	(NOR)

RACES

29/10/2000, Sölden (AUT)
GIANT SLALOM
1.	**HERMANN MAIER**	**(AUT)**
2.	Stephan Eberharter	(AUT)
3.	Fredrik Nyberg	(SWE)

17/11/2000, Park City (USA)
GIANT SLALOM
1.	**MICHAEL VON GRÜNIGEN**	**(SUI)**
2.	Lasse Kjus	(NOR)
3.	Hermann Maier	(AUT)

19/11/2000, Park City (USA)
SLALOM
1.	**HEINZ SCHILCHEGGER**	**(AUT)**
2.	Mario Matt	(AUT)
3.	Kjetil André Aamodt	(NOR)

25/11/2000, Lake Louise (CAN)
DOWNHILL
1.	**STEPHAN EBERHARTER**	**(AUT)**
2.	Silvano Beltrametti	(SUI)
3.	Lasse Kjus	(NOR)

26/11/2000, Lake Louise (CAN)
SUPER-G
1.	**HERMANN MAIER**	**(AUT)**
2.	Lasse Kjus	(NOR)
3.	Andreas Schifferer	(AUT)

02/12/2000, Beaver Creek (USA)
DOWNHILL
1.	**HERMANN MAIER**	**(AUT)**
2.	Lasse Kjus	(NOR)
3.	Stephan Eberharter	(AUT)

03/12/2000, Beaver Creek (USA)
SUPER-G
1.	**FREDRIK NYBERG**	**(SWE)**
2.	Christoph Gruber	(AUT)
3.	Kenneth Sivertsen	(NOR)

09/12/2000, Val-d'Isère (FRA)
DOWNHILL
1.	**HERMANN MAIER**	**(AUT)**
2.	Stephan Eberharter	(AUT)
3.	Fritz Strobl	(AUT)

10/12/2000, Val-d'Isère (FRA)
GIANT SLALOM
1.	**HERMANN MAIER**	**(AUT)**
2.	Heinz Schilchegger	(AUT)
3.	Andreas Schifferer	(AUT)

11/12/2000, Sestriere (ITA)
SLALOM
1.	**HANS PETTER BURAAS**	**(NOR)**
2.	Kilian Albrecht	(AUT)
3.	Pierrick Bourgeat	(FRA)

16/12/2000, Val-d'Isère (FRA)
DOWNHILL
1.	**ALESSANDRO FATTORI**	**(ITA)**
2.	Kristian Ghedina	(ITA)
3.	Roland Fischnaller	(ITA)

17/12/2000, Val-d'Isère (FRA)
GIANT SLALOM

1. **MICHAEL VON GRÜNIGEN** **(SUI)**
2. Heinz Schilchegger (AUT)
3. Bode Miller (USA)

19/12/2000, Madonna di Campiglio (ITA)
SLALOM

1. **MARIO MATT** **(AUT)**
2. Heinz Schilchegger (AUT)
3. Rainer Schönfelder (AUT)

21/12/2000, Bormio (ITA)
GIANT SLALOM

1. **CHRISTOPH GRUBER** **(AUT)**
2. Erik Schlopy (USA)
3. Fredrik Nyberg (SWE)

06/01/2001 Les Arcs (FRA)
GIANT SLALOM

1. **MICHAEL VON GRÜNIGEN** **(SUI)**
2. Benjamin Raich (AUT)
3. Marco Büchel (LIE)

09/01/2001 Adelboden (SUI)
GIANT SLALOM

1. **HERMANN MAIER** **(AUT)**
2. Michael von Grünigen (SUI)
3. Fredrik Nyberg (SWE)

14/01/2001 Wengen (SUI)
SLALOM

1. **BENJAMIN RAICH** **(AUT)**
2. Rainer Schönfelder (AUT)
3. Mario Matt (AUT)

19/01/2001 Kitzbühel (AUT)
SUPER-G

1. **HERMANN MAIER** **(AUT)**
2. Josef Strobl (AUT)
3. Werner Franz (AUT)

20/01/2001 Kitzbühel (AUT)
DOWNHILL

1. **HERMANN MAIER** **(AUT)**
2. Hannes Trinkl (AUT)
3. Stephan Eberharter (AUT)
= Daron Rahlves (USA)

21/01/2001 Kitzbühel (AUT)

SLALOM

1. **BENJAMIN RAICH** **(AUT)**
2. Jure Košir (SLO)
3. Hans Petter Buraas (NOR)

21/01/2001 Kitzbühel (AUT)
COMBINED

1. **LASSE KJUS** **(NOR)**
2. Michael Walchhofer (AUT)
3. Kjetil André Aamodt (NOR)

23/01/2001 Schladming (AUT)
SLALOM

1. **BENJAMIN RAICH** **(AUT)**
2. Hans Petter Buraas (NOR)
3. Mitja Kunc (SLO)

27/01/2001 Garmisch-Partenkirchen (GER)
DOWNHILL

1. **FRITZ STROBL** **(AUT)**
2. Peter Rzehak (AUT)
3. Franco Cavegn (SUI)

28/01/2001 Garmisch-Partenkirchen (GER)
SUPER-G

1. **CHRISTOPH GRUBER** **(AUT)**
2. Hermann Maier (AUT)
3. Didier Cuche (SUI)

15/02/2001 Shigakōgen (JPN)
GIANT SLALOM

1. **HERMANN MAIER** **(AUT)**
2. Marco Büchel (LIE)
3. Benjamin Raich (AUT)

17/02/2001 Shigakōgen (JPN)
SLALOM

1. **PIERRICK BOURGEAT** **(FRA)**
2. Heinz Schilchegger (AUT)
3. Benjamin Raich (AUT)

18/02/2001 Shigakōgen (JPN)
SLALOM

1. **PIERRICK BOURGEAT** **(FRA)**
2. Heinz Schilchegger (AUT)
3. Jure Košir (SLO)

02/03/2001 Kvitfjell (NOR)
DOWNHILL

1. **HERMANN MAIER** **(AUT)**
2. Florian Eckert (GER)

3. Lasse Kjus (NOR)

03/03/2001 Kvitfjell (NOR)
DOWNHILL
1. **STEPHAN EBERHARTER** **(AUT)**
2. Florian Eckert (GER)
3. Fritz Strobl (AUT)

04/03/2001 Kvitfjell (NOR)
SUPER-G
1. **HERMANN MAIER** **(AUT)**
2. Hannes Trinkl (AUT)
3. Stephan Eberharter (AUT)

08/03/2001 Åre (SWE)
DOWNHILL
1. **HERMANN MAIER** **(AUT)**
2. Stephan Eberharter (AUT)
3. Kenneth Sivertsen (NOR)

10/03/2001 Åre (SWE)
GIANT SLALOM
1. **HERMANN MAIER** **(AUT)**
2. Erik Schlopy (USA)
3. Benjamin Raich (AUT)

11/03/2001 Åre (SWE)
SLALOM
1. **BENJAMIN RAICH** **(AUT)**
2. Mario Matt (AUT)
3. Sébastien Amiez (FRA)

2001-02

CUPS

OVERALL
1. **STEPHAN EBERHARTER** **(AUT)**
2. Kjetil André Aamodt (NOR)
3. Didier Cuche (SUI)

SLALOM
1. **IVICA KOSTELIĆ** **(CRO)**
2. Bode Miller (USA)
3. Jean-Pierre Vidal (FRA)

GIANT SLALOM
1. **FRÉDÉRIC COVILI** **(FRA)**
2. Benjamin Raich (AUT)
3. Stephan Eberharter (AUT)

SUPER-G
1. **STEPHAN EBERHARTER** **(AUT)**
2. Didier Cuche (SUI)
3. Fritz Strobl (AUT)

DOWNHILL
1. **STEPHAN EBERHARTER** **(AUT)**
2. Fritz Strobl (AUT)
3. Kristian Ghedina (ITA)

COMBINED
1. **KJETIL ANDRÉ AAMODT** **(NOR)**
2. Lasse Kjus (NOR)
3. Andrej Jerman (SLO)

RACES

28/10/2001 Sölden (AUT)
GIANT SLALOM
1. **FRÉDÉRIC COVILI** **(FRA)**
2. Stephan Eberharter (AUT)
3. Michael von Grünigen (SUI)

25/11/2001 Aspen (USA)
SLALOM
1. **IVICA KOSTELIĆ** **(CRO)**
2. Giorgio Rocca (ITA)
3. Mario Matt (AUT)

26/11/2001 Aspen (USA)
SLALOM

1. **MARIO MATT** (AUT)
2. Bode Miller (USA)
3. Jean-Pierre Vidal (FRA)

07/12/2001 Val-d'Isère (FRA)
SUPER-G
1. **STEPHAN EBERHARTER** (AUT)
2. Didier Cuche (SUI)
3. Silvano Beltrametti (SUI)

08/12/2001 Val-d'Isère (FRA)
DOWNHILL
1. **STEPHAN EBERHARTER** (AUT)
2. Kurt Sulzenbacher (ITA)
3. Michael Walchhofer (AUT)

09/12/2001 Val-d'Isère (FRA)
GIANT SLALOM
1. **BODE MILLER** (USA)
2. Frédéric Covili (FRA)
3. Stephan Eberharter (AUT)

10/12/2001 Madonna di Campiglio (ITA)
SLALOM
1. **BODE MILLER** (USA)
2. Giorgio Rocca (ITA)
3. Tom Stiansen (NOR)

14/12/2001 Val Gardena (ITA)
DOWNHILL
1. **KRISTIAN GHEDINA** (ITA)
2. Lasse Kjus (NOR)
3. Kurt Sulzenbacher (ITA)

15/12/2001 Val Gardena (ITA)
DOWNHILL
1. **STEPHAN EBERHARTER** (AUT)
2. Michael Walchhofer (AUT)
3. Kjetil André Aamodt (NOR)

16/12/2001 Alta Badia (ITA)
GIANT SLALOM
1. **FRÉDÉRIC COVILI** (FRA)
2. Michael von Grünigen (SUI)
3. Sami Uotila (FIN)

20/12/2001 Kranjska Gora (SLO)
GIANT SLALOM
1. **FREDRIK NYBERG** (SWE)
2. Benjamin Raich (AUT)
3. Uroš Pavlovčič (SLO)

21/12/2001 Kranjska Gora (SLO)
GIANT SLALOM
1. **BENJAMIN RAICH** (AUT)
2. Bode Miller (USA)
3. Didier Cuche (SUI)

22/12/2001 Kranjska Gora (SLO)
SLALOM
1. **JEAN-PIERRE VIDAL** (FRA)
2. Mario Matt (AUT)
3. Ivica Kostelić (CRO)

28/12/2001 Bormio (ITA)
DOWNHILL
1. **CHRISTIAN GREBER** (AUT)
2. Fritz Strobl (AUT)
3. Stephan Eberharter (AUT)

29/12/2001 Bormio (ITA)
DOWNHILL
1. **FRITZ STROBL** (AUT)
2. Josef Strobl (AUT)
3. Stephan Eberharter (AUT)

05/01/2002 Adelboden (SUI)
GIANT SLALOM
1. **DIDIER CUCHE** (SUI)
2. Frédéric Covili (FRA)
3. Fredrik Nyberg (SWE)

06/01/2002 Adelboden (SUI)
SLALOM
1. **BODE MILLER** (USA)
2. Ivica Kostelić (CRO)
3. Mitja Kunc (SLO)

12/01/2002 Wengen (SUI)
DOWNHILL
1. **STEPHAN EBERHARTER** (AUT)
2. Hannes Trinkl (AUT)
3. Josef Strobl (AUT)

13/01/2002 Wengen (SUI)
SLALOM
1. **IVICA KOSTELIĆ** (CRO)
2. Mitja Kunc (SLO)
3. Edoardo Zardini (ITA)

13/01/2002 Wengen (SUI)
COMBINED

1. **KJETIL ANDRÉ AAMODT** **(NOR)**
2. Bode Miller (USA)
3. Lasse Kjus (NOR)

18/01/2002 Kitzbühel (AUT)
SUPER-G

1. **STEPHAN EBERHARTER** **(AUT)**
2. Alessandro Fattori (ITA)
3. Didier Cuche (SUI)

19/01/2002 Kitzbühel (AUT)
DOWNHILL

1. **STEPHAN EBERHARTER** **(AUT)**
2. Kjetil André Aamodt (NOR)
3. Hannes Trinkl (AUT)

20/01/2002 Kitzbühel (AUT)
SLALOM

1. **RAINER SCHÖNFELDER** **(AUT)**
2. Kilian Albrecht (AUT)
3. Bode Miller (USA)

20/01/2002 Kitzbühel (AUT)
COMBINED

1. **KJETIL ANDRÉ AAMODT** **(NOR)**
2. Lasse Kjus (NOR)
3. Michael Walchhofer (AUT)

22/01/2002 Schladming (AUT)
SLALOM

1. **BODE MILLER** **(USA)**
2. Jean-Pierre Vidal (FRA)
3. Ivica Kostelić (CRO)

26/01/2002 Garmisch-Partenkirchen (GER)
SUPER-G

1. **FRITZ STROBL** **(AUT)**
2. Didier Cuche (SUI)
3. Stephan Eberharter (AUT)

27/01/2002 Garmisch-Partenkirchen (GER)
SUPER-G

1. **STEPHAN EBERHARTER** **(AUT)**
2. Didier Cuche (SUI)
3. Andreas Schifferer (AUT)

02/02/2002 Sankt Moritz (SUI)
DOWNHILL

1. **STEPHAN EBERHARTER** **(AUT)**
2. Fritz Strobl (AUT)
3. Michael Walchhofer (AUT)

03/02/2002 Sankt Moritz (SUI)
GIANT SLALOM

1. **STEPHAN EBERHARTER** **(AUT)**
2. Didier Cuche (SUI)
3. Hans Knauß (AUT)

02/03/2002 Kvitfjell (NOR)
DOWNHILL

1. **HANNES TRINKL** **(AUT)**
2. Claude Crétier (FRA)
3. Franco Cavegn (SUI)
= Kristian Ghedina (ITA)

03/03/2002 Kvitfjell (NOR)
SUPER-G

1. **ALESSANDRO FATTORI** **(ITA)**
2. Didier Défago (SUI)
3. Stephan Eberharter (AUT)

06/03/2002 Altenmarkt Zauchensee (AUT)
DOWNHILL

1. **STEPHAN EBERHARTER** **(AUT)**
2. Ambrosi Hoffmann (SUI)
3. Hannes Trinkl (AUT)

07/03/2002 Altenmarkt Zauchensee (AUT)
SUPER-G

1. **DIDIER CUCHE** **(SUI)**
2. Fritz Strobl (AUT)
3. Alessandro Fattori (ITA)

09/03/2002 Altenmarkt Zauchensee (AUT)
SLALOM

1. **IVICA KOSTELIĆ** **(CRO)**
2. Bode Miller (USA)
3. Jean-Pierre Vidal (FRA)

10/03/2002 Altenmarkt Zauchensee (AUT)
GIANT SLALOM

1. **MICHAEL VON GRÜNIGEN** **(SUI)**
2. Benjamin Raich (AUT)
3. Stephan Eberharter (AUT)

2002-03

CUPS

OVERALL
1. **STEPHAN EBERHARTER** **(AUT)**
2. Bode Miller (USA)
3. Kjetil André Aamodt (NOR)

SLALOM
1. **KALLE PALANDER** **(FIN)**
2. Ivica Kostelić (CRO)
3. Rainer Schönfelder (AUT)

GIANT SLALOM
1. **MICHAEL VON GRÜNIGEN** **(SUI)**
2. Bode Miller (USA)
3. Hans Knauß (AUT)

SUPER-G
1. **STEPHAN EBERHARTER** **(AUT)**
2. Marco Büchel (LIE)
3. Didier Cuche (SUI)

DOWNHILL
1. **STEPHAN EBERHARTER** **(AUT)**
2. Daron Rahlves (USA)
3. Michael Walchhofer (AUT)

COMBINED
1. **BODE MILLER** **(USA)**
2. Kjetil André Aamodt (NOR)
= Michael Walchhofer (AUT)

RACES

27/10/2002 Sölden (AUT)
GIANT SLALOM
1. **STEPHAN EBERHARTER** **(AUT)**
2. Frédéric Covili (FRA)
3. Michael von Grünigen (SUI)

22/11/2002 Park City (USA)
GIANT SLALOM
1. **MICHAEL VON GRÜNIGEN** **(SUI)**
2. Christian Mayer (AUT)
3. Benjamin Raich (AUT)

24/11/2002 Park City (USA)
SLALOM
1. **RAINER SCHÖNFELDER** **(AUT)**
2. Pierrick Bourgeat (FRA)
3. Benjamin Raich (AUT)

30/11/2002 Lake Louise (CAN)
DOWNHILL
1. **STEPHAN EBERHARTER** **(AUT)**
2. Hannes Trinkl (AUT)
3. Kjetil André Aamodt (NOR)

01/12/2002 Lake Louise (CAN)
SUPER-G
1. **STEPHAN EBERHARTER** **(AUT)**
2. Josef Strobl (AUT)
3. Didier Cuche (SUI)

07/12/2002 Beaver Creek (USA)
DOWNHILL
1. **STEPHAN EBERHARTER** **(AUT)**
2. Michael Walchhofer (AUT)
3. Daron Rahlves (USA)

08/12/2002 Beaver Creek (USA)
SUPER-G
1. **DIDIER CUCHE** **(SUI)**
2. Marco Büchel (LIE)
3. Hannes Trinkl (AUT)

14/12/2002 Val-d'Isère (FRA)
DOWNHILL
1. **STEPHAN EBERHARTER** **(AUT)**
2. Klaus Kröll (AUT)
3. Andreas Schifferer (AUT)

15/12/2002 Val-d'Isère (FRA)
GIANT SLALOM
1. **MICHAEL VON GRÜNIGEN** **(SUI)**
2. Bode Miller (USA)
3. Christoph Gruber (AUT)

16/12/2002 Sestriere (ITA)
SLALOM
1. **IVICA KOSTELIĆ** **(CRO)**
2. Giorgio Rocca (ITA)
3. Truls Ove Karlsen (NOR)

20/12/2002 Val Gardena (ITA)
SUPER-G
1. **DIDIER DÉFAGO** **(SUI)**
2. Hannes Reichelt (AUT)
3. Marco Büchel (LIE)

21/12/2002 Val Gardena (ITA)
DOWNHILL

1.	**ANTOINE DÉNÉRIAZ**	**(FRA)**
2.	Michael Walchhofer	(AUT)
3.	Josef Strobl	(AUT)

22/12/2002 Alta Badia (ITA)
GIANT SLALOM

1.	**BODE MILLER**	**(USA)**
2.	Davide Simoncelli	(ITA)
3.	Christian Mayer	(AUT)

29/12/2002 Bormio (ITA)
DOWNHILL

1.	**DARON RAHLVES**	**(USA)**
2.	Fritz Strobl	(AUT)
3.	Hannes Trinkl	(AUT)

04/01/2003 Kranjska Gora (SLO)
GIANT SLALOM

1.	**BODE MILLER**	**(USA)**
2.	Christian Mayer	(AUT)
3.	Sami Uotila	(FIN)

05/01/2003 Kranjska Gora (SLO)
SLALOM

1.	**IVICA KOSTELIĆ**	**(CRO)**
2.	Rainer Schönfelder	(AUT)
3.	Jean-Pierre Vidal	(FRA)

11/01/2003 Bormio (ITA)
DOWNHILL

1.	**STEPHAN EBERHARTER**	**(AUT)**
2.	Michael Walchhofer	(AUT)
3.	Daron Rahlves	(USA)

12/01/2003 Bormio (ITA)
SLALOM

1.	**IVICA KOSTELIĆ**	**(CRO)**
2.	Bode Miller	(USA)
3.	Hans Petter Buraas	(NOR)

14/01/2003 Adelboden (SUI)
GIANT SLALOM

1.	**HANS KNAUSS**	**(AUT)**
2.	Michael von Grünigen	(SUI)
3.	Kjetil André Aamodt	(NOR)

17/01/2003 Wengen (SUI)
DOWNHILL

1.	**STEPHAN EBERHARTER**	**(AUT)**
2.	Daron Rahlves	(USA)
3.	Bruno Kernen	(SUI)

18/01/2003 Wengen (SUI)
DOWNHILL

1.	**BRUNO KERNEN**	**(SUI)**
2.	Michael Walchhofer	(AUT)
3.	Stephan Eberharter	(AUT)

19/01/2003 Wengen (SUI)
SLALOM

1.	**GIORGIO ROCCA**	**(ITA)**
2.	Akira Sasaki	(JPN)
3.	Ivica Kostelić	(CRO)

19/01/2003 Wengen (SUI)
COMBINED

1.	**KJETIL ANDRÉ AAMODT**	**(NOR)**
2.	Bode Miller	(USA)
3.	Lasse Kjus	(NOR)

25/01/2003 Kitzbühel (AUT)
DOWNHILL

1.	**DARON RAHLVES**	**(USA)**
2.	Didier Cuche	(SUI)
3.	Kjetil André Aamodt	(NOR)

26/01/2003 Kitzbühel (AUT)
SLALOM

1.	**KALLE PALANDER**	**(FIN)**
2.	Rainer Schönfelder	(AUT)
3.	Heinz Schilchegger	(AUT)

26/01/2003 Kitzbühel (AUT)
COMBINED

1.	**MICHAEL WALCHHOFER**	**(AUT)**
2.	Aksel Lund Svindal	(NOR)
3.	Didier Défago	(SUI)

27/01/2003 Kitzbühel (AUT)
SUPER-G

1.	**HERMANN MAIER**	**(AUT)**
2.	Christoph Gruber	(AUT)
3.	Stephan Eberharter	(AUT)

28/01/2003 Schladming (AUT)
SLALOM

1.	**KALLE PALANDER**	**(FIN)**
2.	Benjamin Raich	(AUT)
3.	Hans Petter Buraas	(NOR)

1.	**GIORGIO ROCCA**	**(ITA)**
2.	Kalle Palander	(FIN)
3.	Manfred Pranger	(AUT)

22/02/2003 Garmisch-Partenkirchen (GER)
DOWNHILL
1.	**STEPHAN EBERHARTER**	**(AUT)**
2.	Didier Cuche	(SUI)
3.	Daron Rahlves	(USA)

23/02/2003 Garmisch-Partenkirchen (GER)
SUPER-G
1.	**MARCO BÜCHEL**	**(LIE)**
2.	Stephan Eberharter	(AUT)
3.	Tobias Grünenfelder	(SUI)

01/03/2003 Yongpyong (KOR)
GIANT SLALOM
1.	**MICHAEL VON GRÜNIGEN**	**(SUI)**
2.	Frédéric Covili	(FRA)
3.	Bode Miller	(USA)

02/03/2003 Yongpyong (KOR)
SLALOM
1.	**KALLE PALANDER**	**(FIN)**
2.	Giorgio Rocca	(ITA)
3.	Benjamin Raich	(AUT)

08/03/2003 Shigakōgen (JPN)
SLALOM
1.	**KALLE PALANDER**	**(FIN)**
=	**RAINER SCHÖNFELDER**	**(AUT)**
3.	Giorgio Rocca	(ITA)

12/03/2003 Lillehammer Kvitfjell (NOR)
DOWNHILL
1.	**ANTOINE DÉNÉRIAZ**	**(FRA)**
2.	Stephan Eberharter	(AUT)
3.	Daron Rahlves	(USA)

13/03/2003 Lillehammer Kvitfjell (NOR)
SUPER-G
1.	**STEPHAN EBERHARTER**	**(AUT)**
2.	Lasse Kjus	(NOR)
3.	Hannes Reichelt	(AUT)

15/03/2003 Lillehammer Hafjell (NOR)
GIANT SLALOM
1.	**HANS KNAUSS**	**(AUT)**
2.	Benjamin Raich	(AUT)
3.	Michael von Grünigen	(SUI)

16/03/2003 Lillehammer Hafjell (NOR)
SLALOM

2003-04

CUPS

OVERALL
1. **HERMANN MAIER** **(AUT)**
2. Stephan Eberharter (AUT)
3. Benjamin Raich (AUT)

SLALOM
1. **RAINER SCHÖNFELDER** **(AUT)**
2. Kalle Palander (FIN)
3. Benjamin Raich (AUT)

GIANT SLALOM
1. **BODE MILLER** **(USA)**
2. Kalle Palander (FIN)
3. Massimiliano Blardone (ITA)

SUPER-G
1. **HERMANN MAIER** **(AUT)**
2. Daron Rahlves (USA)
3. Stephan Eberharter (AUT)

DOWNHILL
1. **STEPHAN EBERHARTER** **(AUT)**
2. Daron Rahlves (USA)
3. Hermann Maier (AUT)

COMBINED
1. **BODE MILLER** **(USA)**
2. Benjamin Raich (AUT)
3. Lasse Kjus (NOR)

RACES

26/10/2003 Sölden (AUT)
GIANT SLALOM
1. **BODE MILLER** **(USA)**
2. Frédéric Covili (FRA)
3. Joël Chenal (FRA)

22/11/2003 Park City (USA)
GIANT SLALOM
1. **BODE MILLER** **(USA)**
2. Andreas Schifferer (AUT)
3. Hans Knauß (AUT)

23/11/2003 Park City (USA)
SLALOM
1. **KALLE PALANDER** **(FIN)**
2. Rainer Schönfelder (AUT)
3. Manfred Pranger (AUT)

29/11/2003 Lake Louise (CAN)
DOWNHILL
1. **MICHAEL WALCHHOFER** **(AUT)**
2. Erik Guay (CAN)
3. Antoine Dénériaz (FRA)

30/11/2003 Lake Louise (CAN)
SUPER-G
1. **HERMANN MAIER** **(AUT)**
2. Michael Walchhofer (AUT)
3. Stephan Eberharter (AUT)

05/12/2003 Beaver Creek (USA)
DOWNHILL
1. **DARON RAHLVES** **(USA)**
2. Stephan Eberharter (AUT)
= Bjarne Solbakken (NOR)

06/12/2003 Beaver Creek (USA)
DOWNHILL
1. **HERMANN MAIER** **(AUT)**
2. Hans Knauß (AUT)
3. Andreas Schifferer (AUT)

07/12/2003 Beaver Creek (USA)
SUPER-G
1. **BJARNE SOLBAKKEN** **(NOR)**
2. Hermann Maier (AUT)
3. Hans Knauß (AUT)

14/12/2003 Alta Badia (ITA)
GIANT SLALOM
1. **KALLE PALANDER** **(FIN)**
2. Davide Simoncelli (ITA)
3. Frédéric Covili (FRA)

15/12/2003 Madonna di Campiglio (ITA)
SLALOM
1. **IVICA KOSTELIĆ** **(CRO)**
2. Giorgio Rocca (ITA)
3. Manfred Pranger (AUT)

19/12/2003 Val Gardena (ITA)
SUPER-G
1. **LASSE KJUS** **(NOR)**
2. Stephan Eberharter (AUT)
3. Hermann Maier (AUT)

20/12/2003 Val Gardena (ITA)
DOWNHILL
1. **ANTOINE DÉNÉRIAZ** **(FRA)**
2. Michael Walchhofer (AUT)
3. Hans Knauß (AUT)

21/12/2003 Alta Badia (ITA)
GIANT SLALOM
1. **DAVIDE SIMONCELLI** **(ITA)**
2. Kalle Palander (FIN)
3. Bode Miller (USA)

03/01/2004 Flachau (AUT)
GIANT SLALOM
1. **BENJAMIN RAICH** **(AUT)**
2. Massimiliano Blardone (ITA)
3. Bjarne Solbakken (NOR)

04/01/2004 Flachau (AUT)
SLALOM
1. **KALLE PALANDER** **(FIN)**
2. Manfred Pranger (AUT)
3. Giorgio Rocca (ITA)

10/01/2004 Chamonix (FRA)
DOWNHILL
1. **STEPHAN EBERHARTER** **(AUT)**
2. Lasse Kjus (NOR)
3. Michael Walchhofer (AUT)

11/01/2004 Chamonix (FRA)
SLALOM
1. **GIORGIO ROCCA** **(ITA)**
2. Pierrick Bourgeat (FRA)
3. Bode Miller (USA)

11/01/2004 Chamonix (FRA)
COMBINED
1. **BODE MILLER** **(USA)**
2. Benjamin Raich (AUT)
3. Lasse Kjus (NOR)

18/01/2004 Wengen (SUI)
SLALOM
1. **BENJAMIN RAICH** **(AUT)**
2. Rainer Schönfelder (AUT)
3. Ivica Kostelić (CRO)

22/01/2004 Kitzbühel (AUT)
DOWNHILL

1. **LASSE KJUS** **(NOR)**
2. Stephan Eberharter (AUT)
3. Daron Rahlves (USA)

23/01/2004 Kitzbühel (AUT)
SUPER-G
1. **DARON RAHLVES** **(USA)**
2. Hermann Maier (AUT)
3. Michael Walchhofer (AUT)

24/01/2004 Kitzbühel (AUT)
DOWNHILL
1. **STEPHAN EBERHARTER** **(AUT)**
2. Daron Rahlves (USA)
3. Ambrosi Hoffmann (SUI)

25/01/2004 Kitzbühel (AUT)
SLALOM
1. **KALLE PALANDER** **(FIN)**
2. Thomas Grandi (CAN)
3. Rainer Schönfelder (AUT)

25/01/2004 Kitzbühel (AUT)
COMBINED
1. **BODE MILLER** **(USA)**
2. Benjamin Raich (AUT)
3. Lasse Kjus (NOR)

27/01/2004 Schladming (AUT)
SLALOM
1. **BENJAMIN RAICH** **(AUT)**
2. Manfred Mölgg (ITA)
3. Kalle Palander (FIN)

30/01/2004 Garmisch-Partenkirchen (GER)
DOWNHILL
1. **DIDIER CUCHE** **(SUI)**
2. Daron Rahlves (USA)
3. Stephan Eberharter (AUT)

31/01/2004 Garmisch-Partenkirchen (GER)
DOWNHILL
1. **STEPHAN EBERHARTER** **(AUT)**
2. Fritz Strobl (AUT)
3. Alessandro Fattori (ITA)

01/02/2004 Garmisch-Partenkirchen (GER)
SUPER-G
1. **HERMANN MAIER** **(AUT)**
2. Pierre-Emmanuel Dalcin (FRA)
3. Tobias Grünenfelder (SUI)

07/02/2004 Adelboden (SUI)
GIANT SLALOM
1.	**KALLE PALANDER**	**(FIN)**
2.	Massimiliano Blardone	(ITA)
3.	Christoph Gruber	(AUT)
=	Heinz Schilchegger	(AUT)

08/02/2004 Adelboden (SUI)
SLALOM
1.	**RAINER SCHÖNFELDER**	**(AUT)**
2.	Bode Miller	(USA)
3.	Benjamin Raich	(AUT)

14/02/2004 Sankt Anton am Arlberg (AUT)
DOWNHILL
1.	**HERMANN MAIER**	**(AUT)**
2.	Stephan Eberharter	(AUT)
3.	Hans Grugger	(AUT)

15/02/2004 Sankt Anton am Arlberg (AUT)
SLALOM
1.	**BODE MILLER**	**(USA)**
2.	Kalle Palander	(FIN)
3.	Mario Matt	(AUT)

28/02/2004 Kranjska Gora (SLO)
GIANT SLALOM
1.	**BODE MILLER**	**(USA)**
2.	Alberto Schieppati	(ITA)
3.	Alexander Ploner	(ITA)
=	Fredrik Nyberg	(SWE)

29/02/2004 Kranjska Gora (SLO)
SLALOM
1.	**TRULS OVE KARLSEN**	**(NOR)**
2.	Tom Stiansen	(NOR)
3.	Mario Matt	(AUT)

06/03/2004 Lillehammer Kvitfjell (NOR)
DOWNHILL
1.	**STEPHAN EBERHARTER**	**(AUT)**
2.	Fritz Strobl	(AUT)
3.	Antoine Dénériaz	(FRA)

07/03/2004 Lillehammer Kvitfjell (NOR)
SUPER-G
1.	**DARON RAHLVES**	**(USA)**
2.	Bjarne Solbakken	(NOR)
3.	Hermann Maier	(AUT)

10/03/2004 Sestriere (ITA)
DOWNHILL
1.	**DARON RAHLVES**	**(USA)**
2.	Fritz Strobl	(AUT)
3.	Stephan Eberharter	(AUT)

11/03/2004 Sestriere (ITA)
SUPER-G
1.	**HERMANN MAIER**	**(AUT)**
2.	Stephan Eberharter	(AUT)
3.	Christoph Gruber	(AUT)

14/03/2004 Sestriere (ITA)
SLALOM
1.	**KALLE PALANDER**	**(FIN)**
2.	Rainer Schönfelder	(AUT)
3.	Manfred Pranger	(AUT)

2004-05

CUPS

OVERALL
1.	**BODE MILLER**	**(USA)**
2.	Benjamin Raich	(AUT)
3.	Hermann Maier	(AUT)

SLALOM
1.	**BENJAMIN RAICH**	**(AUT)**
2.	Rainer Schönfelder	(AUT)
3.	Manfred Pranger	(AUT)

GIANT SLALOM
1.	**BENJAMIN RAICH**	**(AUT)**
2.	Bode Miller	(USA)
3.	Thomas Grandi	(CAN)

SUPER-G
1.	**BODE MILLER**	**(USA)**
2.	Hermann Maier	(AUT)
3.	Daron Rahlves	(USA)

DOWNHILL
1.	**MICHAEL WALCHHOFER**	**(AUT)**
2.	Bode Miller	(USA)
3.	Hermann Maier	(AUT)

SUPER COMBINED
1.	**BENJAMIN RAICH**	**(AUT)**
2.	Lasse Kjus	(NOR)
3.	Didier Défago	(SUI)

RACES

26/10/2004 Sölden (AUT)
GIANT SLALOM
1.	**BODE MILLER**	**(USA)**
2.	Massimiliano Blardone	(ITA)
3.	Kalle Palander	(FIN)

27/11/2004 Lake Louise (CAN)
DOWNHILL
1.	**BODE MILLER**	**(USA)**
2.	Antoine Dénériaz	(FRA)
3.	Michael Walchhofer	(AUT)

27/11/2004 Lake Louise (CAN)
SUPER-G
1.	**BODE MILLER**	**(USA)**
2.	Hermann Maier	(AUT)
3.	Michael Walchhofer	(AUT)

02/12/2004 Beaver Creek (USA)
SUPER-G
1.	**STEPHAN GÖRGL**	**(AUT)**
2.	Bode Miller	(USA)
3.	Mario Scheiber	(AUT)

03/12/2004 Beaver Creek (USA)
DOWNHILL
1.	**BODE MILLER**	**(USA)**
2.	Daron Rahlves	(USA)
3.	Michael Walchhofer	(AUT)

04/12/2004 Beaver Creek (USA)
GIANT SLALOM
1.	**LASSE KJUS**	**(NOR)**
2.	Hermann Maier	(AUT)
3.	Benjamin Raich	(AUT)

05/12/2004 Beaver Creek (USA)
SLALOM
1.	**BENJAMIN RAICH**	**(AUT)**
2.	Giorgio Rocca	(ITA)
3.	Rainer Schönfelder	(AUT)

11/12/2004 Val-d'Isère (FRA)
DOWNHILL
1.	**WERNER FRANZ**	**(AUT)**
2.	Marco Büchel	(LIE)
3.	Michael Walchhofer	(AUT)

12/12/2004 Val-d'Isère (FRA)
GIANT SLALOM
1.	**BODE MILLER**	**(USA)**
2.	Lasse Kjus	(NOR)
3.	Hermann Maier	(AUT)

13/12/2004 Sestriere (ITA)
SLALOM
1.	**BODE MILLER**	**(USA)**
2.	Silvan Zurbriggen	(SUI)
3.	Kalle Palander	(FIN)

17/12/2004 Val Gardena (ITA)
SUPER-G
1.	**MICHAEL WALCHHOFER**	**(AUT)**
2.	Hermann Maier	(AUT)
3.	Benjamin Raich	(AUT)

18/12/2004 Val Gardena (ITA)
DOWNHILL

1. **MAX RAUFFER** **(GER)**
2. Jürg Grünenfelder (SUI)
3. Hans Grugger (AUT)

19/12/2004 Alta Badia (ITA)
GIANT SLALOM

1. **THOMAS GRANDI** **(CAN)**
2. Benjamin Raich (AUT)
3. Didier Cuche (SUI)
= Hermann Maier (AUT)

21/12/2004 Flachau (AUT)
GIANT SLALOM

1. **THOMAS GRANDI** **(CAN)**
2. Didier Cuche (SUI)
3. Bode Miller (USA)

22/12/2004 Flachau (AUT)
SLALOM

1. **GIORGIO ROCCA** **(ITA)**
2. Rainer Schönfelder (AUT)
3. Alois Vogl (GER)

29/12/2004 Bormio (ITA)
DOWNHILL

1. **HANS GRUGGER** **(AUT)**
2. Michael Walchhofer (AUT)
3. Fritz Strobl (AUT)

08/01/2005 Chamonix (FRA)
DOWNHILL

1. **HANS GRUGGER** **(AUT)**
2. Kristian Ghedina (ITA)
3. Michael Walchhofer (AUT)

09/01/2005 Chamonix (FRA)
SLALOM

1. **GIORGIO ROCCA** **(ITA)**
2. Benjamin Raich (AUT)
3. Markus Larsson (SWE)

11/01/2005 Adelboden (SUI)
GIANT SLALOM

1. **MASSIMILIANO BLARDONE** **(ITA)**
2. Bode Miller (USA)
3. Kalle Palander (FIN)

14/01/2005 Wengen (SUI)

SUPER COMBINED

1. **BENJAMIN RAICH** **(AUT)**
2. Lasse Kjus (NOR)
3. Didier Défago (SUI)

15/01/2005 Wengen (SUI)
DOWNHILL

1. **MICHAEL WALCHHOFER** **(AUT)**
2. Christoph Gruber (AUT)
3. Bode Miller (USA)

16/01/2005 Wengen (SUI)
SLALOM

1. **ALOIS VOGL** **(GER)**
2. Ivica Kostelić (CRO)
3. Benjamin Raich (AUT)

23/01/2005 Kitzbühel (AUT)
SLALOM

1. **MANFRED PRANGER** **(AUT)**
2. Mario Matt (AUT)
3. Ivica Kostelić (CRO)

24/01/2005 Kitzbühel (AUT)
SUPER-G

1. **HERMANN MAIER** **(AUT)**
2. Daron Rahlves (USA)
3. Fritz Strobl (AUT)

25/01/2005 Schladming (AUT)
SLALOM

1. **MANFRED PRANGER** **(AUT)**
2. Benjamin Raich (AUT)
3. André Myhrer (SWE)

18/02/2005 Garmisch-Partenkirchen (GER)
DOWNHILL

1. **MICHAEL WALCHHOFER** **(AUT)**
2. Hermann Maier (AUT)
3. Bode Miller (USA)

19/02/2005 Garmisch-Partenkirchen (GER)
DOWNHILL

1. **MICHAEL WALCHHOFER** **(AUT)**
2. Mario Scheiber (AUT)
3. Fritz Strobl (AUT)

20/02/2005 Garmisch-Partenkirchen (GER)
SUPER-G

1. **CHRISTOPH GRUBER** **(AUT)**
2. Didier Défago (SUI)

3. François Bourque   (CAN)

26/02/2005 Kranjska Gora (SLO)
GIANT SLALOM
1. **BENJAMIN RAICH** **(AUT)**
2. Hermann Maier (AUT)
3. Kalle Palander (FIN)

27/02/2005 Kranjska Gora (SLO)
SLALOM
1. **GIORGIO ROCCA** **(ITA)**
2. André Myhrer (SWE)
3. Benjamin Raich (AUT)

05/03/2005 Lillehammer Kvitfjell (NOR)
DOWNHILL
1. **HERMANN MAIER** **(AUT)**
2. Mario Scheiber (AUT)
3. Ambrosi Hoffmann (SUI)

06/03/2005 Lillehammer Kvitfjell (NOR)
SUPER-G
1. **HERMANN MAIER** **(AUT)**
2. Didier Défago (SUI)
3. Daron Rahlves (USA)

10/03/2005 Lenzerheide (SUI)
DOWNHILL
1. **LASSE KJUS** **(NOR)**
2. Bode Miller (USA)
3. Fritz Strobl (AUT)

11/03/2005 Lenzerheide (SUI)
SUPER-G
1. **BODE MILLER** **(USA)**
= **DARON RAHLVES** **(USA)**
3, Stephan Görgl (AUT)

12/03/2005 Lenzerheide (SUI)
GIANT SLALOM
1. **STEPHAN GÖRGL** **(AUT)**
2. Bode Miller (USA)
3. Benjamin Raich (AUT)

13/03/2005 Lenzerheide (SUI)
SLALOM
1. **MARIO MATT** **(AUT)**
2. Alois Vogl (GER)
3. Rainer Schönfelder (AUT)

2005-06

CUPS

OVERALL
1. **BENJAMIN RAICH** **(AUT)**
2. Aksel Lund Svindal (NOR)
3. Bode Miller (USA)

SLALOM
1. **GIORGIO ROCCA** **(ITA)**
2. Kalle Palander (FIN)
3. Benjamin Raich (AUT)

GIANT SLALOM
1. **BENJAMIN RAICH** **(AUT)**
2. Massimiliano Blardone (ITA)
3. Fredrik Nyberg (SWE)

SUPER-G
1. **AKSEL LUND SVINDAL** **(NOR)**
2. Hermann Maier (AUT)
3. Daron Rahlves (USA)

DOWNHILL
1. **MICHAEL WALCHHOFER** **(AUT)**
2. Fritz Strobl (AUT)
3. Daron Rahlves (USA)

COMBINED
1. **BENJAMIN RAICH** **(AUT)**
2. Bode Miller (USA)
2. Michael Walchhofer (AUT)

RACES

23/10/2005 Sölden (AUT)
GIANT SLALOM
1. **HERMANN MAIER** **(AUT)**
2. Bode Miller (USA)
3. Rainer Schönfelder (AUT)

26/11/2005 Lake Louise (CAN)
DOWNHILL
1. **FRITZ STROBL** **(AUT)**
2. Kjetil André Aamodt (NOR)
3. Marco Büchel (LIE)

27/11/2005 Lake Louise (CAN)
SUPER-G

1.	**AKSEL LUND SVINDAL**	**(NOR)**
2.	Benjamin Raich	(AUT)
3.	Daron Rahlves	(USA)

01/12/2005 Beaver Creek (USA)
SUPER-G

1.	**HANNES REICHELT**	**(AUT)**
2.	Erik Guay	(CAN)
3.	Matthias Lanzinger	(AUT)

02/12/2005 Beaver Creek (USA)
DOWNHILL

1.	**DARON RAHLVES**	**(USA)**
2.	Bode Miller	(USA)
3.	Hans Grugger	(AUT)

03/12/2005 Beaver Creek (USA)
GIANT SLALOM

1.	**BODE MILLER**	**(USA)**
2.	Daron Rahlves	(USA)
3.	Kalle Palander	(FIN)

04/12/2005 Beaver Creek (USA)
SLALOM

1.	**GIORGIO ROCCA**	**(ITA)**
2.	Stéphane Tissot	(FRA)
3.	Ted Ligety	(USA)

10/12/2005 Val-d'Isère (FRA)
DOWNHILL

1.	**MICHAEL WALCHHOFER**	**(AUT)**
2.	Fritz Strobl	(AUT)
3.	Hans Grugger	(AUT)

11/12/2005 Val-d'Isère (FRA)
SUPER COMBINED

1.	**MICHAEL WALCHHOFER**	**(AUT)**
2.	Rainer Schönfelder	(AUT)
3.	Bode Miller	(USA)

12/12/2005 Madonna di Campiglio (ITA)
SLALOM

1.	**GIORGIO ROCCA**	**(ITA)**
2.	Benjamin Raich	(AUT)
3.	Kalle Palander	(FIN)

16/12/2005 Val Gardena (ITA)
SUPER-G

1.	**HANS GRUGGER**	**(AUT)**
2.	Erik Guay	(CAN)
3.	Ambrosi Hoffmann	(SUI)

17/12/2005 Val Gardena (ITA)
DOWNHILL

1.	**MARCO BÜCHEL**	**(LIE)**
2.	Michael Walchhofer	(AUT)
3.	Erik Guay	(CAN)

18/12/2005 Alta Badia (ITA)
GIANT SLALOM

1.	**MASSIMILIANO BLARDONE**	**(ITA)**
2.	Davide Simoncelli	(ITA)
3.	François Bourque	(CAN)

21/12/2005 Kranjska Gora (SLO)
GIANT SLALOM

1.	**BENJAMIN RAICH**	**(AUT)**
2.	Massimiliano Blardone	(ITA)
3.	Thomas Grandi	(CAN)

22/12/2005 Kranjska Gora (SLO)
SLALOM

1.	**GIORGIO ROCCA**	**(ITA)**
2.	Thomas Grandi	(CAN)
3.	Ted Ligety	(USA)

29/12/2005 Bormio (ITA)
DOWNHILL

1.	**DARON RAHLVES**	**(USA)**
2.	Fritz Strobl	(AUT)
3.	Tobias Grünenfelder	(SUI)

07/01/2006, Adelboden (SUI)
GIANT SLALOM

1.	**BENJAMIN RAICH**	**(AUT)**
2.	Fredrik Nyberg	(SWE)
3.	Stephan Görgl	(AUT)
=	Kalle Palander	(FIN)

08/01/2006, Adelboden (SUI)
SLALOM

1.	**GIORGIO ROCCA**	**(ITA)**
2.	Ted Ligety	(USA)
3.	Benjamin Raich	(AUT)

13/01/2006, Wengen (SUI)
SUPER COMBINED

1.	**BENJAMIN RAICH**	**(AUT)**
2.	Kjetil André Aamodt	(NOR)
3.	Peter Fill	(ITA)

14/01/2006, Wengen (SUI)

DOWNHILL

1.	**DARON RAHLVES**	**(USA)**
2.	Michael Walchhofer	(AUT)
3.	Fritz Strobl	(AUT)

15/01/2006, Wengen (SUI)
SLALOM

1.	**GIORGIO ROCCA**	**(ITA)**
2.	Kalle Palander	(FIN)
3.	Alois Vogl	(GER)

20/01/2006, Kitzbühel (AUT)
SUPER-G

1.	**HERMANN MAIER**	**(AUT)**
2.	Peter Fill	(ITA)
3.	Hannes Reichelt	(AUT)

21/01/2006, Kitzbühel (AUT)
DOWNHILL

1.	**MICHAEL WALCHHOFER**	**(AUT)**
2.	Marco Büchel	(LIE)
3.	Daron Rahlves	(USA)

22/01/2006, Kitzbühel (AUT)
SLALOM

1.	**JEAN-PIERRE VIDAL**	**(FRA)**
2.	Reinfried Herbst	(AUT)
3.	Benjamin Raich	(AUT)

22/01/2006, Kitzbühel (AUT)
COMBINED

1.	**BENJAMIN RAICH**	**(AUT)**
2.	Bode Miller	(USA)
3.	Aksel Lund Svindal	(NOR)

24/01/2006, Schladming (AUT)
SLALOM

1.	**KALLE PALANDER**	**(FIN)**
2.	Akira Sasaki	(JPN)
3.	Benjamin Raich	(AUT)

28/01/2006, Garmisch-Partenkirchen (GER)
DOWNHILL

1.	**HERMANN MAIER**	**(AUT)**
2.	Klaus Kröll	(AUT)
3.	Andreas Buder	(AUT)

29/01/2006, Garmisch-Partenkirchen (GER)
SUPER-G

1.	**CHRISTOPH GRUBER**	**(AUT)**
2.	Scott Macartney	(USA)

3.	Kjetil André Aamodt	(NOR)

03/02/2006, Chamonix (FRA)
SUPER COMBINED

1.	**BENJAMIN RAICH**	**(AUT)**
2.	Rainer Schönfelder	(AUT)
3.	Bode Miller	(USA)

04/03/2006, Yongpyong (KOR)
GIANT SLALOM

1.	**DAVIDE SIMONCELLI**	**(ITA)**
2.	Massimiliano Blardone	(ITA)
3.	Aksel Lund Svindal	(NOR)

05/03/2006, Yongpyong (KOR)
GIANT SLALOM

1.	**TED LIGETY**	**(USA)**
2.	Fredrik Nyberg	(SWE)
=	Kalle Palander (FIN)	

10/03/2006, Shigakōgen (JPN)
SLALOM

1.	**BENJAMIN RAICH**	**(AUT)**
2.	Akira Sasaki	(JPN)
3.	Thomas Grandi	(CAN)

11/03/2006, Shigakōgen (JPN)
SLALOM

1.	**REINFRIED HERBST**	**(AUT)**
=	**KALLE PALANDER**	**(FIN)**
3.	Thomas Grandi	(CAN)

15/03/2006, Åre (SWE)
DOWNHILL

1.	**AKSEL LUND SVINDAL**	**(NOR)**
2.	Bode Miller	(USA)
3.	Peter Fill	(ITA)

16/03/2006, Åre (SWE)
SUPER-G

1.	**BODE MILLER**	**(USA)**
2.	Daron Rahlves	(USA)
3.	Aksel Lund Svindal	(NOR)

17/03/2006, Åre (SWE)
GIANT SLALOM

1.	**BENJAMIN RAICH**	**(AUT)**
2.	Massimiliano Blardone	(ITA)
3.	Fredrik Nyberg	(SWE)

18/03/2006, Åre (SWE)

SLALOM

1.	**MARKUS LARSSON**	**(SWE)**
2.	Stéphane Tissot	(FRA)
3.	Thomas Grandi	(CAN)

2006-07

CUPS

OVERALL

1.	**AKSEL LUND SVINDAL**	**(NOR)**
2.	Benjamin Raich	(AUT)
3.	Didier Cuche	(SUI)

SLALOM

1.	**BENJAMIN RAICH**	**(AUT)**
2.	Mario Matt	(AUT)
3.	Jens Byggmark	(SWE)

GIANT SLALOM

1.	**AKSEL LUND SVINDAL**	**(NOR)**
2.	Massimiliano Blardone	(ITA)
3.	Benjamin Raich	(AUT)

SUPER-G

1.	**BODE MILLER**	**(USA)**
2.	Didier Cuche	(SUI)
3.	John Kucera	(CAN)

DOWNHILL

1.	**DIDIER CUCHE**	**(SUI)**
2.	Marco Büchel	(LIE)
3.	Erik Guay	(CAN)

SUPER COMBINED

1.	**AKSEL LUND SVINDAL**	**(NOR)**
2.	Marc Berthod	(SUI)
3.	Ivica Kostelić	(CRO)

RACES

12/11/2006, Levi (FIN)
SLALOM

1.	**BENJAMIN RAICH**	**(AUT)**
2.	Markus Larsson	(SWE)
3.	Giorgio Rocca	(ITA)

25/11/2006, Lake Louise (CAN)
DOWNHILL

1.	**MARCO BÜCHEL**	**(LIE)**
2.	Manuel Osborne-Paradis	(CAN)
3.	Peter Fill	(ITA)

26/11/2006, Lake Louise (CAN)
SUPER-G

1.	JOHN KUCERA	(CAN)
2.	Mario Scheiber	(AUT)
3.	Patrik Järbyn	(SWE)

30/11/2006, Beaver Creek (USA)
SUPER COMBINED

1.	AKSEL LUND SVINDAL	(NOR)
2.	Marc Berthod	(SUI)
3.	Rainer Schönfelder	(AUT)

01/12/2006, Beaver Creek (USA)
DOWNHILL

1.	BODE MILLER	(USA)
2.	Didier Cuche	(SUI)
3.	Steven Nyman	(USA)

02/12/2006, Beaver Creek (USA)
GIANT SLALOM

1.	MASSIMILIANO BLARDONE	(ITA)
2.	Aksel Lund Svindal	(NOR)
3.	Ted Ligety	(USA)

03/12/2006, Beaver Creek (USA)
SLALOM

1.	ANDRÉ MYHRER	(SWE)
2.	Michael Janyk	(CAN)
3	Felix Neureuther	(GER)

10/12/2006, Reiteralm (AUT)
SUPER COMBINED

1.	IVICA KOSTELIĆ	(CRO)
2.	Romed Baumann	(AUT)
3.	Pierrick Bourgeat	(FRA)

15/12/2006, Val Gardena (ITA)
SUPER-G

1.	BODE MILLER	(USA)
2.	Christoph Gruber	(AUT)
3.	John Kucera	(CAN)

16/12/2006, Val Gardena (ITA)
DOWNHILL

1.	STEVEN NYMAN	(USA)
2.	Didier Cuche	(SUI)
3.	Fritz Strobl	(AUT)

17/12/2006, Alta Badia (ITA)
GIANT SLALOM

1.	KALLE PALANDER	(FIN)
2.	Bode Miller	(USA)
3.	Didier Défago	(SUI)

18/12/2006, Alta Badia (ITA)
SLALOM

1.	MARKUS LARSSON	(SWE)
2.	Ted Ligety	(USA)
3.	Ivica Kostelić	(CRO)

20/12/2006, Hinterstoder (AUT)
SUPER-G

1.	BODE MILLER	(USA)
2.	Peter Fill	(ITA)
3.	Hermann Maier	(AUT)

21/12/2006, Hinterstoder (AUT)
GIANT SLALOM

1.	AKSEL LUND SVINDAL	(NOR)
2.	François Bourque	(CAN)
3.	Kalle Palander	(FIN)

28/12/2006, Bormio (ITA)
DOWNHILL

1.	MICHAEL WALCHHOFER	(AUT)
2.	Didier Cuche	(SUI)
3.	Mario Scheiber	(AUT)

29/12/2006, Bormio (ITA)
DOWNHILL

1.	MICHAEL WALCHHOFER	(AUT)
2.	Peter Fill	(ITA)
3.	Mario Scheiber	(AUT)

06/01/2007, Adelboden (SUI)
GIANT SLALOM

1.	BENJAMIN RAICH	(AUT)
2.	Massimiliano Blardone	(ITA)
3.	Aksel Lund Svindal	(NOR)

07/01/2007, Adelboden (SUI)
SLALOM

1.	MARC BERTHOD	(SUI)
2.	Benjamin Raich	(AUT)
3.	Mario Matt	(AUT)

13/01/2007, Wengen (SUI)
DOWNHILL

1.	BODE MILLER	(USA)
2.	Didier Cuche	(SUI)
3.	Peter Fill	(ITA)

14/01/2007, Wengen (SUI)
SUPER COMBINED

1.	**MARIO MATT**	**(AUT)**
2.	Marc Berthod	(SUI)
3.	Silvan Zurbriggen	(SUI)

20/01/2007, Val-d'Isère (FRA)
DOWNHILL

1.	**PIERRE-EMMANUEL DALCIN**	**(FRA)**
2.	Erik Guay	(CAN)
3.	Manuel Osborne-Paradis	(CAN)

28/01/2007, Kitzbühel (AUT)
SLALOM

1.	**JENS BYGGMARK**	**(SWE)**
2.	Mario Matt	(AUT)
3.	Alois Vogl	(GER)

29/01/2007, Kitzbühel (AUT)
SLALOM

1.	**JENS BYGGMARK**	**(SWE)**
2.	Mario Matt	(AUT)
3.	Manfred Mölgg	(ITA)

30/01/2007, Schladming (AUT)
SLALOM

1.	**BENJAMIN RAICH**	**(AUT)**
2.	Jens Byggmark	(SWE)
3.	Mario Matt	(AUT)

23/02/2007, Garmisch-Partenkirchen (GER)
DOWNHILL

1.	**ANDREJ JERMAN**	**(SLO)**
2.	Hans Grugger	(AUT)
3.	Erik Guay	(CAN)

24/02/2007, Garmisch-Partenkirchen (GER)
DOWNHILL

1.	**ERIK GUAY**	**(CAN)**
2.	Andrej Jerman	(SLO)
3.	Didier Cuche	(SUI)

25/02/2007, Garmisch-Partenkirchen (GER)
SLALOM

1.	**MARIO MATT**	**(AUT)**
2.	Felix Neureuther	(GER)
3.	Benjamin Raich	(AUT)

03/03/2007, Kranjska Gora (SLO)
GIANT SLALOM

1.	**BENJAMIN RAICH**	**(AUT)**
2.	François Bourque	(CAN)
3.	Massimiliano Blardone	(ITA)

04/03/2007, Kranjska Gora (SLO)
SLALOM

1.	**MARIO MATT**	**(AUT)**
2.	Benjamin Raich	(AUT)
3.	Manfred Mölgg	(ITA)

09/03/2007, Lillehammer Kvitfjell (NOR)
SUPER COMBINED

1.	**BENJAMIN RAICH**	**(AUT)**
2.	Silvan Zurbriggen	(SUI)
3.	Aksel Lund Svindal	(NOR)

10/03/2007, Lillehammer Kvitfjell (NOR)
DOWNHILL

1.	**DIDIER CUCHE**	**(SUI)**
2.	Erik Guay	(CAN)
3.	Marco Büchel	(LIE)

11/03/2007, Lillehammer Kvitfjell (NOR)
SUPER-G

1.	**HANS GRUGGER**	**(AUT)**
2.	Mario Scheiber	(AUT)
3.	Didier Cuche	(SUI)

14/03/2007, Lenzerheide (SUI)
DOWNHILL

1.	**AKSEL LUND SVINDAL**	**(NOR)**
2.	Daniel Albrecht	(SUI)
3.	Christoph Gruber	(AUT)

15/03/2007, Lenzerheide (SUI)
SUPER-G

1.	**AKSEL LUND SVINDAL**	**(NOR)**
2.	Benjamin Raich	(AUT)
3.	Erik Guay	(CAN)

17/03/2007, Lenzerheide (SUI)
GIANT SLALOM

1.	**AKSEL LUND SVINDAL**	**(NOR)**
2.	Massimiliano Blardone	(ITA)
3.	Bode Miller	(USA)

18/03/2007, Lenzerheide (SUI)
SLALOM

1.	**BENJAMIN RAICH**	**(AUT)**
2.	Mario Matt	(AUT)
3.	Manfred Mölgg	(ITA)

2007-08

CUPS

OVERALL
1.	**BODE MILLER**	**(USA)**
2.	Benjamin Raich	(AUT)
3.	Didier Cuche	(SUI)

SLALOM
1.	**MANFRED MÖLGG**	**(ITA)**
2.	Jean-Baptiste Grange	(FRA)
3.	Reinfried Herbst	(AUT)

GIANT SLALOM
1.	**TED LIGETY**	**(USA)**
2.	Benjamin Raich	(AUT)
3.	Manfred Mölgg	(ITA)

SUPER-G
1.	**HANNES REICHELT**	**(AUT)**
2.	Didier Cuche	(SUI)
3.	Benjamin Raich	(AUT)

DOWNHILL
1.	**DIDIER CUCHE**	**(SUI)**
2.	Bode Miller	(USA)
3.	Michael Walchhofer	(AUT)

SUPER COMBINED
1.	**BODE MILLER**	**(USA)**
2.	Ivica Kostelić	(CRO)
3.	Daniel Albrecht	(SUI)

RACES

28/10/2007, Sölden (AUT)
GIANT SLALOM
1.	**AKSEL LUND SVINDAL**	**(NOR)**
2.	Ted Ligety	(USA)
3.	Kalle Palander	(FIN)

11/11/2007, Reiteralm (AUT)
SLALOM
1.	**MARC GINI**	**(SUI)**
2.	Kalle Palander	(FIN)
3.	Manfred Mölgg	(ITA)

24/11/2007, Lake Louise (CAN)
DOWNHILL
1.	**JAN HUDEC**	**(CAN)**
2.	Marco Sullivan	(AUT)
3.	Andreas Buder	(AUT)

25/11/2007, Lake Louise (CAN)
SUPER-G
1.	**AKSEL LUND SVINDAL**	**(NOR)**
2.	Benjamin Raich	(AUT)
3.	Didier Cuche	(SUI)

29/11/2007, Beaver Creek (USA)
SUPER COMBINED
1.	**DANIEL ALBRECHT**	**(SUI)**
2.	Jean-Baptiste Grange	(FRA)
3.	Ondřej Bank	(CZE)

30/11/2007, Beaver Creek (USA)
DOWNHILL
1.	**MICHAEL WALCHHOFER**	**(AUT)**
2.	Steven Nyman	(USA)
3.	Didier Cuche	(SUI)

02/12/2007, Beaver Creek (USA)
GIANT SLALOM
1.	**DANIEL ALBRECHT**	**(SUI)**
2.	Mario Matt	(AUT)
3.	Didier Cuche	(SUI)

03/12/2007, Beaver Creek (USA)
SUPER-G
1.	**HANNES REICHELT**	**(AUT)**
2.	Mario Scheiber	(AUT)
3.	Christoph Gruber	(AUT)

08/12/2007, Bad Kleinkirchheim (AUT)
GIANT SLALOM
1.	**MASSIMILIANO BLARDONE**	**(ITA)**
2.	Manfred Mölgg	(ITA)
3.	Ted Ligety	(USA)

09/12/2007, Bad Kleinkirchheim (AUT)
SLALOM
1.	**BENJAMIN RAICH**	**(AUT)**
2.	Jens Byggmark	(SWE)
3.	Manfred Mölgg	(ITA)

14/12/2007, Val Gardena (ITA)
SUPER-G
1.	**DIDIER CUCHE**	**(SUI)**
2.	Bode Miller	(USA)
3.	Marco Büchel	(LIE)

15/12/2007, Val Gardena (ITA)
DOWNHILL

1. **MICHAEL WALCHHOFER** **(AUT)**
2. Didier Cuche (SUI)
3. Scott Macartney (USA)

16/12/2007, Alta Badia (ITA)
GIANT SLALOM

1. **KALLE PALANDER** **(FIN)**
2. Benjamin Raich (AUT)
3. Marc Berthod (SUI)

17/12/2007, Alta Badia (ITA)
SLALOM

1. **JEAN-BAPTISTE GRANGE** **(FRA)**
2. Felix Neureuther (GER)
3. Ted Ligety (USA)

29/12/2007, Bormio (ITA)
DOWNHILL

1. **BODE MILLER** **(USA)**
2. Andreas Buder (AUT)
3. Jan Hudec (CAN)

05/01/2008 Adelboden (SUI)
GIANT SLALOM

1. **MARC BERTHOD** **(SUI)**
2. Daniel Albrecht (SUI)
3. Hannes Reichelt (AUT)

06/01/2008 Adelboden (SUI)
SLALOM

1. **MARIO MATT** **(AUT)**
2. Benjamin Raich (AUT)
3. Felix Neureuther (GER)

11/01/2008 Wengen (SUI)
SUPER COMBINED

1. **JEAN-BAPTISTE GRANGE** **(FRA)**
2. Daniel Albrecht (SUI)
3. Bode Miller (USA)

12/01/2008 Wengen (SUI)
SLALOM

1. **JEAN-BAPTISTE GRANGE** **(FRA)**
2. Jens Byggmark (SWE)
3. Ted Ligety (USA)

13/01/2008 Wengen (SUI)
DOWNHILL

1. **BODE MILLER** **(USA)**
2. Didier Cuche (SUI)
3. Manuel Osborne-Paradis (CAN)

18/01/2008 Kitzbühel (AUT)
SUPER-G

1. **MARCO BÜCHEL** **(LIE)**
2. Hermann Maier (AUT)
3. Didier Cuche (SUI)
= Mario Scheiber (AUT)

19/01/2008 Kitzbühel (AUT)
DOWNHILL

1. **DIDIER CUCHE** **(SUI)**
2. Bode Miller (USA)
= Mario Scheiber (AUT)

20/01/2008 Kitzbühel (AUT)
SLALOM

1. **JEAN-BAPTISTE GRANGE** **(FRA)**
2. Jens Byggmark (SWE)
3. Mario Matt (AUT)

20/01/2008 Kitzbühel (AUT)
COMBINED

1. **BODE MILLER** **(USA)**
2. Benjamin Raich (AUT)
3. Ivica Kostelić (CRO)
= Rainer Schönfelder (AUT)

22/01/2008 Schladming (AUT)
SLALOM

1. **MARIO MATT** **(AUT)**
2. Jean-Baptiste Grange (FRA)
3. Manfred Mölgg (ITA)

26/01/2008 Chamonix (FRA)
DOWNHILL

1. **MARCO SULLIVAN** **(USA)**
2. Didier Cuche (SUI)
3. Andrej Jerman (SLO)

27/01/2008 Chamonix (FRA)
SUPER COMBINED

1. **BODE MILLER** **(USA)**
2. Ivica Kostelić (CRO)
3. Rainer Schönfelder (AUT)

03/02/2008 Val-d'Isère (FRA)
SUPER COMBINED

1. **BODE MILLER** **(USA)**

2. Ivica Kostelić (CRO)
3. Natko Zrnčić-Dim (CRO)

09/02/2008 Garmisch-Partenkirchen (GER)
SLALOM
1. **REINFRIED HERBST** **(AUT)**
2. Manfred Mölgg (ITA)
3. Ivica Kostelić (CRO)

17/02/2008 Zagreb Sljeme (CRO)
SLALOM
1. **MARIO MATT** **(AUT)**
2. Ivica Kostelić (CRO)
3. Reinfried Herbst (AUT)

22/02/2008 Whistler (CAN)
SUPER-G
1. **CHRISTOPH GRUBER** **(AUT)**
2. Hannes Reichelt (AUT)
3. Aleš Gorza (SLO)

24/02/2008 Whistler (CAN)
GIANT SLALOM
1. **HANNES REICHELT** **(AUT)**
2. Didier Cuche (SUI)
3. Benjamin Raich (AUT)

29/02/2008 Lillehammer Kvitfjell (NOR)
DOWNHILL
1. **WERNER HEEL** **(ITA)**
2. Bode Miller (USA)
3. Klaus Kröll (AUT)

01/03/2008 Lillehammer Kvitfjell (NOR)
DOWNHILL
1. **BODE MILLER** **(USA)**
2. Didier Cuche (SUI)
3. Werner Heel (ITA)

02/03/2008 Lillehammer Kvitfjell (NOR)
SUPER-G
1. **GEORG STREITBERGER** **(AUT)**
2. Bode Miller (USA)
3. Didier Cuche (SUI)

08/03/2008 Kranjska Gora (SLO)
GIANT SLALOM
1. **TED LIGETY** **(USA)**
2. Manfred Mölgg (ITA)
3. Massimiliano Blardone (ITA)

08/03/2008 Kranjska Gora (SLO)
SLALOM
1. **MANFRED MÖLGG** **(ITA)**
2. Ivica Kostelić (CRO)
3. Marcel Hirscher (AUT)

13/03/2008 Bormio (ITA)
SUPER-G
1. **HANNES REICHELT** **(AUT)**
2. Didier Défago (SUI)
3. Aleš Gorza (SLO)

14/03/2008 Bormio (ITA)
GIANT SLALOM
1. **TED LIGETY** **(USA)**
2. Benjamin Raich (AUT)
3. Cyprien Richard (FRA)

15/03/2008 Bormio (ITA)
SLALOM
1. **REINFRIED HERBST** **(AUT)**
2. Daniel Albrecht (SUI)
3. Marcel Hirscher (AUT)

2008-09

CUPS

OVERALL

1.	**AKSEL LUND SVINDAL**	**(NOR)**
2.	Benjamin Raich	(AUT)
3.	Didier Cuche	(SUI)

SLALOM

1.	**JEAN-BAPTISTE GRANGE**	**(FRA)**
2.	Ivica Kostelić	(CRO)
3.	Julien Lizeroux	(FRA)

GIANT SLALOM

1.	**DIDIER CUCHE**	**(SUI)**
2.	Benjamin Raich	(AUT)
3.	Ted Ligety	(USA)

SUPER-G

1.	**AKSEL LUND SVINDAL**	**(NOR)**
2.	Werner Heel	(ITA)
3.	Didier Défago	(SUI)

DOWNHILL

1.	**MICHAEL WALCHHOFER**	**(AUT)**
2.	Klaus Kröll	(AUT)
3.	Didier Défago	(SUI)

SUPER COMBINED

1.	**CARLO JANKA**	**(SUI)**
2.	Silvan Zurbriggen	(SUI)
3.	Romed Baumann	(AUT)

RACES

26/10/2008 Sölden (AUT)
GIANT SLALOM

1.	**DANIEL ALBRECHT**	**(SUI)**
2.	Didier Cuche	(SUI)
3.	Ted Ligety	(USA)

16/11/2008 Levi (FIN)
SLALOM

1.	**JEAN-BAPTISTE GRANGE**	**(FRA)**
2.	Bode Miller	(USA)
3.	Mario Matt	(AUT)

29/11/2008 Lake Louise (CAN)
DOWNHILL

1.	**PETER FILL**	**(ITA)**
2.	Carlo Janka	(SUI)
3.	Hans Olsson	(SWE)

30/11/2008 Lake Louise (CAN)
SUPER-G

1.	**HERMANN MAIER**	**(AUT)**
2.	John Kucera	(CAN)
3.	Didier Cuche	(SUI)

05/12/2008 Beaver Creek (USA)
DOWNHILL

1.	**AKSEL LUND SVINDAL**	**(NOR)**
2.	Marco Büchel	(LIE)
3.	Erik Guay	(CAN)

06/12/2008 Beaver Creek (USA)
SUPER-G

1.	**AKSEL LUND SVINDAL**	**(NOR)**
2.	Hermann Maier	(AUT)
3.	Michael Walchhofer	(AUT)

07/12/2008 Beaver Creek (USA)
GIANT SLALOM

1.	**BENJAMIN RAICH**	**(AUT)**
2.	Ted Ligety	(USA)
3.	Aksel Lund Svindal	(NOR)

12/12/2008 Val-d'Isère (FRA)
SUPER COMBINED

1.	**BENJAMIN RAICH**	**(AUT)**
2.	Jean-Baptiste Grange	(FRA)
3.	Marcel Hirscher	(AUT)

13/12/2008 Val-d'Isère (FRA)
GIANT SLALOM

1.	**CARLO JANKA**	**(SUI)**
2.	Massimiliano Blardone	(ITA)
3.	Gauthier de Tessières	(FRA)

19/12/2008 Val Gardena (ITA)
SUPER-G

1.	**WERNER HEEL**	**(ITA)**
2.	Didier Défago	(SUI)
3.	Patrik Järbyn	(SWE)

20/12/2008 Val Gardena (ITA)
DOWNHILL

1.	**MICHAEL WALCHHOFER**	**(AUT)**
2.	Bode Miller	(USA)
3.	Manuel Osborne-Paradis	(CAN)

21/12/2008 Alta Badia (ITA)
GIANT SLALOM

1.	DANIEL ALBRECHT	(SUI)
2.	Ivica Kostelić	(CRO)
3.	Hannes Reichelt	(AUT)

22/12/2008 Alta Badia (ITA)
SLALOM

1.	IVICA KOSTELIĆ	(CRO)
2.	Jean-Baptiste Grange	(FRA)
3.	Benjamin Raich	(AUT)

28/12/2008 Bormio (ITA)
DOWNHILL

1.	CHRISTOF INNERHOFER	(ITA)
2.	Klaus Kröll	(AUT)
3.	Michael Walchhofer	(AUT)

06/01/2009 Zagreb Sljeme (CRO)
SLALOM

1.	JEAN-BAPTISTE GRANGE	(FRA)
2.	Ivica Kostelić	(CRO)
3.	Giuliano Razzoli	(ITA)

10/01/2009 Adelboden (SUI)
GIANT SLALOM

1.	BENJAMIN RAICH	(AUT)
2.	Massimiliano Blardone	(ITA)
3.	Kjetil Jansrud	(NOR)

11/01/2009 Adelboden (SUI)
SLALOM

1.	REINFRIED HERBST	(AUT)
2.	Manfred Pranger	(AUT)
3.	Felix Neureuther	(GER)

16/01/2009 Wengen (SUI)
SUPER COMBINED

1.	CARLO JANKA	(SUI)
2.	Peter Fill	(ITA)
3.	Silvan Zurbriggen	(SUI)

17/01/2009 Wengen (SUI)
DOWNHILL

1.	DIDIER DÉFAGO	(SUI)
2.	Bode Miller	(USA)
3.	Marco Sullivan	(AUT)

18/01/2009 Wengen (SUI)
SLALOM

1.	MANFRED PRANGER	(AUT)
2.	Reinfried Herbst	(AUT)
3.	Ivica Kostelić	(CRO)

23/01/2009 Kitzbühel (AUT)
SUPER-G

1.	KLAUS KRÖLL	(AUT)
2.	Aksel Lund Svindal	(NOR)
3.	Ambrosi Hoffmann	(SUI)

24/01/2009 Kitzbühel (AUT)
DOWNHILL

1.	DIDIER DÉFAGO	(SUI)
2.	Michael Walchhofer	(AUT)
3.	Klaus Kröll	(AUT)

25/01/2009 Kitzbühel (AUT)
SLALOM

1.	JULIEN LIZEROUX	(FRA)
2.	Jean-Baptiste Grange	(FRA)
3.	Patrick Thaler	(ITA)

25/01/2009 Kitzbühel (AUT)
COMBINED

1.	SILVAN ZURBRIGGEN	(SUI)
2.	Ivica Kostelić	(CRO)
3.	Natko Zrnčić-Dim	(CRO)

27/01/2009 Schladming (AUT)
SLALOM

1.	REINFRIED HERBST	(AUT)
2.	Manfred Pranger	(AUT)
3.	Ivica Kostelić	(CRO)

31/01/2009 Garmisch-Partenkirchen (GER)
SLALOM

1.	MANFRED MÖLGG	(ITA)
2.	Giorgio Rocca	(ITA)
3.	Reinfried Herbst	(AUT)

21/02/2009 Sestriere (ITA)
GIANT SLALOM

1.	DIDIER CUCHE	(SUI)
2.	Stephan Görgl	(AUT)
3.	Benjamin Raich	(AUT)

22/02/2009 Sestriere (ITA)
SUPER COMBINED

1.	ROMED BAUMANN	(AUT)
2.	Julien Lizeroux	(FRA)
3.	Christof Innerhofer	(ITA)

= Carlo Janka   (SUI)

28/02/2009 Kranjska Gora (SLO)
GIANT SLALOM

1.	**TED LIGETY**	**(USA)**
2.	Didier Cuche	(SUI)
3.	Massimiliano Blardone	(ITA)

01/03/2009 Kranjska Gora (SLO)
SLALOM

1.	**JULIEN LIZEROUX**	**(FRA)**
2.	Giuliano Razzoli	(ITA)
3.	Felix Neureuther	(GER)

06/03/2009 Lillehammer Kvitfjell (NOR)
DOWNHILL

1.	**MANUEL OSBORNE-PARADIS**	**(CAN)**
2.	Michael Walchhofer	(AUT)
3.	Aksel Lund Svindal	(NOR)

07/03/2009 Lillehammer Kvitfjell (NOR)
DOWNHILL

1.	**KLAUS KRÖLL**	**(AUT)**
2.	Michael Walchhofer	(AUT)
3.	Manuel Osborne-Paradis	(CAN)

11/03/2009 Åre (SWE)
DOWNHILL

1.	**AKSEL LUND SVINDAL**	**(NOR)**
2.	Didier Cuche	(SUI)
3.	Hans Olsson	(SWE)

12/03/2009 Åre (SWE)
SUPER-G

1.	**WERNER HEEL**	**(ITA)**
2.	Aksel Lund Svindal	(NOR)
3.	Christof Innerhofer	(ITA)

13/03/2009 Åre (SWE)
GIANT SLALOM

1.	**BENJAMIN RAICH**	**(AUT)**
2.	Ted Ligety	(USA)
3.	Didier Cuche	(SUI)

14/03/2009 Åre (SWE)
SLALOM

1.	**MARIO MATT**	**(AUT)**
2.	Julien Lizeroux	(FRA)
3.	Jean-Baptiste Grange	(FRA)

2009-10

CUPS

OVERALL

1.	**CARLO JANKA**	**(SUI)**
2.	Benjamin Raich	(AUT)
3.	Didier Cuche	(SUI)

SLALOM

1.	**REINFRIED HERBST**	**(AUT)**
2.	Julien Lizeroux	(FRA)
3.	Silvan Zurbriggen	(SUI)

GIANT SLALOM

1.	**TED LIGETY**	**(USA)**
2.	Carlo Janka	(SUI)
3.	Benjamin Raich	(AUT)

SUPER-G

1.	**ERIK GUAY**	**(CAN)**
2.	Michael Walchhofer	(AUT)
3.	Aksel Lund Svindal	(NOR)

DOWNHILL

1.	**DIDIER CUCHE**	**(SUI)**
2.	Carlo Janka	(SUI)
3.	Werner Heel	(ITA)

SUPER COMBINED

1.	**BENJAMIN RAICH**	**(AUT)**
2.	Carlo Janka	(SUI)
3.	Ivica Kostelić	(CRO)

RACES

25/10/2009 Sölden (AUT)
GIANT SLALOM

1.	**DIDIER CUCHE**	**(SUI)**
2.	Ted Ligety	(USA)
3.	Carlo Janka	(SUI)

15/11/2009 Levi (FIN)
SLALOM

1.	**REINFRIED HERBST**	**(AUT)**
2.	Ivica Kostelić	(CRO)
3.	Jean-Baptiste Grange	(FRA)

28/11/2009 Lake Louise (CAN)
DOWNHILL

1.	**DIDIER CUCHE**	**(SUI)**
2.	Werner Heel	(ITA)
3.	Carlo Janka	(SUI)

29/11/2009 Lake Louise (CAN)
SUPER-G

1.	**MANUEL OSBORNE-PARADIS**	**(CAN)**
2.	Benjamin Raich	(AUT)
3.	Michael Walchhofer	(AUT)

04/12/2009 Beaver Creek (USA)
SUPER COMBINED

1.	**CARLO JANKA**	**(SUI)**
2.	Didier Défago	(SUI)
3.	Natko Zrnčić-Dim	(CRO)

05/12/2009 Beaver Creek (USA)
DOWNHILL

1.	**CARLO JANKA**	**(SUI)**
2.	Didier Cuche	(SUI)
3.	Aksel Lund Svindal	(NOR)

06/12/2009 Beaver Creek (USA)
GIANT SLALOM

1.	**CARLO JANKA**	**(SUI)**
2.	Benjamin Raich	(AUT)
3.	Aksel Lund Svindal	(NOR)

11/12/2009 Val-d'Isère (FRA)
SUPER COMBINED

1.	**BENJAMIN RAICH**	**(AUT)**
2.	Marcel Hirscher	(AUT)
3.	Romed Baumann	(AUT)
=	Manfred Mölgg	(ITA)

12/12/2009 Val-d'Isère (FRA)
SUPER-G

1.	**MICHAEL WALCHHOFER**	**(AUT)**
2.	Ted Ligety	(USA)
3.	Werner Heel	(ITA)

13/12/2009 Val-d'Isère (FRA)
GIANT SLALOM

1.	**MARCEL HIRSCHER**	**(AUT)**
2.	Massimiliano Blardone	(ITA)
3.	Benjamin Raich	(AUT)

18/12/2009 Val Gardena (ITA)
SUPER-G

1.	**AKSEL LUND SVINDAL**	**(NOR)**
2.	Carlo Janka	(SUI)

3.	Patrick Staudacher	(ITA)

19/12/2009 Val Gardena (ITA)
DOWNHILL

1.	**MANUEL OSBORNE-PARADIS**	**(CAN)**
2.	Mario Scheiber	(AUT)
3.	Johan Clarey	(FRA)
=	Ambrosi Hoffmann	(SUI)

20/12/2009 Alta Badia (ITA)
GIANT SLALOM

1.	**MASSIMILIANO BLARDONE**	**(ITA)**
2.	Davide Simoncelli	(ITA)
3.	Cyprien Richard	(FRA)

21/12/2009 Alta Badia (ITA)
SLALOM

1.	**REINFRIED HERBST**	**(AUT)**
2.	Silvan Zurbriggen	(SUI)
3.	Manfred Pranger	(AUT)

29/12/2009 Bormio (ITA)
DOWNHILL

1.	**ANDREJ JERMAN**	**(SLO)**
2.	Didier Défago	(SUI)
3.	Michael Walchhofer	(AUT)

06/01/2010 Zagreb Sljeme (CRO)
SLALOM

1.	**GIULIANO RAZZOLI**	**(ITA)**
2.	Manfred Mölgg	(ITA)
3.	Julien Lizeroux	(FRA)

10/01/2010 Adelboden (SUI)
SLALOM

1.	**JULIEN LIZEROUX**	**(FRA)**
2.	Marcel Hirscher	(AUT)
3.	Ivica Kostelić	(CRO)

15/01/2010 Wengen (SUI)
SUPER COMBINED

1.	**BODE MILLER**	**(USA)**
2.	Carlo Janka	(SUI)
3.	Silvan Zurbriggen	(SUI)

16/01/2010 Wengen (SUI)
DOWNHILL

1.	**CARLO JANKA**	**(SUI)**
2.	Manuel Osborne-Paradis	(CAN)
3.	Marco Büchel	(LIE)

17/01/2010 Wengen (SUI)
SLALOM

1.	**IVICA KOSTELIĆ**	**(CRO)**
2.	André Myhrer	(SWE)
3.	Reinfried Herbst	(AUT)

22/01/2010 Kitzbühel (AUT)
SUPER-G

1.	**DIDIER CUCHE**	**(SUI)**
2.	Michael Walchhofer	(AUT)
3.	Georg Streitberger	(AUT)

23/01/2010 Kitzbühel (AUT)
DOWNHILL

1.	**DIDIER CUCHE**	**(SUI)**
2.	Andrej Šporn	(SLO)
3.	Werner Heel	(ITA)

24/01/2010 Kitzbühel (AUT)
SLALOM

1.	**FELIX NEUREUTHER**	**(GER)**
2.	Julien Lizeroux	(FRA)
3.	Giuliano Razzoli	(ITA)

24/01/2010 Kitzbühel (AUT)
COMBINED

1.	**IVICA KOSTELIĆ**	**(CRO)**
2.	Silvan Zurbriggen	(SUI)
3.	Benjamin Raich	(AUT)

26/01/2010 Schladming (AUT)
SLALOM

1.	**REINFRIED HERBST**	**(AUT)**
2.	Silvan Zurbriggen	(SUI)
3.	Manfred Pranger	(AUT)

29/01/2010 Kranjska Gora (SLO)
GIANT SLALOM

1.	**TED LIGETY**	**(USA)**
2.	Marcel Hirscher	(AUT)
3.	Kjetil Jansrud	(NOR)

30/01/2010 Kranjska Gora (SLO)
GIANT SLALOM

1.	**MARCEL HIRSCHER**	**(AUT)**
2.	Kjetil Jansrud	(NOR)
3.	Ted Ligety	(USA)

31/01/2010 Kranjska Gora (SLO)
SLALOM

1.	**REINFRIED HERBST**	**(AUT)**

2.	Marcel Hirscher	(AUT)
3.	Julien Lizeroux	(FRA)

06/03/2010 Lillehammer Kvitfjell (NOR)
DOWNHILL

1.	**DIDIER CUCHE**	**(SUI)**
2.	Aksel Lund Svindal	(NOR)
3.	Klaus Kröll	(AUT)

07/03/2010 Lillehammer Kvitfjell (NOR)
SUPER-G

1.	**ERIK GUAY**	**(CAN)**
2.	Hannes Reichelt	(AUT)
3.	Tobias Grünenfelder	(SUI)
=	Aksel Lund Svindal	(NOR)

10/03/2010 Garmisch-Partenkirchen (GER)
DOWNHILL

1.	**CARLO JANKA**	**(SUI)**
2.	Mario Scheiber	(AUT)
3.	Erik Guay	(CAN)
=	Patrick Küng	(SUI)

11/03/2010 Garmisch-Partenkirchen (GER)
SUPER-G

1.	**ERIK GUAY**	**(CAN)**
2.	Ivica Kostelić	(CRO)
3.	Aksel Lund Svindal	(NOR)

12/03/2010 Garmisch-Partenkirchen (GER)
GIANT SLALOM

1.	**CARLO JANKA**	**(SUI)**
2.	Davide Simoncelli	(ITA)
3.	Ted Ligety	(USA)
=	Philipp Schörghofer	(AUT)

13/03/2010 Garmisch-Partenkirchen (GER)
SLALOM

1.	**FELIX NEUREUTHER**	**(GER)**
2.	Manfred Pranger	(AUT)
3.	André Myhrer	(SWE)

2010-11

CUPS

OVERALL
1. **IVICA KOSTELIĆ** **(CRO)**
2. Didier Cuche (SUI)
3. Carlo Janka (SUI)

SLALOM
1. **IVICA KOSTELIĆ** **(CRO)**
2. Jean-Baptiste Grange (FRA)
3. André Myhrer (SWE)

GIANT SLALOM
1. **TED LIGETY** **(USA)**
2. Aksel Lund Svindal (NOR)
3. Cyprien Richard (FRA)

SUPER-G
1. **DIDIER CUCHE** **(SUI)**
2. Georg Streitberger (AUT)
3. Ivica Kostelić (CRO)

DOWNHILL
1. **DIDIER CUCHE** **(SUI)**
2. Michael Walchhofer (AUT)
3. Klaus Kröll (AUT)

SUPER COMBINED
1. **IVICA KOSTELIĆ** **(CRO)**
2. Christof Innerhofer (ITA)
3. Kjetil Jansrud (NOR)

RACES

14/11/2010 Levi (FIN)
SLALOM
1. **JEAN-BAPTISTE GRANGE** **(FRA)**
2. André Myhrer (SWE)
3. Ivica Kostelić (CRO)

27/11/2010 Lake Louise (CAN)
DOWNHILL
1. **MICHAEL WALCHHOFER** **(AUT)**
2. Mario Scheiber (AUT)
= Aksel Lund Svindal (NOR)

28/11/2010 Lake Louise (CAN)
SUPER-G
1. **TOBIAS GRÜNENFELDER** **(SUI)**
2. Carlo Janka (SUI)
3. Romed Baumann (AUT)

04/12/2010 Beaver Creek (USA)
SUPER-G
1. **GEORG STREITBERGER** **(AUT)**
2. Adrien Théaux (FRA)
3. Didier Cuche (SUI)

05/12/2010 Beaver Creek (USA)
GIANT SLALOM
1. **TED LIGETY** **(USA)**
2. Kjetil Jansrud (NOR)
3. Marcel Hirscher (AUT)

11/12/2010 Val-d'Isère (FRA)
GIANT SLALOM
1. **TED LIGETY** **(USA)**
2. Aksel Lund Svindal (NOR)
3. Massimiliano Blardone (ITA)

12/12/2010 Val-d'Isère (FRA)
SLALOM
1. **MARCEL HIRSCHER** **(AUT)**
2. Benjamin Raich (AUT)
3. Steve Missillier (FRA)

17/12/2010 Val Gardena (ITA)
SUPER-G
1. **MICHAEL WALCHHOFER** **(AUT)**
2. Stephan Keppler (GER)
3. Erik Guay (CAN)

18/12/2010 Val Gardena (ITA)
DOWNHILL
1. **SILVAN ZURBRIGGEN** **(SUI)**
2. Romed Baumann (AUT)
3. Didier Cuche (SUI)

19/12/2010 Alta Badia (ITA)
GIANT SLALOM
1. **TED LIGETY** **(USA)**
2. Cyprien Richard (FRA)
3. Thomas Fanara (FRA)

29/12/2010 Bormio (ITA)
DOWNHILL
1. **MICHAEL WALCHHOFER** **(AUT)**
2. Silvan Zurbriggen (SUI)
3. Christof Innerhofer (ITA)

02/01/2011 Munich (GER)
PARALLEL SLALOM

1.	**IVICA KOSTELIĆ**	**(CRO)**
2.	Julien Lizeroux	(FRA)
3.	Bode Miller	(USA)

06/01/2011 Zagreb Sljeme (CRO)
SLALOM

1.	**ANDRÉ MYHRER**	**(SWE)**
2.	Ivica Kostelić	(CRO)
3.	Mattias Hargin	(SWE)

08/01/2011 Adelboden (SUI)
GIANT SLALOM

1.	**CYPRIEN RICHARD**	**(FRA)**
=	**AKSEL LUND SVINDAL**	**(NOR)**
3.	Thomas Fanara	(FRA)

09/01/2011 Adelboden (SUI)
SLALOM

1.	**IVICA KOSTELIĆ**	**(CRO)**
2.	Marcel Hirscher	(AUT)
3.	Reinfried Herbst	(AUT)

14/01/2011 Wengen (SUI)
SUPER COMBINED

1.	**IVICA KOSTELIĆ**	**(CRO)**
2.	Carlo Janka	(SUI)
3.	Aksel Lund Svindal	(NOR)

15/01/2011 Wengen (SUI)
DOWNHILL

1.	**KLAUS KRÖLL**	**(AUT)**
2.	Didier Cuche	(SUI)
3.	Carlo Janka	(SUI)

16/01/2011 Wengen (SUI)
SLALOM

1.	**IVICA KOSTELIĆ**	**(CRO)**
2.	Marcel Hirscher	(AUT)
3.	Jean-Baptiste Grange	(FRA)

21/01/2011 Kitzbühel (AUT)
SUPER-G

1.	**IVICA KOSTELIĆ**	**(CRO)**
2.	Georg Streitberger	(AUT)
3.	Aksel Lund Svindal	(NOR)

22/01/2011 Kitzbühel (AUT)
DOWNHILL

1.	**DIDIER CUCHE**	**(SUI)**
2.	Bode Miller	(USA)
3.	Adrien Théaux	(FRA)

23/01/2011 Kitzbühel (AUT)
SLALOM

1.	**JEAN-BAPTISTE GRANGE**	**(FRA)**
2.	Ivica Kostelić	(CRO)
3.	Giuliano Razzoli	(ITA)

23/01/2011 Kitzbühel (AUT)
COMBINED

1.	**IVICA KOSTELIĆ**	**(CRO)**
2.	Silvan Zurbriggen	(SUI)
3.	Romed Baumann	(AUT)

25/01/2011 Schladming (AUT)
SLALOM

1.	**JEAN-BAPTISTE GRANGE**	**(FRA)**
2.	André Myhrer	(SWE)
3.	Mattias Hargin	(SWE)

29/01/2011 Chamonix (FRA)
DOWNHILL

1.	**DIDIER CUCHE**	**(SUI)**
2.	Dominik Paris	(ITA)
3.	Klaus Kröll	(AUT)

30/01/2011 Chamonix (FRA)
SUPER COMBINED

1.	**IVICA KOSTELIĆ**	**(CRO)**
2.	Natko Zrnčić-Dim	(CRO)
3.	Aksel Lund Svindal	(NOR)

05/02/2011 Hinterstoder (AUT)
SUPER-G

1.	**HANNES REICHELT**	**(AUT)**
2.	Benjamin Raich	(AUT)
3.	Bode Miller	(USA)

06/02/2011 Hinterstoder (AUT)
GIANT SLALOM

1.	**PHILIPP SCHÖRGHOFER**	**(AUT)**
2.	Kjetil Jansrud	(NOR)
3.	Carlo Janka	(SUI)

26/02/2011 Bansko (BUL)
SUPER COMBINED

1.	**CHRISTOF INNERHOFER**	**(ITA)**
2.	Felix Neureuther	(GER)
3.	Thomas Mermillod Blondin	(FRA)

27/02/2011 Bansko (BUL)
SLALOM
1.	**MARIO MATT**	**(AUT)**
2.	Reinfried Herbst	(AUT)
3.	Jean-Baptiste Grange	(FRA)

05/03/2011 Kranjska Gora (SLO)
GIANT SLALOM
1.	**CARLO JANKA**	**(SUI)**
2.	Alexis Pinturault	(FRA)
3.	Ted Ligety	(USA)

06/03/2011 Kranjska Gora (SLO)
SLALOM
1.	**MARIO MATT**	**(AUT)**
2.	Axel Bäck	(SWE)
=	Nolan Kasper	(USA)

11/03/2011 Lillehammer Kvitfjell (NOR)
DOWNHILL
1.	**BEAT FEUZ**	**(SUI)**
2.	Erik Guay	(CAN)
3.	Michael Walchhofer	(AUT)

12/03/2011 Lillehammer Kvitfjell (NOR)
DOWNHILL
1.	**MICHAEL WALCHHOFER**	**(AUT)**
2.	Klaus Kröll	(AUT)
3.	Beat Feuz	(SUI)

13/03/2011 Lillehammer Kvitfjell (NOR)
SUPER-G
1.	**DIDIER CUCHE**	**(SUI)**
2.	Klaus Kröll	(AUT)
3.	Joachim Puchner	(AUT)

16/03/2011 Lenzerheide (SUI)
DOWNHILL
1.	**ADRIEN THÉAUX**	**(FRA)**
2.	Joachim Puchner	(AUT)
3.	Aksel Lund Svindal	(NOR)

19/03/2011 Lenzerheide (SUI)
SLALOM
1.	**GIULIANO RAZZOLI**	**(ITA)**
2.	Mario Matt	(AUT)
3.	Felix Neureuther	(GER)

2011-12

CUPS

OVERALL
1.	**MARCEL HIRSCHER**	**(AUT)**
2.	Beat Feuz	(SUI)
3.	Aksel Lund Svindal	(NOR)

SLALOM
1.	**ANDRÉ MYHRER**	**(SWE)**
2.	Ivica Kostelić	(CRO)
3.	Marcel Hirscher	(AUT)

GIANT SLALOM
1.	**MARCEL HIRSCHER**	**(AUT)**
2.	Ted Ligety	(USA)
3.	Massimiliano Blardone	(ITA)

SUPER-G
1.	**AKSEL LUND SVINDAL**	**(NOR)**
2.	Didier Cuche	(SUI)
3.	Beat Feuz	(SUI)

DOWNHILL
1.	**KLAUS KRÖLL**	**(AUT)**
2.	Beat Feuz	(SUI)
3.	Didier Cuche	(SUI)

SUPER COMBINED
1.	**IVICA KOSTELIĆ**	**(CRO)**
2.	Beat Feuz	(SUI)
3.	Romed Baumann	(AUT)

RACES

23/10/2011 Sölden (AUT)
GIANT SLALOM
1.	**TED LIGETY**	**(USA)**
2.	Alexis Pinturault	(FRA)
3.	Philipp Schörghofer	(AUT)

26/11/2011 Lake Louise (CAN)
DOWNHILL
1.	**DIDIER CUCHE**	**(SUI)**
2.	Beat Feuz	(SUI)
3.	Hannes Reichelt	(AUT)

27/11/2011 Lake Louise (CAN)
SUPER-G

1. **AKSEL LUND SVINDAL** **(NOR)**
2. Didier Cuche (SUI)
3. Adrien Théaux (FRA)

02/12/2011 Beaver Creek (USA)
DOWNHILL

1. **BODE MILLER** **(USA)**
2. Beat Feuz (SUI)
3. Klaus Kröll (AUT)

03/12/2011 Beaver Creek (USA)
SUPER-G

1. **SANDRO VILETTA** **(SUI)**
2. Aksel Lund Svindal (NOR)
3. Beat Feuz (SUI)

04/12/2011 Beaver Creek (USA)
GIANT SLALOM

1. **MARCEL HIRSCHER** **(AUT)**
2. Ted Ligety (USA)
3. Fritz Dopfer (GER)

06/12/2011 Beaver Creek (USA)
GIANT SLALOM

1. **TED LIGETY** **(USA)**
2. Marcel Hirscher (AUT)
3. Kjetil Jansrud (NOR)

08/12/2011 Beaver Creek (USA)
SLALOM

1. **IVICA KOSTELIĆ** **(CRO)**
2. Cristian Deville (ITA)
3. Marcel Hirscher (AUT)

16/12/2011 Val Gardena (ITA)
SUPER-G

1. **BEAT FEUZ** **(SUI)**
2. Bode Miller (USA)
3. Kjetil Jansrud (NOR)

18/12/2011 Alta Badia (ITA)
GIANT SLALOM

1. **MASSIMILIANO BLARDONE** **(ITA)**
2. Hannes Reichelt (AUT)
3. Philipp Schörghofer (AUT)

19/12/2011 Alta Badia (ITA)
SLALOM

1. **MARCEL HIRSCHER** **(AUT)**
2. Giuliano Razzoli (ITA)
3. Felix Neureuther (GER)

21/12/2011 Flachau (AUT)
SLALOM

1. **IVICA KOSTELIĆ** **(CRO)**
2. André Myhrer (SWE)
3. Cristian Deville (ITA)

29/12/2011 Bormio (ITA)
DOWNHILL

1. **DIDIER DÉFAGO** **(SUI)**
2. Patrick Küng (SUI)
3. Klaus Kröll (AUT)

05/01/2012 Zagreb Sljeme (CRO)
SLALOM

1. **MARCEL HIRSCHER** **(AUT)**
2. Felix Neureuther (GER)
3. Ivica Kostelić (CRO)

07/01/2012 Adelboden (SUI)
GIANT SLALOM

1. **MARCEL HIRSCHER** **(AUT)**
2. Benjamin Raich (AUT)
3. Massimiliano Blardone (ITA)

08/01/2012 Adelboden (SUI)
SLALOM

1. **MARCEL HIRSCHER** **(AUT)**
2. Ivica Kostelić (CRO)
3. Stefano Gross (ITA)

13/01/2012 Wengen (SUI)
SUPER COMBINED

1. **IVICA KOSTELIĆ** **(CRO)**
2. Beat Feuz (SUI)
3. Bode Miller (USA)

14/01/2012 Wengen (SUI)
DOWNHILL

1. **BEAT FEUZ** **(SUI)**
2. Hannes Reichelt (AUT)
3. Christof Innerhofer (ITA)

15/01/2012 Wengen (SUI)
SLALOM

1. **IVICA KOSTELIĆ** **(CRO)**
2. André Myhrer (SWE)
3. Fritz Dopfer (GER)

21/01/2012 Kitzbühel (AUT)
DOWNHILL

1.	**DIDIER CUCHE**	**(SUI)**
2.	Romed Baumann	(AUT)
3.	Klaus Kröll	(AUT)

22/01/2012 Kitzbühel (AUT)
SLALOM

1.	**CRISTIAN DEVILLE**	**(ITA)**
2.	Mario Matt	(AUT)
3.	Ivica Kostelić	(CRO)

22/01/2012 Kitzbühel (AUT)
COMBINED

1.	**IVICA KOSTELIĆ**	**(CRO)**
2.	Beat Feuz	(SUI)
3.	Silvan Zurbriggen	(SUI)

24/01/2012 Schladming (AUT)
SLALOM

1.	**MARCEL HIRSCHER**	**(AUT)**
2.	Stefano Gross	(ITA)
3.	Mario Matt	(AUT)

28/01/2012 Garmisch-Partenkirchen (GER)
DOWNHILL

1.	**DIDIER CUCHE**	**(SUI)**
2.	Erik Guay	(CAN)
3.	Hannes Reichelt	(AUT)

03/02/2012 Chamonix (FRA)
DOWNHILL

1.	**KLAUS KRÖLL**	**(AUT)**
2.	Bode Miller	(USA)
3.	Didier Cuche	(SUI)

04/02/2012 Chamonix (FRA)
DOWNHILL

1.	**JAN HUDEC**	**(CAN)**
2.	Romed Baumann	(AUT)
3.	Erik Guay	(CAN)

05/02/2012 Chamonix (FRA)
SUPER COMBINED

1.	**ROMED BAUMANN**	**(AUT)**
2.	Alexis Pinturault	(FRA)
3.	Beat Feuz	(SUI)

11/02/2012 Soči Krasnaja Poljana (RUS)
DOWNHILL

1.	**BEAT FEUZ**	**(SUI)**
2.	Benjamin Thomsen	(CAN)
3.	Adrien Théaux	(FRA)

12/02/2012 Soči Krasnaja Poljana (RUS)
SUPER COMBINED

1.	**IVICA KOSTELIĆ**	**(CRO)**
2.	Beat Feuz	(SUI)
3.	Thomas Mermillod Blondin	(FRA)

18/02/2012 Bansko (BUL)
GIANT SLALOM

1.	**MARCEL HIRSCHER**	**(AUT)**
2.	Massimiliano Blardone	(ITA)
3.	Marcel Mathis	(AUT)

19/02/2012 Bansko (BUL)
SLALOM

1.	**MARCEL HIRSCHER**	**(AUT)**
2.	André Myrher	(SWE)
3.	Stefano Gross	(ITA)

21/02/2012 Moscow (RUS)
PARALLEL SLALOM

1.	**ALEXIS PINTURAULT**	**(FRA)**
2.	Felix Neureuther	(GER)
3.	André Myrher	(SWE)

24/02/2012 Crans-Montana (SUI)
SUPER-G

1.	**DIDIER CUCHE**	**(SUI)**
2.	Jan Hudec	(CAN)
3.	Benjamin Raich	(AUT)

25/02/2012 Crans-Montana (SUI)
SUPER-G

1.	**BENJAMIN RAICH**	**(AUT)**
2.	Adrien Théaux	(FRA)
3.	Didier Cuche	(SUI)

26/02/2012 Crans-Montana (SUI)
GIANT SLALOM

1.	**MASSIMILIANO BLARDONE**	**(ITA)**
2.	Marcel Hirscher	(AUT)
3.	Hannes Reichelt	(AUT)

02/03/2012 Lillehammer Kvitfjell (NOR)
SUPER-G

1.	**BEAT FEUZ**	**(SUI)**
=	**KLAUS KRÖLL**	**(AUT)**
3.	Kjetil Jansrud	(NOR)

03/03/2012 Lillehammer Kvitfjell (NOR)
DOWNHILL

1. **KLAUS KRÖLL** (AUT)
2. Kjetil Jansrud (NOR)
3. Aksel Lund Svindal (NOR)

04/03/2012 Lillehammer Kvitfjell (NOR)
SUPER-G
1. **KJETIL JANSRUD** (NOR)
2. Aksel Lund Svindal (NOR)
3. Beat Feuz (SUI)

10/03/2012 Kranjska Gora (SLO)
GIANT SLALOM
1. **TED LIGETY** (USA)
2. Alexis Pinturault (FRA)
3. Marcel Hirscher (AUT)

11/03/2012 Kranjska Gora (SLO)
SLALOM
1. **ANDRÉ MYHRER** (SWE)
2. Cristian Deville (ITA)
3. Alexis Pinturault (FRA)

14/03/2012 Schladming (AUT)
DOWNHILL
1. **AKSEL LUND SVINDAL** (NOR)
2. Beat Feuz (SUI)
3. Hannes Reichelt (AUT)

15/03/2012 Schladming (AUT)
SUPER-G
1. **CHRISTOF INNERHOFER** (ITA)
2. Alexis Pinturault (FRA)
3. Marcel Hirscher (AUT)

17/03/2012 Schladming (AUT)
GIANT SLALOM
1. **MARCEL HIRSCHER** (AUT)
2. Hannes Reichelt (AUT)
3. Marcel Mathis (AUT)

18/03/2012 Schladming (AUT)
SLALOM
1. **ANDRÉ MYHRER** (SWE)
2. Felix Neureuther (GER)
3. Mario Matt (AUT)

2012-13

CUPS

OVERALL
1. **MARCEL HIRSCHER** (AUT)
2. Aksel Lund Svindal (NOR)
3. Ted Ligety (USA)

SLALOM
1. **MARCEL HIRSCHER** (AUT)
2. Felix Neureuther (GER)
3. Ivica Kostelić (CRO)

GIANT SLALOM
1. **TED LIGETY** (USA)
2. Marcel Hirscher (AUT)
3. Alexis Pinturault (FRA)

SUPER-G
1. **AKSEL LUND SVINDAL** (NOR)
2. Matteo Marsaglia (ITA)
3. Matthias Mayer (AUT)

DOWNHILL
1. **AKSEL LUND SVINDAL** (NOR)
2. Klaus Kröll (AUT)
3. Dominik Paris (ITA)

SUPER COMBINED
1. **IVICA KOSTELIĆ** (CRO)
1. **ALEXIS PINTURAULT** (FRA)
3. Thomas Mermillod Blondin (FRA)

RACES

28/10/2012 Sölden (AUT)
GIANT SLALOM
1. **TED LIGETY** (USA)
2. Manfred Mölgg (ITA)
3. Marcel Hirscher (AUT)

11/11/2012 Levi (FIN)
SLALOM
1. **ANDRÉ MYHRER** (SWE)
2. Marcel Hirscher (AUT)
3. Jens Byggmark (SWE)

24/11/2012 Lake Louise (CAN)
DOWNHILL

1.	**AKSEL LUND SVINDAL**	**(NOR)**
2.	Max Franz	(AUT)
3.	Klaus Kröll	(AUT)
=	Marco Sullivan	(AUT)

25/11/2012 Lake Louise (CAN)
SUPER-G
1.	**AKSEL LUND SVINDAL**	**(NOR)**
2.	Adrien Théaux	(FRA)
3.	Joachim Puchner	(AUT)

30/11/2012 Beaver Creek (USA)
DOWNHILL
1.	**CHRISTOF INNERHOFER**	**(ITA)**
2.	Aksel Lund Svindal	(NOR)
3.	Kjetil Jansrud	(NOR)

01/12/2012 Beaver Creek (USA)
SUPER-G
1.	**MATTEO MARSAGLIA**	**(ITA)**
2.	Aksel Lund Svindal	(NOR)
3.	Hannes Reichelt	(AUT)

02/12/2012 Beaver Creek (USA)
GIANT SLALOM
1.	**TED LIGETY**	**(USA)**
2.	Marcel Hirscher	(AUT)
3.	Davide Simoncelli	(ITA)

08/12/2012 Val-d'Isère (FRA)
SLALOM
1.	**ALEXIS PINTURAULT**	**(FRA)**
2.	Felix Neureuther	(GER)
3.	Marcel Hirscher	(AUT)

09/12/2012 Val-d'Isère (FRA)
GIANT SLALOM
1.	**MARCEL HIRSCHER**	**(AUT)**
2.	Stefan Luitz	(GER)
3.	Ted Ligety	(USA)

14/12/2012 Val Gardena (ITA)
SUPER-G
1.	**AKSEL LUND SVINDAL**	**(NOR)**
2.	Matteo Marsaglia	(ITA)
3.	Werner Heel	(ITA)

15/12/2012 Val Gardena (ITA)
DOWNHILL
| 1. | **STEVEN NYMAN** | **(USA)** |
| 2. | Rok Perko | (SLO) |

| 3. | Erik Guay | (CAN) |

16/12/2012 Alta Badia (ITA)
GIANT SLALOM
1.	**TED LIGETY**	**(USA)**
2.	Marcel Hirscher	(AUT)
3.	Thomas Fanara	(FRA)

18/12/2012 Madonna di Campiglio (ITA)
SLALOM
1.	**MARCEL HIRSCHER**	**(AUT)**
2.	Felix Neureuther	(GER)
3.	Naoki Yuasa	(JPN)

29/12/2012 Bormio (ITA)
DOWNHILL
1.	**DOMINIK PARIS**	**(ITA)**
=	**HANNES REICHELT**	**(AUT)**
3.	Aksel Lund Svindal	(NOR)

01/01/2013, Munich (GER)
PARALLEL SLALOM
1.	**FELIX NEUREUTHER**	**(GER)**
2.	Marcel Hirscher	(AUT)
3.	Alexis Pinturault	(FRA)

06/01/2013, Zagreb Sljeme (CRO)
SLALOM
1.	**MARCEL HIRSCHER**	**(AUT)**
2.	André Myhrer	(SWE)
3.	Mario Matt	(AUT)

12/01/2013, Adelboden (SUI)
GIANT SLALOM
1.	**TED LIGETY**	**(USA)**
2.	Fritz Dopfer	(GER)
3.	Felix Neureuther	(GER)

13/01/2013, Adelboden (SUI)
SLALOM
1.	**MARCEL HIRSCHER**	**(AUT)**
2.	Mario Matt	(AUT)
3.	Manfred Mölgg	(ITA)

18/01/2013, Wengen (SUI)
SUPER COMBINED
1.	**ALEXIS PINTURAULT**	**(FRA)**
2.	Ivica Kostelić	(CRO)
3.	Carlo Janka	(SUI)

19/01/2013, Wengen (SUI)

DOWNHILL
1. **CHRISTOF INNERHOFER** **(ITA)**
2. Klaus Kröll (AUT)
3. Hannes Reichelt (AUT)

20/01/2013, Wengen (SUI)
SLALOM
1. **FELIX NEUREUTHER** **(GER)**
2. Marcel Hirscher (AUT)
3. Ivica Kostelić (CRO)

24/01/2013, Kitzbühel (AUT)
SUPER-G
1. **AKSEL LUND SVINDAL** **(NOR)**
2. Matthias Mayer (AUT)
3. Christof Innerhofer (ITA)

26/01/2013, Kitzbühel (AUT)
DOWNHILL
1. **DOMINIK PARIS** **(ITA)**
2. Erik Guay (CAN)
3. Hannes Reichelt (AUT)

27/01/2013, Kitzbühel (AUT)
SLALOM
1. **MARCEL HIRSCHER** **(AUT)**
2. Felix Neureuther (GER)
3. Ivica Kostelić (CRO)

27/01/2013, Kitzbühel (AUT)
COMBINED
1. **IVICA KOSTELIĆ** **(CRO)**
2. Alexis Pinturault (FRA)
3. Thomas Mermillod Blondin (FRA)

29/01/2013, Moscow (RUS)
PARALLEL SLALOM
1. **MARCEL HIRSCHER** **(AUT)**
2. André Myhrer (SWE)
3. Ivica Kostelić (CRO)

23/02/2013, Garmisch-Partenkirchen (GER)
DOWNHILL
1. **CHRISTOF INNERHOFER** **(ITA)**
2. Georg Streitberger (AUT)
3. Klaus Kröll (AUT)

24/02/2013, Garmisch-Partenkirchen (GER)
GIANT SLALOM
1. **ALEXIS PINTURAULT** **(FRA)**
2. Marcel Hirscher (AUT)

3. Ted Ligety (USA)

02/03/2013, Lillehammer Kvitfjell (NOR)
DOWNHILL
1. **ADRIEN THÉAUX** **(FRA)**
2. Aksel Lund Svindal (NOR)
3. Klaus Kröll (AUT)

03/03/2013, Lillehammer Kvitfjell (NOR)
SUPER-G
1. **AKSEL LUND SVINDAL** **(NOR)**
2. Georg Streitberger (AUT)
3. Werner Heel (ITA)

09/03/2013, Kranjska Gora (SLO)
GIANT SLALOM
1. **TED LIGETY** **(USA)**
2. Marcel Hirscher (AUT)
3. Alexis Pinturault (FRA)

10/03/2013, Kranjska Gora (SLO)
SLALOM
1. **IVICA KOSTELIĆ** **(CRO)**
2. Marcel Hirscher (AUT)
3. Mario Matt (AUT)

16/03/2013, Lenzerheide (SUI)
GIANT SLALOM
1. **TED LIGETY** **(USA)**
2. Marcel Hirscher (AUT)
3. Alexis Pinturault (FRA)

17/03/2013, Lenzerheide (SUI)
SLALOM
1. **FELIX NEUREUTHER** **(GER)**
2. Marcel Hirscher (AUT)
3. Ivica Kostelić (CRO)

2013-14

CUPS

OVERALL
1.	**MARCEL HIRSCHER**	**(AUT)**
2.	Aksel Lund Svindal	(NOR)
3.	Alexis Pinturault	(FRA)

SLALOM
1.	**MARCEL HIRSCHER**	**(AUT)**
2.	Felix Neureuther	(GER)
3.	Henrik Kristoffersen	(NOR)

GIANT SLALOM
1.	**TED LIGETY**	**(USA)**
2.	Marcel Hirscher	(AUT)
3.	Alexis Pinturault	(FRA)

SUPER-G
1.	**AKSEL LUND SVINDAL**	**(NOR)**
2.	Kjetil Jansrud	(NOR)
3.	Patrick Küng	(SUI)

DOWNHILL
1.	**AKSEL LUND SVINDAL**	**(NOR)**
2.	Hannes Reichelt	(AUT)
3.	Erik Guay	(CAN)

SUPER COMBINED
1.	**TED LIGETY**	**(USA)**
1.	**ALEXIS PINTURAULT**	**(FRA)**
3.	Thomas Mermillod Blondin	(FRA)

RACES

27/10/2013, Sölden (AUT)
GIANT SLALOM
1.	**TED LIGETY**	**(USA)**
2.	Alexis Pinturault	(FRA)
3.	Marcel Hirscher	(AUT)

17/11/2013, Levi (FIN)
SLALOM
1.	**MARCEL HIRSCHER**	**(AUT)**
2.	Mario Matt	(AUT)
3.	Henrik Kristoffersen	(NOR)

30/11/2013, Lake Louise (CAN)
DOWNHILL
1.	**DOMINIK PARIS**	**(ITA)**
2.	Klaus Kröll	(AUT)
3.	Adrien Théaux	(FRA)

01/12/2013, Lake Louise (CAN)
SUPER-G
1.	**AKSEL LUND SVINDAL**	**(NOR)**
2.	Matthias Mayer	(AUT)
3.	Georg Streitberger	(AUT)

06/12/2013, Beaver Creek (USA)
DOWNHILL
1.	**AKSEL LUND SVINDAL**	**(NOR)**
2.	Hannes Reichelt	(AUT)
3.	Peter Fill	(ITA)

07/12/2013, Beaver Creek (USA)
SUPER-G
1.	**PATRICK KÜNG**	**(SUI)**
2.	Otmar Striedinger	(AUT)
3.	Peter Fill	(ITA)
=	Hannes Reichelt	(AUT)

08/12/2013, Beaver Creek (USA)
GIANT SLALOM
1.	**TED LIGETY**	**(USA)**
2.	Bode Miller	(USA)
3.	Marcel Hirscher	(AUT)

14/12/2013, Val-d'Isère (FRA)
GIANT SLALOM
1.	**MARCEL HIRSCHER**	**(AUT)**
2.	Thomas Fanara	(FRA)
3.	Stefan Luitz	(GER)

15/12/2013, Val-d'Isère (FRA)
SLALOM
1.	**MARIO MATT**	**(AUT)**
2.	Mattias Hargin	(SWE)
3.	Patrick Thaler	(ITA)

20/12/2013, Val Gardena (ITA)
SUPER-G
1.	**AKSEL LUND SVINDAL**	**(NOR)**
2.	Jan Hudec	(CAN)
3.	Adrien Théaux	(FRA)

21/12/2013, Val Gardena (ITA)
DOWNHILL
1.	**ERIK GUAY**	**(CAN)**
2.	Kjetil Jansrud	(NOR)

3. Johan Clarey   (FRA)

22/12/2013, Alta Badia (ITA)
GIANT SLALOM
1. **MARCEL HIRSCHER**   **(AUT)**
2. Alexis Pinturault   (FRA)
3. Ted Ligety   (USA)

29/12/2013, Bormio (ITA)
DOWNHILL
1. **AKSEL LUND SVINDAL**   **(NOR)**
2. Hannes Reichelt   (AUT)
3. Erik Guay   (CAN)

06/01/2014, Bormio (ITA)
SLALOM
1. **FELIX NEUREUTHER**   **(GER)**
2. Marcel Hirscher   (AUT)
3. Manfred Mölgg   (ITA)

11/01/2014, Adelboden (SUI)
GIANT SLALOM
1. **FELIX NEUREUTHER**   **(GER)**
2. Thomas Fanara   (FRA)
3. Marcel Hirscher   (AUT)

12/01/2014, Adelboden (SUI)
SLALOM
1. **MARCEL HIRSCHER**   **(AUT)**
2. André Myhrer   (SWE)
3. Henrik Kristoffersen   (NOR)

17/01/2014, Wengen (SUI)
SUPER COMBINED
1. **TED LIGETY**   **(USA)**
2. Alexis Pinturault   (FRA)
3. Natko Zrnčić-Dim   (CRO)

17/01/2014, Wengen (SUI)
DOWNHILL
1. **PATRICK KÜNG**   **(SUI)**
2. Hannes Reichelt   (AUT)
3. Aksel Lund Svindal   (NOR)

19/01/2014, Wengen (SUI)
SLALOM
1. **ALEXIS PINTURAULT**   **(FRA)**
2. Felix Neureuther   (GER)
3. Marcel Hirscher   (AUT)

24/01/2014, Kitzbühel (AUT)

SLALOM
1. **FELIX NEUREUTHER**   **(GER)**
2. Henrik Kristoffersen   (NOR)
3. Patrick Thaler   (ITA)

25/01/2014, Kitzbühel (AUT)
DOWNHILL
1. **HANNES REICHELT**   **(AUT)**
2. Aksel Lund Svindal   (NOR)
3. Bode Miller   (USA)

26/01/2014, Kitzbühel (AUT)
SUPER-G
1. **DIDIER DÉFAGO**   **(SUI)**
2. Bode Miller   (USA)
3. Max Franz   (AUT)
=   Aksel Lund Svindal   (NOR)

26/01/2014, Kitzbühel (AUT)
SUPER COMBINED
1. **ALEXIS PINTURAULT**   **(FRA)**
2. Ted Ligety   (USA)
3. Marcel Hirscher   (AUT)

28/01/2014, Schladming (AUT)
SLALOM
1. **HENRIK KRISTOFFERSEN**   **(NOR)**
2. Marcel Hirscher   (AUT)
3. Felix Neureuther   (GER)

02/02/2014, Sankt Moritz (SUI)
GIANT SLALOM
1. **TED LIGETY**   **(USA)**
2. Marcel Hirscher   (AUT)
3. Alexis Pinturault   (FRA)

28/02/2014, Lillehammer Kvitfjell (NOR)
DOWNHILL
1. **KJETIL JANSRUD**   **(NOR)**
=   **GEORG STREITBERGER**   **(AUT)**
3. Travis Ganong   (USA)

01/03/2014, Lillehammer Kvitfjell (NOR)
DOWNHILL
1. **ERIK GUAY**   **(CAN)**
2. Johan Clarey   (FRA)
3. Matthias Mayer   (AUT)

02/03/2014, Lillehammer Kvitfjell (NOR)
SUPER-G
1. **KJETIL JANSRUD**   **(NOR)**

2.	Patrick Küng	(SUI)
3.	Matthias Mayer	(AUT)

08/03/2014, Kranjska Gora (SLO)
GIANT SLALOM

1.	**TED LIGETY**	**(USA)**
2.	Benjamin Raich	(AUT)
3.	Henrik Kristoffersen	(NOR)

09/03/2014, Kranjska Gora (SLO)
SLALOM

1.	**FELIX NEUREUTHER**	**(GER)**
2.	Fritz Dopfer	(GER)
3.	Henrik Kristoffersen	(NOR)

12/03/2014, Lenzerheide (SUI)
DOWNHILL

1.	**MATTHIAS MAYER**	**(AUT)**
2.	Christof Innerhofer	(ITA)
=	Ted Ligety	(USA)

13/03/2014, Lenzerheide (SUI)
SUPER-G

1.	**ALEXIS PINTURAULT**	**(FRA)**
2.	Thomas Mermillod Blondin	(FRA)
3.	Bode Miller	(USA)

15/03/2014, Lenzerheide (SUI)
GIANT SLALOM

1.	**TED LIGETY**	**(USA)**
2.	Alexis Pinturault	(FRA)
3.	Felix Neureuther	(GER)

16/03/2014, Lenzerheide (SUI)
SLALOM

1.	**MARCEL HIRSCHER**	**(AUT)**
2.	Felix Neureuther	(GER)
3.	Mario Matt	(AUT)

2014-15

CUPS

OVERALL

1.	**MARCEL HIRSCHER**	**(AUT)**
2.	Kjetil Jansrud	(NOR)
3.	Alexis Pinturault	(FRA)

SLALOM

1.	**MARCEL HIRSCHER**	**(AUT)**
2.	Felix Neureuther	(GER)
3.	Aleksandr Chorošilov	(RUS)

GIANT SLALOM

1.	**MARCEL HIRSCHER**	**(AUT)**
2.	Alexis Pinturault	(FRA)
3.	Ted Ligety	(USA)

SUPER-G

1.	**KJETIL JANSRUD**	**(NOR)**
2.	Dominik Paris	(ITA)
3.	Matthias Mayer	(AUT)

DOWNHILL

1.	**KJETIL JANSRUD**	**(NOR)**
2.	Hannes Reichelt	(AUT)
3.	Guillermo Fayed	(FRA)

SUPER COMBINED

1.	**CARLO JANKA**	**(SUI)**
2.	Alexis Pinturault	(FRA)
3.	Victor Muffat-Jeandet	(FRA)

RACES

26/10/2014, Sölden (AUT)
GIANT SLALOM

1.	**MARCEL HIRSCHER**	**(AUT)**
2.	Fritz Dopfer	(GER)
3.	Alexis Pinturault	(FRA)

16/11/2014, Levi (FIN)
SLALOM

1.	**HENRIK KRISTOFFERSEN**	**(NOR)**
2.	Marcel Hirscher	(AUT)
3.	Felix Neureuther	(GER)

29/11/2014, Lake Louise (CAN)
DOWNHILL

1. **KJETIL JANSRUD** (NOR)
2. Guillermo Fayed (FRA)
= Manuel Osborne-Paradis (CAN)

30/11/2014, Lake Louise (CAN)
SUPER-G
1. **KJETIL JANSRUD** (NOR)
2. Matthias Mayer (AUT)
3. Dominik Paris (ITA)

05/12/2014, Beaver Creek (USA)
DOWNHILL
1. **KJETIL JANSRUD** (NOR)
2. Beat Feuz (SUI)
3. Steven Nyman (USA)

06/12/2014, Beaver Creek (USA)
SUPER-G
1. **HANNES REICHELT** (AUT)
2. Kjetil Jansrud (NOR)
3. Alexis Pinturault (FRA)

07/12/2014, Beaver Creek (USA)
GIANT SLALOM
1. **TED LIGETY** (USA)
2. Alexis Pinturault (FRA)
3. Marcel Hirscher (AUT)

12/12/2014, Åre (SWE)
GIANT SLALOM
1. **MARCEL HIRSCHER** (AUT)
2. Ted Ligety (USA)
3. Stefan Luitz (GER)

14/12/2014, Åre (SWE)
SLALOM
1. **MARCEL HIRSCHER** (AUT)
2. Felix Neureuther (GER)
3. Aleksandr Chorošilov (RUS)

19/12/2014, Val Gardena (ITA)
DOWNHILL
1. **STEVEN NYMAN** (USA)
2. Kjetil Jansrud (NOR)
3. Dominik Paris (ITA)

20/12/2014, Val Gardena (ITA)
SUPER-G
1. **KJETIL JANSRUD** (NOR)
2. Dominik Paris (ITA)
3. Hannes Reichelt (AUT)

21/12/2014, Alta Badia (ITA)
GIANT SLALOM
1. **MARCEL HIRSCHER** (AUT)
2. Ted Ligety (USA)
3. Thomas Fanara (FRA)

22/12/2014, Madonna di Campiglio (ITA)
SLALOM
1. **FELIX NEUREUTHER** (GER)
2. Fritz Dopfer (GER)
3. Jens Byggmark (SWE)

28/12/2014, Santa Caterina Valfurva (ITA)
DOWNHILL
1. **TRAVIS GANONG** (USA)
2. Matthias Mayer (AUT)
3. Dominik Paris (ITA)

06/01/2015, Zagreb Sljeme (CRO)
SLALOM
1. **MARCEL HIRSCHER** (AUT)
2. Felix Neureuther (GER)
3. Sebastian Foss Solevåg (NOR)

10/01/2015, Adelboden (SUI)
GIANT SLALOM
1. **MARCEL HIRSCHER** (AUT)
2. Alexis Pinturault (FRA)
3. Henrik Kristoffersen (NOR)

11/01/2015, Adelboden (SUI)
SLALOM
1. **STEFANO GROSS** (ITA)
2. Fritz Dopfer (GER)
3. Marcel Hirscher (AUT)

16/01/2015, Wengen (SUI)
ALPINE COMBINED
1. **CARLO JANKA** (SUI)
2. Victor Muffat Jeandet (FRA)
3. Ivica Kostelić (CRO)

17/01/2015, Wengen (SUI)
SLALOM
1. **FELIX NEUREUTHER** (GER)
2. Stefano Gross (ITA)
3. Henrik Kristoffersen (NOR)

18/01/2015, Wengen (SUI)
DOWNHILL

1. **HANNES REICHELT** **(AUT)**
2. Beat Feuz (SUI)
3. Carlo Janka (SUI)

23/01/2015, Kitzbühel (AUT)
SUPER-G

1. **DOMINIK PARIS** **(ITA)**
2. Matthias Mayer (AUT)
3. Georg Streitberger (AUT)

23/01/2015, Kitzbühel (AUT)
ALPINE COMBINED

1. **ALEXIS PINTURAULT** **(FRA)**
2. Marcel Hirscher (AUT)
3. Ondřej Bank (CZE)

24/01/2015, Kitzbühel (AUT)
DOWNHILL

1. **KJETIL JANSRUD** **(NOR)**
2. Dominik Paris (ITA)
3. Guillermo Fayed (FRA)

25/01/2015, Kitzbühel (AUT)
SLALOM

1. **MATTIAS HARGIN** **(SWE)**
2. Marcel Hirscher (AUT)
3. Felix Neureuther (GER)

27/01/2015, Schladming (AUT)
SLALOM

1. **ALEKSANDR CHOROŠILOV** **(RUS)**
2. Stefano Gross (ITA)
3. Felix Neureuther (GER)

21/02/2015, Saalbach-Hinterglemm (AUT)
DOWNHILL

1. **MATTHIAS MAYER** **(AUT)**
2. Max Franz (AUT)
3. Hannes Reichelt (AUT)

22/02/2015, Saalbach-Hinterglemm (AUT)
SUPER-G

1. **MATTHIAS MAYER** **(AUT)**
2. Adrien Théaux (FRA)
3. Kjetil Jansrud (NOR)

28/02/2015, Garmisch-Partenkirchen (GER)
DOWNHILL

1. **HANNES REICHELT** **(AUT)**
2. Romed Baumann (AUT)
3. Matthias Mayer (AUT)

01/03/2015, Garmisch-Partenkirchen (GER)
GIANT SLALOM

1. **MARCEL HIRSCHER** **(AUT)**
2. Felix Neureuther (GER)
3. Benjamin Raich (AUT)

07/03/2015, Lillehammer Kvitfjell (NOR)
DOWNHILL

1. **HANNES REICHELT** **(AUT)**
2. Manuel Osborne-Paradis (CAN)
3. Werner Heel (ITA)

08/03/2015, Lillehammer Kvitfjell (NOR)
SUPER-G

1. **KJETIL JANSRUD** **(NOR)**
2. Vincent Kriechmayr (AUT)
3. Dustin Cook (CAN)

14/03/2015, Kranjska Gora (SLO)
GIANT SLALOM

1. **ALEXIS PINTURAULT** **(FRA)**
2. Marcel Hirscher (AUT)
3. Thomas Fanara (FRA)

15/03/2015, Kranjska Gora (SLO)
SLALOM

1. **HENRIK KRISTOFFERSEN** **(NOR)**
2. Giuliano Razzoli (ITA)
3. Mattias Hargin (SWE)

18/03/2015, Méribel (FRA)
DOWNHILL

1. **KJETIL JANSRUD** **(NOR)**
2. Didier Défago (SUI)
3. Georg Streitberger (AUT)

19/03/2015, Méribel (FRA)
SUPER-G

1. **DUSTIN COOK** **(CAN)**
2. Kjetil Jansrud (NOR)
3. Brice Roger (FRA)

21/03/2015, Méribel (FRA)
GIANT SLALOM

1. **HENRIK KRISTOFFERSEN** **(NOR)**
2. Fritz Dopfer (GER)
3. Thomas Fanara (FRA)

22/03/2015, Méribel (FRA)
SLALOM

1.	**MARCEL HIRSCHER**	**(AUT)**
2.	Giuliano Razzoli	(ITA)
3.	Aleksandr Chorošilov	(RUS)

2015-16

CUPS

OVERALL

1.	**MARCEL HIRSCHER**	**(AUT)**
2.	Henrik Kristoffersen	(NOR)
3.	Alexis Pinturault	(FRA)

SLALOM

1.	**HENRIK KRISTOFFERSEN**	**(NOR)**
2.	Marcel Hirscher	(AUT)
3.	Felix Neureuther	(GER)

GIANT SLALOM

1.	**MARCEL HIRSCHER**	**(AUT)**
2.	Alexis Pinturault	(FRA)
3.	Henrik Kristoffersen	(NOR)

SUPER-G

1.	**ALEKSANDER AAMODT KILDE**	**(NOR)**
2.	Kjetil Jansrud	(NOR)
3.	Aksel Lund Svindal	(NOR)

DOWNHILL

1.	**PETER FILL**	**(ITA)**
2.	Aksel Lund Svindal	(NOR)
3.	Dominik Paris	(ITA)

COMBINED

1.	**ALEXIS PINTURAULT**	**(FRA)**
2.	Thomas Mermillod Blondin	(FRA)
3.	Kjetil Jansrud	(NOR)

RACES

25/10/2015, Sölden (AUT)
GIANT SLALOM

1.	**TED LIGETY**	**(USA)**
2.	Thomas Fanara	(FRA)
3.	Marcel Hirscher	(AUT)

28/11/2015, Lake Louise (CAN)
DOWNHILL

1.	**AKSEL LUND SVINDAL**	**(NOR)**
2.	Peter Fill	(ITA)
3.	Travis Ganong	(USA)

29/11/2015, Lake Louise (CAN)
SUPER-G

1. **AKSEL LUND SVINDAL** **(NOR)**
2. Matthias Mayer (AUT)
3. Peter Fill (ITA)

04/12/2015, Beaver Creek (USA)
DOWNHILL
1. **AKSEL LUND SVINDAL** **(NOR)**
2. Kjetil Jansrud (NOR)
3. Guillermo Fayed (FRA)

05/12/2015, Beaver Creek (USA)
SUPER-G
1. **MARCEL HIRSCHER** **(AUT)**
2. Ted Ligety (USA)
3. Andrew Weibrecht (USA)

06/12/2015, Beaver Creek (USA)
GIANT SLALOM
1. **MARCEL HIRSCHER** **(AUT)**
2. Victor Muffat Jeandet (FRA)
3. Henrik Kristoffersen (NOR)

12/12/2015, Val-d'Isère (FRA)
GIANT SLALOM
1. **MARCEL HIRSCHER** **(AUT)**
2. Felix Neureuther (GER)
3. Victor Muffat Jeandet (FRA)

13/12/2015, Val-d'Isère (FRA)
SLALOM
1. **HENRIK KRISTOFFERSEN** **(NOR)**
2. Marcel Hirscher (AUT)
3. Felix Neureuther (GER)

18/12/2015, Val Gardena (ITA)
SUPER-G
1. **AKSEL LUND SVINDAL** **(NOR)**
2. Kjetil Jansrud (NOR)
3. Aleksander Aamodt Kilde (NOR)

19/12/2015, Val Gardena (ITA)
DOWNHILL
1. **AKSEL LUND SVINDAL** **(NOR)**
2. Guillermo Fayed (FRA)
3. Kjetil Jansrud (NOR)

20/12/2015, Alta Badia (ITA)
GIANT SLALOM
1. **MARCEL HIRSCHER** **(AUT)**
2. Henrik Kristoffersen (NOR)
3. Victor Muffat Jeandet (FRA)

21/12/2015, Alta Badia (ITA)
PARALLEL GIANT SLALOM
1. **KJETIL JANSRUD** **(NOR)**
2. Aksel Lund Svindal (NOR)
3. André Myhrer (SWE)

22/12/2015, Madonna di Campiglio (ITA)
SLALOM
1. **HENRIK KRISTOFFERSEN** **(NOR)**
2. Marcel Hirscher (AUT)
3. Marco Schwarz (AUT)

29/12/2015, Santa Caterina Valfurva (ITA)
DOWNHILL
1. **ADRIEN THÉAUX** **(FRA)**
2. Hannes Reichelt (AUT)
3. David Poisson (FRA)

06/01/2016, Santa Caterina Valfurva (ITA)
SLALOM
1. **MARCEL HIRSCHER** **(AUT)**
2. Henrik Kristoffersen (NOR)
3. Aleksandr Chorošilov (RUS)

10/01/2016, Adelboden (SUI)
SLALOM
1. **HENRIK KRISTOFFERSEN** **(NOR)**
2. Marcel Hirscher (AUT)
3. Aleksandr Chorošilov (RUS)

15/01/2016, Wengen (SUI)
ALPINE COMBINED
1. **KJETIL JANSRUD** **(NOR)**
2. Aksel Lund Svindal (NOR)
3. Adrien Théaux (FRA)

16/01/2016, Wengen (SUI)
DOWNHILL
1. **AKSEL LUND SVINDAL** **(NOR)**
2. Hannes Reichelt (AUT)
3. Klaus Kröll (AUT)

17/01/2016, Wengen (SUI)
SLALOM
1. **HENRIK KRISTOFFERSEN** **(NOR)**
2. Giuliano Razzoli (ITA)
3. Stefano Gross (ITA)

22/01/2016, Kitzbühel (AUT)
SUPER-G

1. **AKSEL LUND SVINDAL** **(NOR)**
2. Andrew Weibrecht (USA)
3. Hannes Reichelt (AUT)

22/01/2016, Kitzbühel (AUT)
ALPINE COMBINED
1. **ALEXIS PINTURAULT** **(FRA)**
2. Victor Muffat Jeandet (FRA)
3. Thomas Mermillod Blondin (FRA)

23/01/2016, Kitzbühel (AUT)
DOWNHILL
1. **PETER FILL** **(ITA)**
2. Beat Feuz (SUI)
3. Carlo Janka (SUI)

24/01/2016, Kitzbühel (AUT)
SLALOM
1. **HENRIK KRISTOFFERSEN** **(NOR)**
2. Marcel Hirscher (AUT)
3. Fritz Dopfer (GER)

26/01/2016, Schladming (AUT)
SLALOM
1. **HENRIK KRISTOFFERSEN** **(NOR)**
2. Marcel Hirscher (AUT)
3. Aleksandr Chorošilov (RUS)

30/01/2016, Garmisch-Partenkirchen (GER)
DOWNHILL
1. **ALEKSANDER AAMODT KILDE** **(NOR)**
2. Boštjan Kline (SLO)
3. Beat Feuz (SUI)

06/02/2016, Jeongseon (KOR)
DOWNHILL
1. **KJETIL JANSRUD** **(NOR)**
2. Dominik Paris (ITA)
3. Steven Nyman (USA)

07/02/2016, Jeongseon (KOR)
SUPER-G
1. **CARLO JANKA** **(SUI)**
2. Christof Innerhofer (ITA)
3. Vincent Kriechmayr (AUT)

13/02/2016, Naeba (JPN)
GIANT SLALOM
1. **ALEXIS PINTURAULT** **(FRA)**
2. Mathieu Faivre (FRA)
3. Massimiliano Blardone (ITA)

14/02/2016, Naeba (JPN)
SLALOM
1. **FELIX NEUREUTHER** **(GER)**
2. André Myrher (SWE)
3. Marco Schwarz (AUT)

19/02/2016, Chamonix (FRA)
ALPINE COMBINED
1. **ALEXIS PINTURAULT** **(FRA)**
2. Dominik Paris (ITA)
3. Thomas Mermillod Blondin (FRA)

20/02/2016, Chamonix (FRA)
DOWNHILL
1. **DOMINIK PARIS** **(ITA)**
2. Steven Nyman (USA)
3. Beat Feuz (SUI)

23/02/2016, Stockholm (SWE)
PARALLEL SLALOM
1. **MARCEL HIRSCHER** **(AUT)**
2. André Myrher (SWE)
3. Stefano Gross (ITA)

26/02/2016, Hinterstoder (AUT)
GIANT SLALOM
1. **ALEXIS PINTURAULT** **(FRA)**
2. Marcel Hirscher (AUT)
3. Thomas Fanara (FRA)

27/02/2016, Hinterstoder (AUT)
SUPER-G
1. **ALEKSANDER AAMODT KILDE** **(NOR)**
2. Boštjan Kline (SLO)
3. Marcel Hirscher (AUT)

28/02/2016, Hinterstoder (AUT)
GIANT SLALOM
1. **ALEXIS PINTURAULT** **(FRA)**
2. Marcel Hirscher (AUT)
3. Henrik Kristoffersen (NOR)

04/03/2016, Kranjska Gora (SLO)
GIANT SLALOM
1. **ALEXIS PINTURAULT** **(FRA)**
2. Philipp Schörghofer (AUT)
3. Marcel Hirscher (AUT)

05/03/2016, Kranjska Gora (SLO)
GIANT SLALOM

1.	**MARCEL HIRSCHER**	**(AUT)**
2.	Alexis Pinturault	(FRA)
3.	Henrik Kristoffersen	(NOR)

06/03/2016, Kranjska Gora (SLO)
SLALOM

1.	**MARCEL HIRSCHER**	**(AUT)**
2.	Henrik Kristoffersen	(NOR)
3.	Stefano Gross	(ITA)

12/03/2016, Kvitfjell (NOR)
DOWNHILL

1.	**DOMINIK PARIS**	**(ITA)**
2.	Valentin Giraud Moine	(FRA)
3.	Steven Nyman	(USA)

13/03/2016, Kvitfjell (NOR)
SUPER-G

1.	**KJETIL JANSRUD**	**(NOR)**
2.	Vincent Kriechmayr	(AUT)
3.	Dominik Paris	(ITA)

16/03/2016, Sankt Moritz (SUI)
DOWNHILL

1.	**BEAT FEUZ**	**(SUI)**
2.	Steven Nyman	(USA)
3.	Erik Guay	(CAN)

17/03/2016, Sankt Moritz (SUI)
SUPER-G

1.	**BEAT FEUZ**	**(SUI)**
2.	Kjetil Jansrud	(NOR)
=	Aleksander Aamodt Kilde	(NOR)

19/03/2016, Sankt Moritz (SUI)
GIANT SLALOM

1.	**THOMAS FANARA**	**(FRA)**
2.	Alexis Pinturault	(FRA)
3.	Mathieu Faivre	(FRA)

20/03/2016, Sankt Moritz (SUI)
SLALOM

1.	**ANDRÉ MYHRER**	**(SWE)**
2.	Marcel Hirscher	(AUT)
3.	Sebastian Foss Solevåg	(NOR)

2016-17

CUPS

OVERALL

1.	**MARCEL HIRSCHER**	**(AUT)**
2.	Kjetil Jansrud	(NOR)
3.	Henrik Kristoffersen	(NOR)

SLALOM

1.	**MARCEL HIRSCHER**	**(AUT)**
2.	Henrik Kristoffersen	(NOR)
3.	Manfred Mölgg	(ITA)

GIANT SLALOM

1.	**MARCEL HIRSCHER**	**(AUT)**
2.	Mathieu Faivre	(FRA)
3.	Alexis Pinturault	(FRA)

SUPER-G

1.	**KJETIL JANSRUD**	**(NOR)**
2.	Hannes Reichelt	(AUT)
3.	Aleksander Aamodt Kilde	(NOR)

DOWNHILL

1.	**PETER FILL**	**(ITA)**
2.	Kjetil Jansrud	(NOR)
3.	Dominik Paris	(ITA)

COMBINED

1.	**ALEXIS PINTURAULT**	**(FRA)**
2.	Niels Hintermann	(SUI)
3.	Aleksander Aamodt Kilde	(NOR)

RACES

23/10/2016, Sölden (AUT)
GIANT SLALOM

1.	**ALEXIS PINTURAULT**	**(FRA)**
2.	Marcel Hirscher	(AUT)
3.	Felix Neureuther	(GER)

13/11/2016, Levi (FIN)
SLALOM

1.	**MARCEL HIRSCHER**	**(AUT)**
2.	Michael Matt	(AUT)
3.	Manfred Mölgg	(ITA)

02/12/2016, Val-d'Isère (FRA)
SUPER-G

1. **KJETIL JANSRUD** **(NOR)**
2. Aksel Lund Svindal (NOR)
3. Dominik Paris (ITA)

03/12/2016, Val-d'Isère (FRA)
DOWNHILL
1. **KJETIL JANSRUD** **(NOR)**
2. Peter Fill (ITA)
3. Aksel Lund Svindal (NOR)

04/12/2016, Val-d'Isère (FRA)
GIANT SLALOM
1. **MATHIEU FAIVRE** **(FRA)**
2. Marcel Hirscher (AUT)
3. Alexis Pinturault (FRA)

10/12/2016, Val-d'Isère (FRA)
GIANT SLALOM
1. **ALEXIS PINTURAULT** **(FRA)**
2. Marcel Hirscher (AUT)
3. Henrik Kristoffersen (NOR)

11/12/2016, Val-d'Isère (FRA)
SLALOM
1. **HENRIK KRISTOFFERSEN** **(NOR)**
2. Marcel Hirscher (AUT)
3. Aleksandr Chorošilov (RUS)

16/12/2016, Val Gardena (ITA)
SUPER-G
1. **KJETIL JANSRUD** **(NOR)**
2. Aleksander Aamodt Kilde (NOR)
3. Erik Guay (CAN)

17/12/2016, Val Gardena (ITA)
DOWNHILL
1. **MAX FRANZ** **(AUT)**
2. Aksel Lund Svindal (NOR)
3. Steven Nyman (USA)

18/12/2016, Alta Badia (ITA)
GIANT SLALOM
1. **MARCEL HIRSCHER** **(AUT)**
2. Mathieu Faivre (FRA)
3. Florian Eisath (ITA)

19/12/2016, Alta Badia (ITA)
PARALLEL GIANT SLALOM
1. **CYPRIEN SARRAZIN** **(FRA)**
2. Carlo Janka (SUI)
3. Kjetil Jansrud (NOR)

22/12/2016, Madonna di Campiglio (ITA)
SLALOM
1. **HENRIK KRISTOFFERSEN** **(NOR)**
2. Marcel Hirscher (AUT)
3. Stefano Gross (ITA)

27/12/2016, Santa Caterina Valfurva (ITA)
SUPER-G
1. **KJETIL JANSRUD** **(NOR)**
2. Hannes Reichelt (AUT)
3. Dominik Paris (ITA)

29/12/2016, Santa Caterina Valfurva (ITA)
ALPINE COMBINED
1. **ALEXIS PINTURAULT** **(FRA)**
2. Marcel Hirscher (AUT)
3. Aleksander Aamodt Kilde (NOR)

05/01/2017, Zagreb Sljeme (CRO)
SLALOM
1. **MANFRED MÖLGG** **(ITA)**
2. Felix Neureuther (GER)
3. Henrik Kristoffersen (NOR)

07/01/2017, Adelboden (SUI)
GIANT SLALOM
1. **ALEXIS PINTURAULT** **(FRA)**
2. Marcel Hirscher (AUT)
3. Philipp Schörghofer (AUT)

08/01/2017, Adelboden (SUI)
SLALOM
1. **HENRIK KRISTOFFERSEN** **(NOR)**
2. Manfred Mölgg (ITA)
3. Marcel Hirscher (AUT)

13/01/2017, Wengen (SUI)
ALPINE COMBINED
1. **NIELS HINTERMANN** **(SUI)**
2. Maxence Muzaton (FRA)
3. Frederic Berthold (AUT)

15/01/2017, Wengen (SUI)
SLALOM
1. **HENRIK KRISTOFFERSEN** **(NOR)**
2. Marcel Hirscher (AUT)
3. Felix Neureuther (GER)

20/01/2017, Kitzbühel (AUT)
SUPER-G

1. **MATTHIAS MAYER** (AUT)
2. Christof Innerhofer (ITA)
3. Beat Feuz (SUI)

21/01/2017, Kitzbühel (AUT)
DOWNHILL
1. **DOMINIK PARIS** (ITA)
2. Valentin Giraud Moine (FRA)
3. Johan Clarey (FRA)

22/01/2017, Kitzbühel (AUT)
SLALOM
1. **MARCEL HIRSCHER** (AUT)
2. Dave Ryding (GBR)
3. Aleksandr Chorošilov (RUS)

24/01/2017, Schladming (AUT)
SLALOM
1. **HENRIK KRISTOFFERSEN** (NOR)
2. Marcel Hirscher (AUT)
3. Aleksandr Chorošilov (RUS)

27/01/2017, Garmisch-Partenkirchen (GER)
DOWNHILL
1. **TRAVIS GANONG** (USA)
2. Kjetil Jansrud (NOR)
3. Peter Fill (ITA)

28/01/2017, Garmisch-Partenkirchen (GER)
DOWNHILL
1. **HANNES REICHELT** (AUT)
2. Peter Fill (ITA)
3. Beat Feuz (SUI)

29/01/2017, Garmisch-Partenkirchen (GER)
GIANT SLALOM
1. **MARCEL HIRSCHER** (AUT)
2. Matts Olsson (SWE)
3. Stefan Luitz (GER)

31/01/2017, Stockholm (SWE)
PARALLEL SLALOM
1. **LINUS STRASSER** (GER)
2. Alexis Pinturault (FRA)
3. Mattias Hargin (SWE)

24/02/2017, Kvitfjell (NOR)
DOWNHILL
1. **BOŠTJAN KLINE** (SLO)
2. Matthias Mayer (AUT)
3. Kjetil Jansrud (NOR)

25/02/2017, Kvitfjell (NOR)
DOWNHILL
1. **KJETIL JANSRUD** (NOR)
2. Peter Fill (ITA)
3. Beat Feuz (SUI)

26/02/2017, Kvitfjell (NOR)
SUPER-G
1. **PETER FILL** (ITA)
2. Hannes Reichelt (AUT)
3. Erik Guay (CAN)

04/03/2017, Kranjska Gora (SLO)
GIANT SLALOM
1. **MARCEL HIRSCHER** (AUT)
2. Leif Kristian Haugen (NOR)
3. Matts Olsson (SWE)

05/03/2017, Kranjska Gora (SLO)
SLALOM
1. **MICHAEL MATT** (AUT)
2. Stefano Gross (ITA)
3. Felix Neureuther (GER)

15/03/2017, Aspen (USA)
DOWNHILL
1. **DOMINIK PARIS** (ITA)
2. Peter Fill (ITA)
3. Carlo Janka (SUI)

16/03/2017, Aspen (USA)
SUPER-G
1. **HANNES REICHELT** (AUT)
2. Dominik Paris (ITA)
3. Mauro Caviezel (SUI)
= Aleksander Aamodt Kilde (NOR)

18/03/2017, Aspen (USA)
GIANT SLALOM
1. **MARCEL HIRSCHER** (AUT)
2. Felix Neureuther (GER)
3. Mathieu Faivre (FRA)

19/03/2017, Aspen (USA)
SLALOM
1. **ANDRÉ MYHRER** (SWE)
2. Felix Neureuther (GER)
3. Michael Matt (AUT)

2017-18

CUPS

OVERALL
1.	**MARCEL HIRSCHER**	**(AUT)**
2.	Henrik Kristoffersen	(NOR)
3.	Aksel Lund Svindal	(NOR)

SLALOM
1.	**MARCEL HIRSCHER**	**(AUT)**
2.	Henrik Kristoffersen	(NOR)
3.	André Myhrer	(SWE)

GIANT SLALOM
1.	**MARCEL HIRSCHER**	**(AUT)**
2.	Henrik Kristoffersen	(NOR)
3.	Alexis Pinturault	(FRA)

SUPER-G
1.	**KJETIL JANSRUD**	**(NOR)**
2.	Vincent Kriechmayr	(AUT)
3.	Aksel Lund Svindal	(NOR)

DOWNHILL
1.	**BEAT FEUZ**	**(SUI)**
2.	Aksel Lund Svindal	(NOR)
3.	Thomas Dreßen	(GER)

COMBINED
1.	**PETER FILL**	**(ITA)**
2.	Kjetil Jansrud	(NOR)
3.	Victor Muffat-Jeandet	(FRA)

RACES

12/11/2017, Levi (FIN)
SLALOM
1.	**FELIX NEUREUTHER**	**(GER)**
2.	Henrik Kristoffersen	(NOR)
3.	Mattias Hargin	(SWE)

25/11/2017, Lake Louise (CAN)
DOWNHILL
1.	**BEAT FEUZ**	**(SUI)**
2.	Matthias Mayer	(AUT)
3.	Aksel Lund Svindal	(NOR)

26/11/2017, Lake Louise (CAN)
SUPER-G
1.	**KJETIL JANSRUD**	**(NOR)**
2.	Max Franz	(AUT)
3.	Hannes Reichelt	(AUT)

01/12/2017, Beaver Creek (USA)
SUPER-G
1.	**VINCENT KRIECHMAYR**	**(AUT)**
2.	Kjetil Jansrud	(NOR)
3.	Hannes Reichelt	(AUT)

02/12/2017, Beaver Creek (USA)
DOWNHILL
1.	**AKSEL LUND SVINDAL**	**(NOR)**
2.	Beat Feuz	(SUI)
3.	Thomas Dreßen	(GER)

03/12/2017, Beaver Creek (USA)
GIANT SLALOM
1.	**MARCEL HIRSCHER**	**(AUT)**
2.	Henrik Kristoffersen	(NOR)
3.	Stefan Luitz	(GER)

09/12/2017, Val-d'Isère (FRA)
GIANT SLALOM
1.	**ALEXIS PINTURAULT**	**(FRA)**
2.	Stefan Luitz	(GER)
3.	Marcel Hirscher	(AUT)

10/12/2017, Val-d'Isère (FRA)
SLALOM
1.	**MARCEL HIRSCHER**	**(AUT)**
2.	Henrik Kristoffersen	(NOR)
3.	André Myhrer	(SWE)

15/12/2017, Val Gardena (ITA)
SUPER-G
1.	**JOSEF FERSTL**	**(GER)**
2.	Max Franz	(AUT)
3.	Matthias Mayer	(AUT)

16/12/2017, Val Gardena (ITA)
DOWNHILL
1.	**AKSEL LUND SVINDAL**	**(NOR)**
2.	Kjetil Jansrud	(NOR)
3.	Max Franz	(AUT)

17/12/2017, Alta Badia (ITA)
GIANT SLALOM
1.	**MARCEL HIRSCHER**	**(AUT)**
2.	Henrik Kristoffersen	(NOR)
3.	Žan Kranjec	(SLO)

18/12/2017, Alta Badia (ITA)
PARALLEL GIANT SLALOM
1. **MATTS OLSSON** **(SWE)**
2. Henrik Kristoffersen (NOR)
3. Marcel Hirscher (AUT)

22/12/2017, Madonna di Campiglio (ITA)
SLALOM
1. **MARCEL HIRSCHER** **(AUT)**
2. Luca Aerni (SUI)
3. Henrik Kristoffersen (NOR)

28/12/2017, Bormio (ITA)
DOWNHILL
1. **DOMINIK PARIS** **(ITA)**
2. Aksel Lund Svindal (NOR)
3. Kjetil Jansrud (NOR)

29/12/2017, Bormio (ITA)
ALPINE COMBINED
1. **ALEXIS PINTURAULT** **(FRA)**
2. Peter Fill (ITA)
3. Kjetil Jansrud (NOR)

01/01/2018, Oslo (NOR)
PARALLEL SLALOM
1. **ANDRÉ MYHRER** **(SWE)**
2. Michael Matt (AUT)
3. Linus Straßer (GER)

04/01/2018, Zagreb Sljeme (CRO)
SLALOM
1. **MARCEL HIRSCHER** **(AUT)**
2. Michael Matt (AUT)
3. Henrik Kristoffersen (NOR)

06/01/2018, Adelboden (SUI)
GIANT SLALOM
1. **MARCEL HIRSCHER** **(AUT)**
2. Henrik Kristoffersen (NOR)
3. Alexis Pinturault (FRA)

07/01/2018, Adelboden (SUI)
SLALOM
1. **MARCEL HIRSCHER** **(AUT)**
2. Michael Matt (AUT)
3. Henrik Kristoffersen (NOR)

12/01/2018, Wengen (SUI)
ALPINE COMBINED
1. **VICTOR MUFFAT JEANDET** **(FRA)**
2. Pavel Trichičev (RUS)
3. Peter Fill (ITA)

13/01/2018, Wengen (SUI)
DOWNHILL
1. **BEAT FEUZ** **(SUI)**
2. Aksel Lund Svindal (NOR)
3. Matthias Mayer (AUT)

14/01/2018, Wengen (SUI)
SLALOM
1. **MARCEL HIRSCHER** **(AUT)**
2. Henrik Kristoffersen (NOR)
3. André Myhrer (SWE)

19/01/2018, Kitzbühel (AUT)
SUPER-G
1. **AKSEL LUND SVINDAL** **(NOR)**
2. Kjetil Jansrud (NOR)
3. Matthias Mayer (AUT)

20/01/2018, Kitzbühel (AUT)
DOWNHILL
1. **THOMAS DRESSEN** **(GER)**
2. Beat Feuz (SUI)
3. Hannes Reichelt (AUT)

21/01/2018, Kitzbühel (AUT)
SLALOM
1. **HENRIK KRISTOFFERSEN** **(NOR)**
2. Marcel Hirscher (AUT)
3. Daniel Yule (SUI)

23/01/2018, Schladming (AUT)
SLALOM
1. **MARCEL HIRSCHER** **(AUT)**
2. Henrik Kristoffersen (NOR)
3. Daniel Yule (SUI)

27/01/2018, Garmisch-Partenkirchen (GER)
DOWNHILL
1. **BEAT FEUZ** **(SUI)**
2. Vincent Kriechmayr (AUT)
= Dominik Paris (ITA)

28/01/2018, Garmisch-Partenkirchen (GER)
GIANT SLALOM
1. **MARCEL HIRSCHER** **(AUT)**
2. Manuel Feller (AUT)
3. Ted Ligety (USA)

30/01/2018, Stockholm (SWE)
PARALLEL SLALOM

1. **RAMON ZENHÄUSERN** **(SUI)**
2. André Myhrer (SWE)
3. Linus Straßer (GER)

03/03/2018, Kranjska Gora (SLO)
GIANT SLALOM

1. **MARCEL HIRSCHER** **(AUT)**
2. Henrik Kristoffersen (NOR)
3. Alexis Pinturault (FRA)

04/03/2018, Kranjska Gora (SLO)
SLALOM

1. **MARCEL HIRSCHER** **(AUT)**
2. Henrik Kristoffersen (NOR)
3. Ramon Zenhäusern (SUI)

10/03/2018, Kvitfjell (NOR)
DOWNHILL

1. **THOMAS DRESSEN** **(GER)**
2. Beat Feuz (SUI)
3. Aksel Lund Svindal (NOR)

11/03/2018, Kvitfjell (NOR)
SUPER-G

1. **KJETIL JANSRUD** **(NOR)**
2. Beat Feuz (SUI)
3. Brice Roger (FRA)

14/03/2018, Åre (SWE)
DOWNHILL

1. **VINCENT KRIECHMAYR** **(AUT)**
= **MATTHIAS MAYER** **(AUT)**
3. Beat Feuz (SUI)

15/03/2018, Åre (SWE)
SUPER-G

1. **VINCENT KRIECHMAYR** **(AUT)**
2. Christof Innerhofer (ITA)
3. Thomas Dreßen (GER)
= Aksel Lund Svindal (NOR)

17/03/2018, Åre (SWE)
GIANT SLALOM

1. **MARCEL HIRSCHER** **(AUT)**
2. Henrik Kristoffersen (NOR)
3. Victor Muffat Jeandet (FRA)

2018-19

CUPS

OVERALL

1. **MARCEL HIRSCHER** **(AUT)**
2. Alexis Pinturault (FRA)
3. Henrik Kristoffersen (NOR)

SLALOM

1. **MARCEL HIRSCHER** **(AUT)**
2. Clément Noël (FRA)
3. Daniel Yule (SUI)

GIANT SLALOM

1. **MARCEL HIRSCHER** **(AUT)**
2. Henrik Kristoffersen (NOR)
3. Alexis Pinturault (FRA)

SUPER-G

1. **DOMINIK PARIS** **(ITA)**
2. Vincent Kriechmayr (AUT)
3. Mauro Caviezel (SUI)

DOWNHILL

1. **BEAT FEUZ** **(SUI)**
2. Dominik Paris (ITA)
3. Vincent Kriechmayr (AUT)

COMBINED

1. **ALEXIS PINTURAULT** **(FRA)**
2. Marco Schwarz (AUT)
3. Mauro Caviezel (SUI)

RACES

18/11/2018, Levi (FIN)
SLALOM

1. **MARCEL HIRSCHER** **(AUT)**
2. Henrik Kristoffersen (NOR)
3. André Myhrer (SWE)

24/11/2018, Lake Louise (CAN)
DOWNHILL

1. **MAX FRANZ** **(AUT)**
2. Christof Innerhofer (ITA)
3. Dominik Paris (ITA)

25/11/2018, Lake Louise (CAN)
SUPER-G

1. **KJETIL JANSRUD** **(NOR)**
2. Vincent Kriechmayr (AUT)
3. Mauro Caviezel (SUI)

30/11/2018, Beaver Creek (USA)
DOWNHILL

1. **BEAT FEUZ** **(SUI)**
2. Mauro Caviezel (SUI)
3. Aksel Lund Svindal (NOR)

01/12/2018, Beaver Creek (USA)
SUPER-G

1. **MAX FRANZ** **(AUT)**
2. Mauro Caviezel (SUI)
3. Aleksander Aamodt Kilde (NOR)
= Dominik Paris (ITA)
= Aksel Lund Svindal (NOR)

02/12/2018, Beaver Creek (USA)
GIANT SLALOM

1. **STEFAN LUITZ** **(GER)**
2. Marcel Hirscher (AUT)
3. Thomas Tumler (SUI)

08/12/2018, Val-d'Isère (FRA)
GIANT SLALOM

1. **MARCEL HIRSCHER** **(AUT)**
2. Henrik Kristoffersen (NOR)
3. Matts Olsson (SWE)

14/12/2018, Val Gardena (ITA)
SUPER-G

1. **AKSEL LUND SVINDAL** **(NOR)**
2. Christof Innerhofer (ITA)
3. Kjetil Jansrud (NOR)

15/12/2018, Val Gardena (ITA)
DOWNHILL

1. **ALEKSANDER AAMODT KILDE** **(NOR)**
2. Max Franz (AUT)
3. Beat Feuz (SUI)

16/12/2018, Alta Badia (ITA)
GIANT SLALOM

1. **MARCEL HIRSCHER** **(AUT)**
2. Thomas Fanara (FRA)
3. Alexis Pinturault (FRA)

17/12/2018, Alta Badia (ITA)
PARALLEL GIANT SLALOM

1. **MARCEL HIRSCHER** **(AUT)**

2. Thibaut Favrot (FRA)
3. Alexis Pinturault (FRA)

19/12/2018, Saalbach-Hinterglemm (AUT)
GIANT SLALOM

1. **ŽAN KRANJEC** **(SLO)**
2. Loïc Meillard (SUI)
3. Mathieu Faivre (FRA)

20/12/2018, Saalbach-Hinterglemm (AUT)
SLALOM

1. **MARCEL HIRSCHER** **(AUT)**
2. Loïc Meillard (SUI)
3. Henrik Kristoffersen (NOR)

22/12/2018, Madonna di Campiglio (ITA)
SLALOM

1. **DANIEL YULE** **(SUI)**
2. Marco Schwarz (AUT)
3. Michael Matt (AUT)

28/12/2018, Bormio (ITA)
DOWNHILL

1. **DOMINIK PARIS** **(ITA)**
2. Christof Innerhofer (ITA)
3. Beat Feuz (SUI)

29/12/2018, Bormio (ITA)
SUPER-G

1. **DOMINIK PARIS** **(ITA)**
2. Matthias Mayer (AUT)
3. Aleksander Aamodt Kilde (NOR)

01/01/2019, Oslo (NOR)
PARALLEL SLALOM

1. **MARCO SCHWARZ** **(AUT)**
2. Dave Ryding (GBR)
3. Ramon Zenhäusern (SUI)

06/01/2019, Zagreb Sljeme (CRO)
SLALOM

1. **MARCEL HIRSCHER** **(AUT)**
2. Alexis Pinturault (FRA)
3. Manuel Feller (AUT)

12/01/2019, Adelboden (SUI)
GIANT SLALOM

1. **MARCEL HIRSCHER** **(AUT)**
2. Henrik Kristoffersen (NOR)
3. Thomas Fanara (FRA)

13/01/2019, Adelboden (SUI)
SLALOM
1. **MARCEL HIRSCHER** **(AUT)**
2. Clément Noël (FRA)
3. Henrik Kristoffersen (NOR)

18/01/2019, Wengen (SUI)
ALPINE COMBINED
1. **MARCO SCHWARZ** **(AUT)**
2. Victor Muffat Jeandet (FRA)
3. Alexis Pinturault (FRA)

19/01/2019, Wengen (SUI)
DOWNHILL
1. **VINCENT KRIECHMAYR** **(AUT)**
2. Beat Feuz (SUI)
3. Aleksander Aamodt Kilde (NOR)

20/01/2019, Wengen (SUI)
SLALOM
1. **CLÉMENT NOËL** **(FRA)**
2. Manuel Feller (AUT)
3. Marcel Hirscher (AUT)

25/01/2019, Kitzbühel (AUT)
DOWNHILL
1. **DOMINIK PARIS** **(ITA)**
2. Beat Feuz (SUI)
3. Otmar Striedinger (AUT)

26/01/2019, Kitzbühel (AUT)
SLALOM
1. **CLÉMENT NOËL** **(FRA)**
2. Marcel Hirscher (AUT)
3. Alexis Pinturault (FRA)

27/01/2019, Kitzbühel (AUT)
SUPER-G
1. **JOSEF FERSTL** **(GER)**
2. Johan Clarey (FRA)
3. Dominik Paris (ITA)

29/01/2019, Schladming (AUT)
SLALOM
1. **MARCEL HIRSCHER** **(AUT)**
2. Alexis Pinturault (FRA)
3. Daniel Yule (SUI)

19/02/2019, Stockholm (SWE)
PARALLEL SLALOM
1. **RAMON ZENHÄUSERN** **(SUI)**

2. André Myhrer (SWE)
3. Marco Schwarz (AUT)

22/02/2019, Bansko (BUL)
ALPINE COMBINED
1. **ALEXIS PINTURAULT** **(FRA)**
2. Marcel Hirscher (AUT)
3. Štefan Hadalin (SLO)

24/02/2019, Bansko (BUL)
GIANT SLALOM
1. **HENRIK KRISTOFFERSEN** **(NOR)**
2. Marcel Hirscher (AUT)
3. Thomas Fanara (FRA)

02/03/2019, Kvitfjell (NOR)
DOWNHILL
1. **DOMINIK PARIS** **(ITA)**
2. Beat Feuz (SUI)
3. Matthias Mayer (AUT)

03/03/2019, Kvitfjell (NOR)
SUPER-G
1. **DOMINIK PARIS** **(ITA)**
2. Kjetil Jansrud (NOR)
3. Beat Feuz (SUI)

09/03/2019, Kranjska Gora (SLO)
GIANT SLALOM
1. **HENRIK KRISTOFFERSEN** **(NOR)**
2. Rasmus Windingstad (NOR)
3. Marco Odermatt (SUI)

10/03/2019, Kranjska Gora (SLO)
SLALOM
1. **RAMON ZENHÄUSERN** **(SUI)**
2. Henrik Kristoffersen (NOR)
3. Marcel Hirscher (AUT)

13/03/2019, Soldeu (AND)
DOWNHILL
1. **DOMINIK PARIS** **(ITA)**
2. Kjetil Jansrud (NOR)
3. Otmar Striedinger (AUT)

14/03/2019, Soldeu (AND)
SUPER-G
1. **DOMINIK PARIS** **(ITA)**
2. Mauro Caviezel (SUI)
3. Vincent Kriechmayr (AUT)

16/03/2019, Soldeu (AND)
GIANT SLALOM

1. **ALEXIS PINTURAULT** **(FRA)**
2. Marco Odermatt (SUI)
3. Žan Kranjec (SLO)

17/03/2019, Soldeu (AND)
SLALOM

1. **CLÉMENT NOËL** **(FRA)**
2. Manuel Feller (AUT)
3. Daniel Yule (SUI)

2019-20

CUPS

OVERALL

1. **ALEKSANDER AAMODT KILDE** **(NOR)**
2. Alexis Pinturault (FRA)
3. Henrik Kristoffersen (NOR)

SLALOM

1. **HENRIK KRISTOFFERSEN** **(NOR)**
2. Clément Noël (FRA)
3. Daniel Yule (SUI)

GIANT SLALOM

1. **HENRIK KRISTOFFERSEN** **(NOR)**
2. Alexis Pinturault (FRA)
3. Filip Zubčić (CRO)

SUPER-G

1. **MAURO CAVIEZEL** **(SUI)**
2. Vincent Kriechmayr (AUT)
3. Aleksander Aamodt Kilde (NOR)

DOWNHILL

1. **BEAT FEUZ** **(SUI)**
2. Thomas Dreßen (GER)
3. Matthias Mayer (AUT)

COMBINED

1. **ALEXIS PINTURAULT** **(FRA)**
2. Aleksander Aamodt Kilde (NOR)
3. Matthias Mayer (AUT)

PARALLEL SLALOM

1. **LOÏC MEILLARD** **(SUI)**
2. Rasmus Windingstad (NOR)
3. Stefan Luitz (GER)

RACES

27/10/2019, Sölden (AUT)
GIANT SLALOM

1. **ALEXIS PINTURAULT** **(FRA)**
2. Mathieu Faivre (FRA)
3. Žan Kranjec (SLO)

24/11/2019, Levi (FIN)
SLALOM

1. **HENRIK KRISTOFFERSEN** **(NOR)**

2. Clément Noël (FRA)
3. Daniel Yule (SUI)

30/11/2019, Lake Louise (CAN)
DOWNHILL
1. **THOMAS DRESSEN** **(GER)**
2. Dominik Paris (ITA)
3. Beat Feuz (SUI)
= Carlo Janka (SUI)

01/12/2019, Lake Louise (CAN)
SUPER-G
1. **MATTHIAS MAYER** **(AUT)**
2. Dominik Paris (ITA)
3. Mauro Caviezel (SUI)
= Vincent Kriechmayr (AUT)

06/12/2019, Beaver Creek (USA)
SUPER-G
1. **MARCO ODERMATT** **(SUI)**
2. Aleksander Aamodt Kilde (NOR)
3. Matthias Mayer (AUT)

07/12/2019, Beaver Creek (USA)
DOWNHILL
1. **BEAT FEUZ** **(SUI)**
2. Johan Clarey (FRA)
= Vincent Kriechmayr (AUT)

08/12/2019, Beaver Creek (USA)
GIANT SLALOM
1. **TOMMY FORD** **(USA)**
2. Henrik Kristoffersen (NOR)
3. Leif Kristian Haugen (NOR)

15/12/2019, Val-d'Isère (FRA)
SLALOM
1. **ALEXIS PINTURAULT** **(FRA)**
2. André Myhrer (SWE)
3. Stefano Gross (ITA)

20/12/2019, Val Gardena (ITA)
SUPER-G
1. **VINCENT KRIECHMAYR** **(AUT)**
2. Kjetil Jansrud (NOR)
3. Thomas Dreßen (GER)

22/12/2019, Alta Badia (ITA)
GIANT SLALOM
1. **HENRIK KRISTOFFERSEN** **(NOR)**
2. Cyprien Sarrazin (FRA)

3. Žan Kranjec (SLO)

23/12/2019, Alta Badia (ITA)
PARALLEL GIANT SLALOM
1. **RASMUS WINDINGSTAD** **(NOR)**
2. Stefan Luitz (GER)
3. Roland Leitinger (AUT)

27/12/2019, Bormio (ITA)
DOWNHILL
1. **DOMINIK PARIS** **(ITA)**
2. Beat Feuz (SUI)
3. Matthias Mayer (AUT)

28/12/2019, Bormio (ITA)
DOWNHILL
1. **DOMINIK PARIS** **(ITA)**
2. Urs Kryenbühl (SUI)
3. Beat Feuz (SUI)

29/12/2019, Bormio (ITA)
ALPINE COMBINED
1. **ALEXIS PINTURAULT** **(FRA)**
2. Aleksander Aamodt Kilde (NOR)
3. Loïc Meillard (FRA)

05/01/2020, Zagreb Sljeme (CRO)
SLALOM
1. **CLÉMENT NOËL** **(FRA)**
2. Ramon Zenhäusern (SUI)
3. Alex Vinatzer (ITA)

08/01/2020, Madonna di Campiglio (ITA)
SLALOM
1. **DANIEL YULE** **(SUI)**
2. Henrik Kristoffersen (NOR)
3. Clément Noël (FRA)

11/01/2020, Adelboden (SUI)
GIANT SLALOM
1. **ŽAN KRANJEC** **(SLO)**
2. Filip Zubčić (CRO)
3. Henrik Kristoffersen (NOR)
= Victor Muffat Jeandet (FRA)

12/01/2020, Adelboden (SUI)
SLALOM
1. **DANIEL YULE** **(SUI)**
2. Henrik Kristoffersen (NOR)
3. Marco Schwarz (AUT)

17/01/2020, Wengen (SUI)
ALPINE COMBINED

1. **MATTHIAS MAYER** **(AUT)**
2. Alexis Pinturault (FRA)
3. Victor Muffat Jeandet (FRA)

18/01/2020, Wengen (SUI)
DOWNHILL

1. **BEAT FEUZ** **(SUI)**
2. Dominik Paris (ITA)
3. Thomas Dreßen (GER)

19/01/2020, Wengen (SUI)
SLALOM

1. **CLÉMENT NOËL** **(FRA)**
2. Henrik Kristoffersen (NOR)
3. Aleksandr Chorošilov (RUS)

24/01/2020, Kitzbühel (AUT)
SUPER-G

1. **KJETIL JANSRUD** **(NOR)**
2. Aleksander Aamodt Kilde (NOR)
= Matthias Mayer (AUT)

25/01/2020, Kitzbühel (AUT)
DOWNHILL

1. **MATTHIAS MAYER** **(AUT)**
2. Beat Feuz (SUI)
= Vincent Kriechmayr (AUT)

26/01/2020, Kitzbühel (AUT)
SLALOM

1. **DANIEL YULE** **(SUI)**
2. Marco Schwarz (AUT)
3. Clément Noël (FRA)

28/01/2020, Schladming (AUT)
SLALOM

1. **HENRIK KRISTOFFERSEN** **(NOR)**
2. Alexis Pinturault (FRA)
3. Daniel Yule (SUI)

01/02/2020, Garmisch-Partenkirchen (GER)
DOWNHILL

1. **THOMAS DRESSEN** **(GER)**
2. Aleksander Aamodt Kilde (NOR)
3. Johan Clarey (FRA)

02/02/2020, Garmisch-Partenkirchen (GER)
GIANT SLALOM

1. **ALEXIS PINTURAULT** **(FRA)**

2. Loïc Meillard (SUI)
3. Leif Kristian Haugen (NOR)

08/02/2020, Chamonix (FRA)
SLALOM

1. **CLÉMENT NOËL** **(FRA)**
2. Timon Haugan (NOR)
3. Adrian Pertl (AUT)

09/02/2020, Chamonix (FRA)
PARALLEL GIANT SLALOM

1. **LOÏC MEILLARD** **(SUI)**
2. Thomas Tumler (SUI)
3. Alexander Schmid (GER)

13/02/2020, Saalbach-Hinterglemm (AUT)
DOWNHILL

1. **THOMAS DRESSEN** **(GER)**
2. Beat Feuz (SUI)
3. Mauro Caviezel (SUI)

14/02/2020, Saalbach-Hinterglemm (AUT)
SUPER-G

1. **ALEKSANDER AAMODT KILDE** **(NOR)**
2. Mauro Caviezel (SUI)
3. Thomas Dreßen (GER)

22/02/2020, Naeba (JPN)
GIANT SLALOM

1. **FILIP ZUBČIĆ** **(CRO)**
2. Marco Odermatt (SUI)
3. Tommy Ford (USA)

29/02/2020, Hinterstoder (AUT)
SUPER-G

1. **VINCENT KRIECHMAYR** **(AUT)**
2. Mauro Caviezel (SUI)
3. Matthias Mayer (AUT)

01/03/2020, Hinterstoder (AUT)
ALPINE COMBINED

1. **ALEXIS PINTURAULT** **(FRA)**
2. Mauro Caviezel (SUI)
3. Aleksander Aamodt Kilde (NOR)

02/03/2020, Hinterstoder (AUT)
GIANT SLALOM

1. **ALEXIS PINTURAULT** **(FRA)**
2. Filip Zubčić (CRO)
3. Henrik Kristoffersen (NOR)

07/03/2020, Kvitfjell (NOR)

DOWNHILL

1. **MATTHIAS MAYER** **(AUT)**
2. Aleksander Aamodt Kilde (NOR)
3. Carlo Janka (SUI)

2020-21

CUPS

OVERALL

1. **ALEXIS PINTURAULT** **(FRA)**
2. Marco Odermatt (SUI)
3. Marco Schwarz (AUT)

SLALOM

1. **MARCO SCHWARZ** **(AUT)**
2. Clément Noël (FRA)
3. Ramon Zenhäusern (SUI)

GIANT SLALOM

1. **ALEXIS PINTURAULT** **(FRA)**
2. Marco Odermatt (SUI)
3. Filip Zubčić (CRO)

SUPER-G

1. **VINCENT KRIECHMAYR** **(AUT)**
2. Marco Odermatt (SUI)
3. Matthias Mayer (AUT)

DOWNHILL

1. **BEAT FEUZ** **(SUI)**
2. Matthias Mayer (AUT)
3. Dominik Paris (ITA)

PARALLEL SLALOM

1. **ALEXIS PINTURAULT** **(FRA)**
2. Henrik Kristoffersen (NOR)
3. Alexander Schmid (GER)

RACES

18/10/2020, Sölden (AUT)

GIANT SLALOM

1. **LUCAS BRAATHEN** **(NOR)**
2. Marco Odermatt (SUI)
3. Gino Caviezel (SUI)

27/11/2020, Lech/Zürs (AUT)

PARALLEL SLALOM

1. **ALEXIS PINTURAULT** **(FRA)**
2. Henrik Kristoffersen (NOR)
3. Alexander Schmid (GER)

05/12/2020, Santa Caterina Valfurva (ITA)

GIANT SLALOM

1. **FILIP ZUBČIĆ** **(CRO)**
2. Žan Kranjec (SLO)
3. Marco Odermatt (SUI)

07/12/2020, Santa Caterina Valfurva (ITA)
GIANT SLALOM
1. **MARCO ODERMATT** **(SUI)**
2. Tommy Ford (USA)
3. Filip Zubčić (CRO)

12/12/2020, Val-d'Isère (FRA)
SUPER-G
1. **MAURO CAVIEZEL** **(SUI)**
2. Adrian Smiseth Sejersted (NOR)
3. Christian Walder (AUT)

13/12/2020, Val-d'Isère (FRA)
DOWNHILL
1. **MARTIN ČATER** **(SLO)**
2. Otmar Striedinger (AUT)
3. Urs Kryenbühl (SUI)

18/12/2020, Val Gardena (ITA)
SUPER-G
1. **ALEKSANDER AAMODT KILDE** **(NOR)**
2. Mauro Caviezel (SUI)
3. Kjetil Jansrud (NOR)

19/12/2020, Val Gardena (ITA)
DOWNHILL
1. **ALEKSANDER AAMODT KILDE** **(NOR)**
2. Ryan Cochran-Siegle (USA)
3. Beat Feuz (SUI)

20/12/2020, Alta Badia (ITA)
GIANT SLALOM
1. **ALEXIS PINTURAULT** **(FRA)**
2. Atle Lie McGrath (NOR)
3. Justin Murisier (SUI)

21/12/2020, Alta Badia (ITA)
SLALOM
1. **RAMON ZENHÄUSERN** **(SUI)**
2. Manuel Feller (AUT)
3. Marco Schwarz (AUT)

22/12/2020, Madonna di Campiglio (ITA)
SLALOM
1. **HENRIK KRISTOFFERSEN** **(NOR)**
2. Sebastian Foss Solevåg (NOR)
3. Alex Vinatzer (ITA)

29/12/2020, Bormio (ITA)
SUPER-G
1. **RYAN COCHRAN-SIEGLE** **(USA)**
2. Vincent Kriechmayr (AUT)
3. Adrian Smiseth Sejersted (NOR)

30/12/2020, Bormio (ITA)
DOWNHILL
1. **MATTHIAS MAYER** **(AUT)**
2. Vincent Kriechmayr (AUT)
3. Urs Kryenbühl (SUI)

06/01/2021, Zagreb Sljeme (CRO)
SLALOM
1. **LINUS STRASSER** **(GER)**
2. Manuel Feller (AUT)
3. Marco Schwarz (AUT)

08/01/2021, Adelboden (SUI)
GIANT SLALOM
1. **ALEXIS PINTURAULT** **(FRA)**
2. Filip Zubčić (CRO)
3. Marco Odermatt (SUI)

09/01/2021, Adelboden (SUI)
GIANT SLALOM
1. **ALEXIS PINTURAULT** **(FRA)**
2. Filip Zubčić (CRO)
3. Loïc Meillard (FRA)

10/01/2021, Adelboden (SUI)
SLALOM
1. **MARCO SCHWARZ** **(AUT)**
2. Linus Straßer (GER)
3. Dave Ryding (GBR)

16/01/2021, Flachau (AUT)
SLALOM
1. **MANUEL FELLER** **(AUT)**
2. Clément Noël (FRA)
3. Marco Schwarz (AUT)

17/01/2021, Flachau (AUT)
SLALOM
1. **SEBASTIAN FOSS SOLEVÅG** **(NOR)**
2. Marco Schwarz (AUT)
3. Alexis Pinturault (FRA)

22/01/2021, Kitzbühel (AUT)
DOWNHILL

1. **BEAT FEUZ** (SUI)
2. Matthias Mayer (AUT)
3. Dominik Paris (ITA)

24/01/2021, Kitzbühel (AUT)
DOWNHILL
1. **BEAT FEUZ** (SUI)
2. Johan Clarey (FRA)
3. Matthias Mayer (AUT)

25/01/2021, Kitzbühel (AUT)
SUPER-G
1. **VINCENT KRIECHMAYR** (AUT)
2. Marco Odermatt (SUI)
3. Matthias Mayer (AUT)

26/01/2021, Schladming (AUT)
SLALOM
1. **MARCO SCHWARZ** (AUT)
2. Clément Noël (FRA)
3. Alexis Pinturault (FRA)

30/01/2021, Chamonix (FRA)
SLALOM
1. **CLÉMENT NOËL** (FRA)
2. Ramon Zenhäusern (SUI)
3. Marco Schwarz (AUT)

31/01/2021, Chamonix (FRA)
SLALOM
1. **HENRIK KRISTOFFERSEN** (NOR)
2. Ramon Zenhäusern (SUI)
3. Sandro Simonet (SUI)

05/02/2021, Garmisch-Partenkirchen (GER)
DOWNHILL
1. **DOMINIK PARIS** (ITA)
2. Beat Feuz (SUI)
3. Matthias Mayer (AUT)

06/02/2021, Garmisch-Partenkirchen (GER)
SUPER-G
1. **VINCENT KRIECHMAYR** (AUT)
2. Matthias Mayer (AUT)
3. Marco Odermatt (SUI)

27/02/2021, Bansko (BUL)
GIANT SLALOM
1. **FILIP ZUBČIĆ** (CRO)
2. Mathieu Faivre (FRA)
3. Stefan Brennsteiner (AUT)

28/02/2021, Bansko (BUL)
GIANT SLALOM
1. **MATHIEU FAIVRE** (FRA)
2. Marco Odermatt (SUI)
3. Alexis Pinturault (FRA)

06/03/2021, Saalbach-Hinterglemm (AUT)
DOWNHILL
1. **VINCENT KRIECHMAYR** (AUT)
2. Beat Feuz (SUI)
3. Matthias Mayer (AUT)

07/03/2021, Saalbach-Hinterglemm (AUT)
SUPER-G
1. **MARCO ODERMATT** (SUI)
2. Matthieu Bailet (FRA)
3. Vincent Kriechmayr (AUT)

13/03/2021, Kranjska Gora (SLO)
GIANT SLALOM
1. **MARCO ODERMATT** (SUI)
2. Loïc Meillard (SUI)
3. Stefan Brennsteiner (AUT)

14/03/2021, Kranjska Gora (SLO)
SLALOM
1. **CLÉMENT NOËL** (FRA)
2. Victor Muffat Jeandet (FRA)
3. Ramon Zenhäusern (SUI)

20/03/2021, Lenzerheide (SUI)
GIANT SLALOM
1. **ALEXIS PINTURAULT** (FRA)
2. Filip Zubčić (CRO)
3. Mathieu Faivre (FRA)

21/03/2021, Lenzerheide (SUI)
SLALOM
1. **MANUEL FELLER** (AUT)
2. Clément Noël (FRA)
3. Alexis Pinturault (FRA)

2021-22

CUPS

OVERALL
1. **MARCO ODERMATT** **(SUI)**
2. Aleksander Aamodt Kilde (NOR)
3. Henrik Kristoffersen (NOR)

SLALOM
1. **HENRIK KRISTOFFERSEN** **(NOR)**
2. Manuel Feller (AUT)
3. Atle Lie McGrath (NOR)

GIANT SLALOM
1. **MARCO ODERMATT** **(SUI)**
2. Henrik Kristoffersen (NOR)
3. Manuel Feller (AUT)

SUPER-G
1. **ALEKSANDER AAMODT KILDE** **(NOR)**
2. Marco Odermatt (SUI)
3. Vincent Kriechmayr (AUT)

DOWNHILL
1. **ALEKSANDER AAMODT KILDE** **(NOR)**
2. Beat Feuz (SUI)
3. Dominik Paris (ITA)

PARALLEL SLALOM
1. **CHRISTIAN HIRSCHBÜHL** **(AUT)**
2. Dominik Raschner (AUT)
3. Atle Lie McGrath (NOR)

RACES

24/10/2021, Sölden (AUT)
GIANT SLALOM
1. **MARCO ODERMATT** **(SUI)**
2. Roland Leitinger (AUT)
3. Žan Kranjec (SLO)

14/11/2021, Lech/Zürs (AUT)
PARALLEL GIANT SLALOM
1. **CHRISTIAN HIRSCHBÜHL** **(AUT)**
2. Dominik Raschner (AUT)
3. Atle Lie McGrath (NOR)

27/11/2021, Lake Louise (CAN)
DOWNHILL
1. **MATTHIAS MAYER** **(AUT)**
2. Vincent Kriechmayr (AUT)
3. Beat Feuz (SUI)

02/12/2021, Beaver Creek (USA)
SUPER-G
1. **MARCO ODERMATT** **(SUI)**
2. Matthias Mayer (AUT)
3. Broderick Thompson (CAN)

03/12/2021, Beaver Creek (USA)
SUPER-G
1. **ALEKSANDER AAMODT KILDE** **(NOR)**
2. Marco Odermatt (SUI)
3. Travis Ganong (USA)

04/12/2021, Beaver Creek (USA)
DOWNHILL
1. **ALEKSANDER AAMODT KILDE** **(NOR)**
2. Matthias Mayer (AUT)
3. Beat Feuz (SUI)

11/12/2021, Val-d'Isère (FRA)
GIANT SLALOM
1. **MARCO ODERMATT** **(SUI)**
2. Alexis Pinturault (FRA)
3. Manuel Feller (AUT)

12/12/2021, Val-d'Isère (FRA)
SLALOM
1. **CLÉMENT NOËL** **(FRA)**
2. Kristoffer Jakobsen (SWE)
3. Filip Zubčić (CRO)

17/12/2021, Val Gardena (ITA)
SUPER-G
1. **ALEKSANDER AAMODT KILDE** **(NOR)**
2. Matthias Mayer (AUT)
3. Vincent Kriechmayr (AUT)

18/12/2021, Val Gardena (ITA)
DOWNHILL
1. **BRYCE BENNETT** **(USA)**
2. Otmar Striedinger (AUT)
3. Niels Hintermann (SUI)

19/12/2021, Alta Badia (ITA)
GIANT SLALOM
1. **HENRIK KRISTOFFERSEN** **(NOR)**
2. Marco Odermatt (SUI)
3. Manuel Feller (AUT)

20/12/2021, Alta Badia (ITA)
GIANT SLALOM

1. **MARCO ODERMATT** **(SUI)**
2. Luca De Aliprandini (ITA)
3. Alexander Schmid (GER)

22/12/2021, Madonna di Campiglio (ITA)
SLALOM

1. **SEBASTIAN FOSS SOLEVÅG** **(NOR)**
2. Alexis Pinturault (FRA)
3. Kristoffer Jakobsen (SWE)

28/12/2021, Bormio (ITA)
DOWNHILL

1. **DOMINIK PARIS** **(ITA)**
2. Marco Odermatt (SUI)
3. Niels Hintermann (SUI)

29/12/2021, Bormio (ITA)
SUPER-G

1. **ALEKSANDER AAMODT KILDE** **(NOR)**
2. Raphael Haaser (AUT)
3. Vincent Kriechmayr (AUT)

08/01/2022, Adelboden (SUI)
GIANT SLALOM

1. **MARCO ODERMATT** **(SUI)**
2. Manuel Feller (AUT)
3. Alexis Pinturault (FRA)

09/01/2022, Adelboden (SUI)
SLALOM

1. **JOHANNES STROLZ** **(AUT)**
2. Manuel Feller (AUT)
3. Linus Straßer (GER)

13/01/2022, Wengen (SUI)
SUPER-G

1. **MARCO ODERMATT** **(SUI)**
2. Aleksander Aamodt Kilde (NOR)
3. Matthias Mayer (AUT)

14/01/2022, Wengen (SUI)
DOWNHILL

1. **ALEKSANDER AAMODT KILDE** **(NOR)**
2. Marco Odermatt (SUI)
3. Beat Feuz (SUI)

15/01/2022, Wengen (SUI)
DOWNHILL

1. **VINCENT KRIECHMAYR** **(AUT)**
2. Beat Feuz (SUI)
3. Dominik Paris (ITA)

16/01/2022, Wengen (SUI)
SLALOM

1. **LUCAS BRAATHEN** **(NOR)**
2. Daniel Yule (SUI)
3. Giuliano Razzoli (ITA)

21/01/2022, Kitzbühel (AUT)
DOWNHILL

1. **ALEKSANDER AAMODT KILDE** **(NOR)**
2. Johan Clarey (FRA)
3. Blaise Giezendanner (FRA)

22/01/2022, Kitzbühel (AUT)
SLALOM

1. **DAVE RYDING** **(GBR)**
2. Lucas Braathen (NOR)
3. Henrik Kristoffersen (NOR)

23/01/2022, Kitzbühel (AUT)
DOWNHILL

1. **BEAT FEUZ** **(SUI)**
2. Marco Odermatt (SUI)
3. Daniel Hemetsberger (AUT)

25/01/2022, Schladming (AUT)
SLALOM

1. **LINUS STRASSER** **(GER)**
2. Atle Lie McGrath (NOR)
3. Manuel Feller (AUT)

26/02/2022, Garmisch-Partenkirchen (GER)
SLALOM

1. **HENRIK KRISTOFFERSEN** **(NOR)**
2. Loïc Meillard (SUI)
3. Manuel Feller (AUT)

27/02/2022, Garmisch-Partenkirchen (GER)
SLALOM

1. **HENRIK KRISTOFFERSEN** **(NOR)**
2. Dave Ryding (GBR)
3. Linus Straßer (GER)

04/03/2022, Kvitfjell (NOR)
DOWNHILL

1. **CAMERON ALEXANDER** **(CAN)**
= **NIELS HINTERMANN** **(SUI)**
3. Matthias Mayer (AUT)

05/03/2022, Kvitfjell (NOR)
DOWNHILL

1.	**DOMINIK PARIS**	**(ITA)**
2.	Aleksander Aamodt Kilde	(NOR)
3.	Beat Feuz	(SUI)
=	Niels Hintermann	(SUI)

06/03/2022, Kvitfjell (NOR)
SUPER-G

1.	**ALEKSANDER AAMODT KILDE**	**(NOR)**
2.	James Crawford	(CAN)
3.	Matthias Mayer	(AUT)

09/03/2022, Flachau (AUT)
SLALOM

1.	**ATLE LIE MCGRATH**	**(NOR)**
2.	Clément Noël	(FRA)
3.	Daniel Yule	(SUI)

12/03/2022, Kranjska Gora (SLO)
GIANT SLALOM

1.	**HENRIK KRISTOFFERSEN**	**(NOR)**
2.	Lucas Braathen	(NOR)
=	Marco Odermatt	(SUI)

13/03/2022, Kranjska Gora (SLO)
GIANT SLALOM

1.	**HENRIK KRISTOFFERSEN**	**(NOR)**
2.	Stefan Brennsteiner	(AUT)
3.	Marco Odermatt	(SUI)

16/03/2022, Courchevel (FRA)
DOWNHILL

1.	**VINCENT KRIECHMAYR**	**(AUT)**
2.	Marco Odermatt	(SUI)
3.	Beat Feuz	(SUI)

17/03/2022, Courchevel (FRA)
SUPER-G

1.	**VINCENT KRIECHMAYR**	**(AUT)**
2.	Marco Odermatt	(SUI)
3.	Gino Caviezel	(SUI)

19/03/2022, Méribel (FRA)
GIANT SLALOM

1.	**MARCO ODERMATT**	**(SUI)**
2.	Lucas Braathen	(NOR)
3.	Loïc Meillard	(FRA)

20/03/2022, Méribel (FRA)

SLALOM

1.	**ATLE LIE MCGRATH**	**(NOR)**
2.	Henrik Kristoffersen	(NOR)
3.	Manuel Feller	(AUT)

2022-23

CUPS

OVERALL
1. **MARCO ODERMATT** **(SUI)**
2. Aleksander Aamodt Kilde (NOR)
3. Henrik Kristoffersen (NOR)

SLALOM
1. **LUCAS BRAATHEN** **(NOR)**
2. Henrik Kristoffersen (NOR)
3. Ramon Zenhäusern (SUI)

GIANT SLALOM
1. **MARCO ODERMATT** **(SUI)**
2. Henrik Kristoffersen (NOR)
3. Žan Kranjec (SLO)

SUPER-G
1. **MARCO ODERMATT** **(SUI)**
2. Aleksander Aamodt Kilde (NOR)
3. Vincent Kriechmayr (AUT)

DOWNHILL
1. **ALEKSANDER AAMODT KILDE** **(NOR)**
2. Vincent Kriechmayr (AUT)
3. Marco Odermatt (SUI)

RACES

23/10/2022, Sölden (AUT)
GIANT SLALOM
1. **MARCO ODERMATT** **(SUI)**
2. Žan Kranjec (SLO)
3. Henrik Kristoffersen (NOR)

26/11/2022, Lake Louise (CAN)
DOWNHILL
1. **ALEKSANDER AAMODT KILDE** **(NOR)**
2. Daniel Hemetsberger (AUT)
3. Marco Odermatt (SUI)

27/11/2022, Lake Louise (CAN)
SUPER-G
1. **MARCO ODERMATT** **(SUI)**
2. Aleksander Aamodt Kilde (NOR)
3. Matthias Mayer (AUT)

03/12/2022, Beaver Creek (USA)
DOWNHILL
1. **ALEKSANDER AAMODT KILDE** **(NOR)**
2. Marco Odermatt (SUI)
3. James Crawford (CAN)

04/12/2022, Beaver Creek (USA)
SUPER-G
1. **ALEKSANDER AAMODT KILDE** **(NOR)**
2. Marco Odermatt (SUI)
3. Alexis Pinturault (FRA)

10/12/2022, Val-d'Isère (FRA)
GIANT SLALOM
1. **MARCO ODERMATT** **(SUI)**
2. Manuel Feller (AUT)
3. Žan Kranjec (SLO)

11/12/2022, Val-d'Isère (FRA)
SLALOM
1. **LUCAS BRAATHEN** **(NOR)**
2. Manuel Feller (AUT)
3. Loïc Meillard (SUI)

15/12/2022, Val Gardena (ITA)
DOWNHILL
1. **VINCENT KRIECHMAYR** **(AUT)**
2. Marco Odermatt (SUI)
3. Matthias Mayer (AUT)

17/12/2022, Val Gardena (ITA)
DOWNHILL
1. **ALEKSANDER AAMODT KILDE** **(NOR)**
2. Johan Clarey (FRA)
3. Mattia Casse (ITA)

18/12/2022, Alta Badia (ITA)
GIANT SLALOM
1. **LUCAS BRAATHEN** **(NOR)**
2. Henrik Kristoffersen (NOR)
3. Marco Odermatt (SUI)

19/12/2022, Alta Badia (ITA)
GIANT SLALOM
1. **MARCO ODERMATT** **(SUI)**
2. Henrik Kristoffersen (NOR)
3. Žan Kranjec (SLO)

22/12/2022, Madonna di Campiglio (ITA)
SLALOM
1. **DANIEL YULE** **(SUI)**
2. Henrik Kristoffersen (NOR)

3. Linus Straßer (GER)

28/12/2022, Bormio (ITA)
DOWNHILL
1. **VINCENT KRIECHMAYR** **(AUT)**
2. James Crawford (CAN)
3. Aleksander Aamodt Kilde (NOR)

29/12/2022, Bormio (ITA)
SUPER-G
1. **MARCO ODERMATT** **(SUI)**
2. Vincent Kriechmayr (AUT)
3. Loïc Meillard (SUI)

04/01/2023, Garmisch-Partenkirchen (GER)
SLALOM
1. **HENRIK KRISTOFFERSEN** **(NOR)**
2. Manuel Feller (AUT)
3. Clément Noël (FRA)

07/01/2023, Adelboden (SUI)
GIANT SLALOM
1. **MARCO ODERMATT** **(SUI)**
2. Henrik Kristoffersen (NOR)
3. Loïc Meillard (SUI)

08/01/2023, Adelboden (SUI)
SLALOM
1. **LUCAS BRAATHEN** **(NOR)**
2. Atle Lie McGrath (NOR)
3. Linus Straßer (GER)

13/01/2023, Wengen (SUI)
SUPER-G
1. **ALEKSANDER AAMODT KILDE** **(NOR)**
2. Stefan Rogentin (SUI)
3. Marco Odermatt (SUI)

14/01/2023, Wengen (SUI)
DOWNHILL
1. **ALEKSANDER AAMODT KILDE** **(NOR)**
2. Marco Odermatt (SUI)
3. Mattia Casse (ITA)

15/01/2023, Wengen (SUI)
SLALOM
1. **HENRIK KRISTOFFERSEN** **(NOR)**
2. Loïc Meillard (SUI)
3. Lucas Braathen (NOR)

20/01/2023, Kitzbühel (AUT)
DOWNHILL
1. **VINCENT KRIECHMAYR** **(AUT)**
2. Florian Schieder (ITA)
3. Niels Hintermann (SUI)

21/01/2023, Kitzbühel (AUT)
DOWNHILL
1. **ALEKSANDER AAMODT KILDE** **(NOR)**
2. Johan Clarey (FRA)
3. Travis Ganong (USA)

22/01/2023, Kitzbühel (AUT)
SLALOM
1. **DANIEL YULE** **(SUI)**
2. Dave Ryding (GBR)
3. Lucas Braathen (NOR)

24/01/2023, Schladming (AUT)
SLALOM
1. **CLÉMENT NOËL** **(FRA)**
2. Ramon Zenhäusern (SUI)
3. Lucas Braathen (NOR)

25/01/2023, Schladming (AUT)
GIANT SLALOM
1. **LOÏC MEILLARD** **(SUI)**
2. Gino Caviezel (SUI)
3. Marco Schwarz (AUT)

28/01/2023, Cortina d'Ampezzo (ITA)
SUPER-G
1. **MARCO ODERMATT** **(SUI)**
2. Aleksander Aamodt Kilde (NOR)
3. Mattia Casse (ITA)

29/01/2023, Cortina d'Ampezzo (ITA)
SUPER-G
1. **MARCO ODERMATT** **(SUI)**
2. Dominik Paris (ITA)
3. Daniel Hemetsberger (AUT)

04/02/2023, Chamonix (FRA)
SLALOM
1. **RAMON ZENHÄUSERN** **(SUI)**
2. AJ Ginnis (GRE)
3. Daniel Yule (SUI)

25/02/2023, Palisades Tahoe (USA)
GIANT SLALOM
1. **MARCO SCHWARZ** **(AUT)**
2. Marco Odermatt (SUI)

3. Rasmus Windingstad   (NOR)

26/02/2023, Palisades Taohe (USA)
SLALOM

1. **ALEXANDER STEEN OLSEN** **(NOR)**
2. Timon Haugan (NOR)
3. Clément Noël (FRA)
= Alberto Popov BUL)

04/03/2023, Aspen (USA)
DOWNHILL

1. **ALEKSANDER AAMODT KILDE** **(NOR)**
2. James Crawford (CAN)
3. Marco Odermatt (SUI)

05/03/2023, Aspen (USA)
SUPER-G

1. **MARCO ODERMATT** **(SUI)**
2. Andreas Sander (GER)
3. Aleksander Aamodt Kilde (NOR)

11/03/2023, Kranjska Gora (SLO)
GIANT SLALOM

1. **MARCO ODERMATT** **(SUI)**
2. Alexis Pinturault (FRA)
3. Henrik Kristoffersen (NOR)

12/03/2023, Kranjska Gora (SLO)
GIANT SLALOM

1. **MARCO ODERMATT** **(SUI)**
2. Henrik Kristoffersen (NOR)
3. Alexis Pinturault (FRA)

15/03/2023, Soldeu (AND)
DOWNHILL

1. **VINCENT KRIECHMAYR** **(AUT)**
2. Romed Baumann (GER)
3. Andreas Sander (GER)

16/03/2023, Soldeu (AND)
SUPER-G

1. **MARCO ODERMATT** **(SUI)**
2. Marco Schwarz (AUT)
3. Aleksander Aamodt Kilde (NOR)

18/03/2023, Soldeu (AND)
GIANT SLALOM

1. **MARCO ODERMATT** **(SUI)**
2. Henrik Kristoffersen (NOR)
3. Marco Schwarz (AUT)

19/03/2023, Soldeu (AND)
SLALOM

1. **RAMON ZENHÄUSERN** **(SUI)**
2. Lucas Braathen (NOR)
3. Henrik Kristoffersen (NOR)

COUNTRY CODES

AND	Andorra	Andorre	Andorra	Andorra	Andorra
ARG	Argentina	Argentine	Argentinien	Argentina	Argentina
AUS	Australia	Australie	Australien	Australia	Australia
AUT	Austria	Autriche	Österreich	Austria	Austria
BUL	Bulgaria	Bulgarie	Bulgarien	Bulgaria	Bulgaria
CAN	Canada	Canada	Kanada	Canadá	Canada
CRO	Croatia	Croatie	Kroatien	Croacia	Croazia
CZE	Czech Republic	Rép. chèque	Tschechische Rep.	República Checa	Repubblica Ceca
ESP	Spain	Espagne	Spanien	España	Spagna
FIN	Finland	Finlande	Finnland	Finlandia	Finlandia
FRA	France	France	Frankreich	Francia	Francia
FRG	West Germany	Allemagne Ouest	Westdeutschland	Alemania Occid.	Germania Ovest
GBR	Great Britain	Grande-Bretagne	Großbritannien	Reino Unido	Gran Bretagna
GER	Germany	Allemagne	Deutschland	Alemania	Germania
GRE	Greece	Grèce	Griechenland	Grecia	Grecia
HUN	Hungary	Hongrie	Ungarn	Hungría	Ungheria
IRI	Iran	Iran	Iran	Irán	Iran
ISL	Iceland	Islande	Island	Islandia	Islanda
ITA	Italy	Italie	Italien	Italia	Italia
JPN	Japan	Japon	Japan	Japón	Giappone
KOR	South Korea	Corée du Sud	Südkorea	Corea del Sur	Corea del Sud
LIE	Liechtenstein	Liechtenstein	Liechtenstein	Liechtenstein	Liechtenstein
LUX	Luxembourg	Luxembourg	Luxemburg	Luxemburgo	Lussemburgo
NOR	Norway	Norvège	Norwegen	Noruega	Norvegia
NZL	New Zealand	Nouvelle-Zélande	Neuseeland	Nueva Zelanda	Nuova Zelanda
POL	Poland	Pologne	Polen	Polonia	Polonia
RUS	Russia	Russie	Russland	Rusia	Russia
SLO	Slovenia	Slovénie	Slowenien	Eslovenia	Slovenia
SUI	Switzerland	Suisse	Schweiz	Suiza	Svizzera
SVK	Slovakia	Slovaquie	Slowakei	Eslovaquia	Slovacchia
SWE	Sweden	Suède	Schweden	Suecia	Svezia
TCH	Czechoslovakia	Tchécoslovaquie	Tschechoslowakei	Checoslovaquia	Cecoslovacchia
URS	Soviet Union	Union Soviétique	Sowjetunion	Unión Soviética	Unione Sovietica

Made in the USA
Monee, IL
15 January 2024

51858929R00081